TURKISH POLITICS AND 'THE PEOPLE'

TURKISH POLITICS AND 'THE PEOPLE'

Mass Mobilisation and Populism

Spyros A. Sofos

EDINBURGH
University Press

Edinburgh University Press is one of the leading university presses in the UK. We publish academic books and journals in our selected subject areas across the humanities and social sciences, combining cutting-edge scholarship with high editorial and production values to produce academic works of lasting importance. For more information visit our website: edinburghuniversitypress.com

© Spyros A. Sofos, 2022

Edinburgh University Press Ltd
The Tun – Holyrood Road
12 (2f) Jackson's Entry
Edinburgh EH8 8PJ

Typeset in 11/15 Adobe Garamond by
IDSUK (DataConnection) Ltd, and
printed and bound in Great Britain

A CIP record for this book is available from the British Library

ISBN 978 1 3995 0285 6 (hardback)
ISBN 978 1 3995 0287 0 (webready PDF)
ISBN 978 1 3995 0288 7 (epub)

The right of Spyros A. Sofos to be identified as author of this work has been asserted in accordance with the Copyright, Designs and Patents Act 1988 and the Copyright and Related Rights Regulations 2003 (SI No. 2498).

CONTENTS

ACKNOWLEDGEMENTS

In my idiosyncratic reading of *Labyrinths*, written by Jorge Luis Borges – one of my favourite writers – writing is a form of perilous travelling, of exploring, getting lost and finding oneself again. Writing this book represents indeed a very long labyrinthine journey, replete with treacherous routes, detours, dead ends and moments when the destination figured unattainable.

In mid-2020, five years after the original idea behind this book was just that – a vague, exciting notion – the manuscript was finally being completed in the midst of a pandemic, with working from home measures in place and travel having been relegated to the fuzzy realm of utopia. Several months of working almost alone can create a false sense of self-sufficiency, but, as is the case in most intellectual work, this book has been the culmination of intellectual and human exchanges. *Turkish Politics and 'The People'* would not have been possible without the numerous interlocutors and friends who have made an input to the intellectual content of this book.

Catharina Raudvere has been a most supportive colleague, friend and interlocutor, and without her keen interest and encouragement I have no doubt that I would still be lost in the dead ends of this route. Paul Levin and Bahar Baser Özturk provided extensive and invaluable feedback on the contents of this book as did the two anonymous Edinburgh University Press reviewers. Emma Rees, the Press's commissioning editor, and Alp Özerdem and Erdi Öztürk, the series editors, offered advice and placed their confidence in this volume. I am grateful to them for their support and enthusiasm.

Various interlocutors were at times unaware that our conversations would eventually find their way into this particular book. Nicolas Demertzis has been a good friend, interlocutor and invaluable mentor for as long as I can remember. Our casual and more formal conversations on nationalism, populism, the political, psychoanalysis and, as this manuscript was being prepared, emotion in politics have informed ideas that underpin the argument of this book. My ideas on populism and nationalism, especially the distinction between 'the popular' and 'the populist' have been taking shape over decades and thus my intellectual debt extends way back. A number of exchanges with the late Stuart Hall on hegemony and authoritarian populism, and with the late Ernesto Laclau on populism and the concept of hegemony, have helped me sketch the contours of my current argument on populism and the popular, and, although elements of some of these ideas found their way into earlier work, my discussion of populism in this book benefits from these conversations. My intellectual debt encompasses earlier conversations with Glenn Bowman on constitutive violence, post-Marxism and post-foundationalism; and John Breuilly's work on nationalism and his reminders of the importance of historical perspective in any theoretical endeavour. The late Rosemary Bechler gave me the invaluable opportunity to test my ideas in public in the aftermath of the 2016 failed coup in Turkey, and later on, as we embarked on the adventure of the *rethinkingPopulism* project from the pages of *openDemocracy* was a considerate and constructive interlocutor. Conversations and exchanges with Dibyesh Anand, Albena Azmanova, Seyla Benhabib, Paula Biglieri, Luciana Cadahia, Rodrigo Echecopar, Paolo Gerbaudo, Jeremy Gilbert, Catarina Kinnvall, Grigoris Markou, Chantal Mouffe, James Schneider, Guy Standing and Cihan Tuğal provided much needed food for thought with regard to formulating the contours of my understanding of populism. My reading of Turkish politics and society has benefited from exchanges with Ayhan Aktar, Isa Blumi, Pinar Dinç, Zeynep Direk, Ayhan Kaya, Mehmet Kırık, Özge Özdüzen, İnan Ruma, Ömer Tekdemir, Ömer Turan (who also very generously pointed me out to some hard-to-locate literature), Maria Varaki and Jenny White. I am also grateful to Miray Keskin, who has provided invaluable research assistance in Turkey.

Oscar Hemer, Hans Åke Persson and Thomas Tufte gave me the opportunity to test my thoughts on Turkish politics in the course of a MICS/

Örecomm Centre for Communication and Social Change workshop held at the Swedish Research Institute in Istanbul back in May 2015, and David Shankland and Natalie Martin invited me to a roundtable at the Royal Anthropological Institute in April 2018, discussing recent political developments in Turkey with parliamentarians and policy-makers. The Human Rights Summer School of the Swedish Research Institute in Istanbul, where I taught over several years, has always provided a space for intellectual experimentation, and the Institute itself has been a home to me, while its staff and visitors have extended warm collegiality and a stimulating intellectual environment on several occasions. İlhami Alkan Olsson of the Raoul Wallenberg Institute for Human Rights and Humanitarian Law (Turkey office) has offered me the opportunity to combine aspects of my research with a programme on Democratic Dialogue in Turkey, which I coordinated together with Zeynep Direk and Mehmet Kırık. The Istanbul Roundtables that we organised within the framework of this programme have been the most gratifying and fascinating interdisciplinary experiences, and I am grateful to İlhami and my co-organisers as well as the participants for exploring with us the notion of trust from a theoretical perspective and its empirical application in the Turkish context. I also wish to thank the Centre for Advanced Middle Eastern Studies, Lund University, which, prior to my move to the Middle East Centre, London School of Economics, was home to me, and was where most of the research for this book was conducted. Finally, I could not have wished for more supportive colleagues than my co-workers at the LSE Middle East Centre, and for a more intellectually stimulating research environment than the Centre itself as I concluded this manuscript.

My parents have been intimately involved in this endeavour from the very start; there are no words that can even begin to describe my gratitude and love for their having been there for me, their unconditional support, encouragement and confidence in me. My late father sadly passed away prematurely, yet part of the aspiration and perseverance embodied in this book is due to the fact that he has always remained with me. My brother, Alexandros, who was in his mid-teens when I left Greece to study and, later, work in the UK has always made the distance separating us seem short and inconsequential. I am grateful to him for braving the distance, and being there in so many ways. I have been immensely privileged to have shared this journey with my lovely children, Iason and Roxana, who are now young adults. They have been, and are, a source of joy, pride and strength and have brought to this long process immensely invaluable moments of respite, affection and love.

Finally, Nazanin, you have been a veritable *yoldaş*, braving adversity with me, making the journey bearable and helping me see the destination.

1

'THE PEOPLE': LEGITIMACY AND MOBILISATION IN TURKISH POLITICS

> To throw some light on discussions about the 'people' and the 'popular', one need only bear in mind that the 'people' or the 'popular' ('popular art', 'popular religion', 'popular medicine', etc.) is first of all one of the things at stake in the struggle between intellectuals. The fact of being or feeling authorized to speak about the 'people' or of speaking for (in both senses of the word) the 'people' may constitute, in itself, a force in the struggles within different fields, political, religious, artistic, etc.: a force that is all the greater the weaker the relative autonomy of the field under consideration.
>
> *In Other Words: Essays Towards a Reflexive Sociology*, Pierre Bourdieu

The Notion of 'The People'

The use notion of 'the people' in the discourse of the social sciences is indeed one that has eluded consensus. Distinctions between 'the serious' and 'the popular' in, say, aesthetics and cultural studies, have for a long time informed connotations of a lowbrow, naïve or shallow quality for the products of popular creativity. The 'serious/popular' dichotomy sustained a series of other distinctions: 'the people' were distinguished from the elites, and, by extension, their more 'refined' tastes and cultural production, their more serious predispositions. As Derrida suggests, meaning is often defined in terms of binary oppositions, where 'one of the two terms governs the other'; integrated in such binary schemata, concepts are categorised and hierarchised (Derrida 1992:41). Thus, to return to the fields of cultural studies and aesthetics where

I

'the people' became the subject of contestation and debate, the notion of 'the popular' became one of the central preoccupations for members of the Frankfurt School, mainly in the context of what was then referred to as 'mass culture', or the culture industry. In the work of Horkheimer and Adorno (1944), 'the popular' was often approached as a field comprising practices, ideologies and cultural products that debased the masses, or even flattered their 'shallowness'. Dismayed at the state of mass culture, and equating it with popular culture, they produced a very pessimistic account of how ordinary people became passive consumers of culture industry products. Coming from a different intellectual background, British elitism, as expounded by Matthew Arnold (2006) and his followers, sought to insulate 'the best of what was thought and said', the high culture of the time, from the debasing influence of the popular commercial press and mass culture in general. For the British elitist school, to be interested in popular things was to be base and common, a philosophy that was later endorsed by public institutions such as the BBC which, during its early years, shunned popular culture and sought to civilise the masses. Against this background of pessimism regarding popular culture, or disdain and contempt for it, the work of the Birmingham school (see Turner 2002) engaged critically with these intellectual traditions and went a long way towards rehabilitating the notion of 'the popular', focusing on a host of manifestations of popular cultural production and consumption, looking for a politics of the prophane, the mundane and the vernacular. This engagement of academics and intellectuals with the cultural dimensions of 'the popular' has not been, and is, not a neutral intellectual exercise; it constitutes a field of debate, or, even better, struggle where hierarchies of meaning are established, contested, deconstructed. And, what is more, they have tangible, material implications such as the aforementioned impact of British elitism on the ethos and remit of the early BBC, or, to come closer to the focus of this thesis, the policies of suppressing vernacular cultures in republican Turkey, premised on the assumption that they were belated and primitive.

The fields of politics and other social sciences have not, of course, constituted an exception in this respect. The notion of 'the popular' and its intersection with politics became the object of debate and intellectual interrogation from the nineteenth century when scholars attempted to unpack the dynamics of the revolutions and mass mobilisations that left their imprint on

European politics. Against the influence of work on the crowd influenced by Le Bon's elitist perspective (1897), social historians such as E. P. Thompson attempted to develop more nuanced approaches that could make sense of the complexity of crowd psychology and explore the issue of agency that was largely absent from elitist perspectives. Thompson's work focused on the politics of the English crowd (1978) and the plebeian cultures (1971; 1974) that emanated from these in an effort to better understand the way in which notions of 'the people' shaped political discourses and action in early modernity and opened up new avenues for exploring 'the popular'.

Others used the term 'populism' to refer to political traditions in ways that markedly contrasted with the much maligned articulation of 'the popular' in politics, the roots of which go back to Le Bon's work. American social historian Lawrence Goodwyn, in his *Democratic Promise: The Populist Moment in America* (1976), explores the origins and rise of the People's Party and the democratic influence it had on US politics, and set the leitmotif of a long US-located tradition that also informed a strand of critical theory best exemplified by the circle of intellectuals around the *Telos Quarterly*, marking a cultural turn that sought to integrate the focus on the emancipatory tradition of populism as identified by Goodwyn with insights from Western Marxism and the Frankfurt School as well as civic action possibilities derived from Carl Schmitt's analysis of liberal democracy. Similarly, political scientists like Laclau (1977) and Mouffe (2018; 2020) explored populist politics as a progressive form of mobilisation, and, more recently, Biglieri and Cadahia (2021) made a case for recognising in populism an intrinsic emancipatory quality that can bring progressive change and counter emerging right-wing trends, including the types of politics often recognised by scholars as right-wing populism. The very same term was used by Camus and Lebourg (2017) to explore the far-right dimensions of populism and the exclusivist politics associated with it, while Müller (2017) has argued that at the core of populism is a rejection of pluralism and associated populist governance to nationalism, occasionally tinted with elements of racism.

Turkish Politics and 'The People' is intended to make a contribution to ongoing efforts to enhance our understanding of 'the popular' in the study of politics through a critical examination of the uses and constructions of 'the people' in Turkish politics since the establishment of the Turkish Republic in 1923, to the present. As such, this volume aspires to provide a grounded engagement with conceptual, theoretical and empirical research on 'the popular' in politics. The long-durée focus of the book makes it possible to sketch the contours of a genealogy, of the process of the 'constitution of knowledges, discourses, domains of objects' (Foucault 2003:306), especially those that we tend to consider as without history, in the context of particular power configurations over time (Foucault 1977:139). *Turkish Politics and 'The People'* thus distinguishes between different traditions and modalities of appeals to 'the people', establishing convergences and divergences between them, reconstructing the social-historical and power contexts in which 'the people' and 'discourses about the people' emerge and change over time and making sense of them from sociological, cultural and social psychological perspectives.

The choice of Turkey is by no means accidental. The notion of 'the people' has been central in the political discourse of the Republic, and even in the late Ottoman era. The new nation state of Turkey declared that it was a 'populist' state, with a strong anti-elitist and emancipatory emphasis and a promise of radical equality in its founding principles. 'The people' has adorned the names of some of the key parties and many of the peripheral ones in the history of the Republic, including some of the ones that sprang out of the Kurdish national movements. And, finally, the politics of the past twenty years have been described by researchers and the media as 'populist', so much so that Turkey has become for many a textbook case of populist politics. Critically exploring how the notion of 'the people', and the allied notions of 'the national' and 'the plebeian/vernacular' have been shaped by the history of the Republic, and, in turn, have informed ways of visualising society and politics, and have framed the parameters and repertoires of political action in the social-historical context of Turkey, can provide valuable insights for deepening our understanding of Turkish politics, but also contribute to a theoretically nuanced and historicised understanding of populism.

Appeals to 'the people' (often conflated with 'the nation', as the words *halk* (people) and *millet* (nation) are often used interchangeably) have been central in Turkish political discourse both left and right, secular, nationalist and Islamist and have been used both as a pretext for legitimising curtailments of the democratic process and for the perpetration of human rights abuses on the one hand, and as a means of democratic political mobilisation on the other, yet the term *people* has been used to refer to diverse parts of the population and to denote diverse political values and cultures in time and space. It is only relatively recently, however, that students of Turkish politics and society started using the concept of populism as a means of making sense of Turkish political culture and political developments in the country (Baykan 2018; Erdoğan et al. 2018; Erçetin and Erdoğan 2018; Gürsoy 2021; Kandiyoti 2015; Tekdemir 2018; Yabanci 2016, to mention but a few). Yet several of these attempts to make use of the theoretical and methodological toolkits available for the study of populism, despite admittedly shedding light on hitherto less studied aspects of Turkish politics, have been plagued by some of the key problems endemic in the general debate on populism and, in turn, have not avoided reproducing them. Regardless of their theoretical perspective for example, the underlying concepts in Erdoğan et al. (2018), or Tekdemir (2018) open the way to referring to all major participants in Turkish political life, from the secularist Republican People's Party (Cumhuriyet Halk Partisi, CHP), to the ultra-nationalist Nationalist Action Party (Milliyetçi Hareket Partisi, MHP), the conservative Justice and Development Party (Adalet ve Kalkınma Partisi, AKP) and the left-leaning pro-minority People's Democratic Party (Halkların Demokratik Partisi, HDP) – and, in Tekdemir's analysis, even the Gezi mobilisations in addition to all others. The repercussions of such conceptual laxity are obvious: if every political actor, every mobilisation, every discourse can be considered populist, then what is the heuristic, critical and analytical use of the term/concept? To be sure, this is by no means a problem faced only by scholars of Turkish politics; work on populism in general has also suffered as our conceptual toolkits have not been rigorously tested and carefully deployed.

The Popular and the Populist

An influential strand of work on 'the popular' originates in the commentary of late nineteenth-century European, especially French and Italian, chroniclers, sociologists, psychologists and criminologists who, having witnessed or experienced polarisation in their societies, lived and remembered the revolutionary upheavals of that period as a monumental crisis. For them the assertiveness of protesters and the mass politics that challenged the idea of a public sphere as an exclusive locus underpinned by consensus, constituted not responses to social injustice but pathological symptoms of a society that was degenerating – socialism, anarchism, feminism were not seen as expressions of the wish of the proletarian class and subordinate segments of society to gain a political voice, but were coupled with disease, insanity and alcoholism and relegated to societal pathologies. The work of Scipio Sighele on the intelligence of the crowd (1903) and Gabriel Tarde (1903) on its criminal predispositions, as well as the *Origines de la France contemporaine* written by historian, philosopher, and literary critic Hippolyte Taine (1876–8), especially his account of the French Revolution and the role of the people (i.e. the crowd) in it, contributed to intertwining the fear of revolution and the social concern with criminality.

Drawing on Taine's account of the September Massacres – a series of killings of prison inmates in Paris that lasted four days in September 1792 and constituted the prelude of the period of intense violence known as the Reign of Terror during the French Revolution – Gustave Le Bon developed his outline of crowd psychology (1897). Le Bon attributes to 'the people' or the 'plebs' particular propensities that are reinforced in the course of the mass action such that characterised the politics of the nineteenth century in the pursuit of popular sovereignty. These include 'incapacity to reason, and the absence of judgement of the critical spirit' (1897:16), and 'openness to suggestion, credulity, mobility, the exaggeration of the sentiments good or bad, the manifestation of certain forms of morality' (1897:165).

Le Bon and his followers, whose elitism influenced the Turkish nationalist elite of the early twentieth century as I suggest later in this volume (Chapter 4), were unable, or unwilling, to come to grips with the increasing inseparability of the crowd from bourgeois democracy, to reconcile the corporeal vibrancy of the politics of the former with 'principled', 'orderly' bourgeois politics. The putative irrationality and susceptibility of the crowd opened the way to dismissing popular mobilisations of the long nineteenth century and representing them as a marker of infancy, savagery and lack of sophistication. This original stigmatisation of popular politics as an aberration has found its way into theories that have left an indelible mark in the social sciences. In his *Group Psychology and the Analysis of the Ego* (1955), Freud built upon Le Bon's association of the crowd with irrationality encapsulated in the latter's notion of 'group mind'. Freud thus sought to identify in crowd action particular psychological mechanisms that enable individuals to set themselves free of the pressures of the existing social order and make it possible for a heterogeneous and temporary entity such as the masses to momentarily exist and act. In the context of the affective ecology of this momentary union of effective strangers, Freud argues, the individual's conscious personality recedes to the extent that the masses, with their impulsiveness, volatility and irritability, are governed largely by the unconscious.

Elements of this approach can be further discerned in the effort of members of the Frankfurt School to make sense of the success of fascism in winning the masses in the interwar period, and later on, to shed light on the logics underpinning the 'culture industry'. Despite his scepticism over Freud's approach to the masses and the latter's irrationality, Adorno, for example, maintained the idea of psychological mechanisms that give the unconscious free rein as, in his opinion, fascism mobilised 'irrational, unconscious, regressive processes' (1982:123–34).

Not directly connected to the elitist school of Le Bon, but equally sceptical with regard to popular mobilisations, was the work of Richard Hofstadter, perhaps one of the most influential critics of US populism and reformism. Hofstadter (1948; 1955; 1963) advances a reading of the American Populist movement of the end of the nineteenth century as a highly regressive, provincial, bigoted, nativist and anti-Semitic insurgency, a movement marked by moral absolutism and status anxiety of a rural elite bent on preserving the benefits of an era of prosperity. Hofstadter's intentional misreading of the Populist insurgency, refuted by Woodward (1955) and Goodwyn (1976), did not affect his influence on the academic debate and contributed substantially to the development of arguments against styles of politics that involved popular mobilisation, and of stereotypes that associated 'the people's' engagement in politics with the erosion of liberal democracy. Hofstadter's binary distinction was between backward traditionalism – which in his opinion was often espoused by popular movements – and forward-looking liberalism, untainted by popular activism, which was mirrored in the political development theories of the time. His distinction between anti-modern politics (left and right) and politics inspired by what Almond and Verba (1963) termed civic culture and its liberal Cold War connotations left its mark on intellectual engagement with popular politics and often served to delegitimise radical movements as susceptible to 'agitators with paranoid tendencies, who are able to make a vocational asset out of their psychic disturbances' (Hofstadter 1955:71).

A common thread connecting these approaches is a mistrust of 'the people' whose entry to politics is registered as the rule of 'the crowd', largely irrational, uncritical, impulsive and volatile. Premised on a binary juxtaposition of 'the people' and 'the elite' that also permeates approaches to populism as I suggest later on in this chapter, it denies 'the people' the capacity that is allegedly possessed by the elites to reason and engage in crucial decision-making processes that require the ability to keep emotion at bay.

A more nuanced approach is advanced by Germani in his discussion of mass mobilisation in Argentina under Juán Perón. Germani saw Perón's followers as 'the passive, manipulated urban masses which emerge in the course of an incomplete modernisation process' (1963:187, 230), and considered their 'irrational' support for Perón's authoritarian leadership a feature of the rapid socioeconomic transition that Argentinian society was undergoing at the time. Although he does not explicitly preclude the possibility of the masses behaving rationally under other circumstances, he nonetheless invests the entry of the masses in politics with a diminished capacity and dependence on the *Lider*. He thus refuses to entertain the possibility of strategic and rational choice in the 'passivity' of the masses and their 'deference' to Perón given that his authoritarianism 'provided the quickest and most rational means of satisfying the desires of the lower class' (Smith 1969:34).

And moving to the present, contemporary commentators have identified in political developments of the past decade (which have been marked by a critique of liberal democracy from what has been called the populist left and right alike and the emergence of leaders who can be characterised as charismatic or demagogues) a similar moment to the ones that prompted Hofstadter's aversion towards the 'popularisation' of politics. Mishra (2018) subsumes the politics of populism in the broader sociopolitical constellation that he calls 'the age of anger', a time when those who have felt excluded from the enjoyment of the promises of modernity have channelled their frustration and rage into politics and have increasingly become susceptible to demagogues who articulate a promise of empowerment. Mbembe (2019) makes a similar argument as he argues that contemporary politics is marked by a radical change in the fundamental mechanisms of affective life. New technologies have not only made possible new strategies in the formation of masses but have also brought about what he calls 'virtual hordes'. Drawing uncritically on Freud's discussion of mass psychology, Mbembe argues that today's virtual hordes are excited by spectacularised politics and drawn to authoritarian solutions. Mbembe laments the end of 'the age of humanism', as he contends that this politics of the virtual hordes is incompatible with the logic of liberal democracy, which, already considerably ground down by the forces of capital, technology and militarism, is on the retreat.

Such approaches have been bundled together under the rubric of 'anti-populism' by critics (see, for example, Stavrakakis 2014, Markou 2021). Critics of anti-populism are right in warning that anti-populism has an anti-democratic potential, especially as it can be used as a means of delegitimising 'non-centrist politics', political radicalism and attempts to engage critically with deficiencies of today's technocratised democratic processes. Yet the sharp binary divide between populism and anti-populism reduces popular mobilisations and activism to populist politics, and does a disservice to the diversity of forms of popular organisation and struggle. This misrecognition of all modalities of popular politics for populism is grounded in the particular ways in which critics of anti-populism have understood and defined the latter. Conflating critiques of populism with a more general disdain at popular involvement in politics and of popular mobilisations (which, admittedly, many proponents of what has been termed anti-populism espouse), close the critical space in which evocations, interpellations and mobilisations of 'the people' can be explored, nuanced and differentiated, as not all kinds of evocation/inclusion of the people have an emancipatory potential, or, more importantly, intent. Definitions of populism such as the one deployed by critics of anti-populism lack theoretical rigour and, as such, fail to advance our understanding of the phenomenon.

A different, historically informed perspective in the study of popular mobilisations but also everyday life was cast by social historians influenced by the work of E. P. Thompson (1971; 1974; 1978; 1991; also see Breaugh 2013), which focused on history unfolding 'from below'. Thompson turned his attention to the lifeworld of agricultural workers displaced by the social and technological changes associated with the transition to capitalism as well as that of the urban workers who supplied their labour to the emerging industrial bourgeoisie of nineteenth-century England. The former possessed skills that were no longer in demand and started moving to the cities joining an early working class that was not yet able to narrate and make sense of its own dispossession; and Thompson tried to make sense of the ways this highly diverse melting pot of the early industrial era gave rise to disruptive possibilities, mainly at times of acute food scarcity, and slowly built a sense of self-awareness and self-worth. The plebeians of the eighteenth and early nineteenth centuries, Thompson argues, should not be confused with the working class that emerged as modernity and industrialisation took hold as they had not developed a 'class consciousness' or any specific idea of their political objectives, other than a vague sense of being distinct from the patricians of the period. Having said that, Thompson shed light on the plebeians as political actors, as evidenced by the upheavals they brought about through non-deference and direct action (Thompson 1991:64). The value of Thompson's analysis is that it challenges the elitist assumptions about the lack of agency in popular culture and action without erring towards the mythicisation of 'the people' allowing us to examine plebeian cultures as distinct from the more politicised versions of 'class', 'the people' and 'the nation' that emerged in the nineteenth and twentieth centuries (such as at the time of the emergence of Turkish republican nationalism) and explore their interrelations.

Others attempt to dissect the nature of more contemporary plebeian struggles and juxtapose them to class as well as populist politics by drawing parallels between the early modern crowds in Europe studied by Thompson and those of the aboriginal populations in Amazonia, Bolivia or other parts of the globe and their resistance to the multinationals and states that destroy their habitats and their communities in the pursuit of resource extraction, or contemporary urban and rural crowds as diverse as the 1989 Caracazo in Venezuela, or protests by the vast unorganised popular mass of the *forajidos* (outlaws) in Ecuador in 2005, or, as I argue later in this volume, the Gezi protests in Turkey in 2013, to name but a few. Among them, extending Breaugh's work on the plebeian experience (2013), Peñafiel (2012) coins the term 'plebeian interpellation' to refer to a mode of momentary subjectification, or 'subjectification without subject', of these masses resembling Thompson's crowds that fill streets and squares to protest against injustice, but without seeking to become insiders in the political arena. His reference to 'subjectification without subject' can be construed as an attempt to render intelligible both the 'instant', 'momentary' character of plebeian mobilisations and the unwillingness of the plebs to conform to political norms and form a durable presence in the political arena. Moulier-Boutang (2014), builds on this attempt to identify, not the people, but the plebeian masses. He argues that they 'come from outside and remain there' (p. 216), with the rural plebs 'seeking to restore their rights to ancient commons . . . clashing with the industrial, energy and agro-industrial projects of multinationals and states, with land and biodiversity resources as their confrontation grounds' and their urban counterparts setting claim on 'new digital common goods, public services, transport, health, access to knowledge' (p. 219). Corten (2012), reflecting on the failure or, perhaps, unwillingness, on the part of these plebeian masses to translate their energy and mobilisation into political power argues that their claim to sovereignty is 'instant' and does not lead to becoming sovereign in terms of 'capturing' the state (p. 49), while Huart (2012) suggested that the actions of the plebeians do not aim to gain the status of 'totality' or 'to be proposing an alternative political arrangement to the dominant one' (pp. 62–3). Similarly, in my attempt to contextualise the Gezi protests during 2013 in Turkey in social-historical terms, I proposed to see them as a 'happening', or, following Badiou (2005), an 'event', as characterised by rupture and liminality (Turner 1967, 1974), located outside the linear time and conventional topography of Turkish politics, and suggested that they should be interpreted as a brief but powerful moment of rupture in a political system where both the incumbent political forces and the opposition are resisting change and consider extra-institutional 'anti-politics' a threat to them (Sofos 2018a:83).

This book examines 'the popular' at a time when the concept of *populism* dominates discussions in political science and political sociology and has become the main prism through which 'the people' is examined in these disciplines. It also encounters and navigates a scholarly field where *populism* has become a catch-all term, used to describe all sorts of manifestations of authoritarian politics, majoritarian logics or political discourses that revolve around the notion of 'the people' as a political subject, so much so that it runs the danger of losing its critical edge and value. In one of the first attempts to conduct an extensive comparative analysis of the concept, Gellner and

Ionescu (1969) back in the late 1960s convey the sense of the challenge faced by students of populism:

> There can, at present, be no doubt about the importance of populism. But no one is quite clear just what it is. As a doctrine or as a movement, it is elusive and protean. It bobs up everywhere, but in many and contradictory shapes. Does it have any underlying unity? Or does one name cover a multitude of unconnected tendencies? The challenge of defining populism is at least partially due to the fact that the term has been used to describe political movements, parties, ideologies, and leaders across geographical, historical, and ideological contexts. (1969:1)

Indeed, the social-historical moments in which the term was used have varied considerably in their geography, as well as the social and political constellations that endowed the term with relevance and meaning. From the Russian Narodniki (Von Laue 1954) and the somewhat relevant East European experience of the nineteenth century, to the American agrarian movement that Goodwyn described (1976), to the Latin American experience, the Iranian Revolution or the Southern European and later on East-Central European movements of the 1980s and 1990s, to today's global wave of far-right and nativist movements from Europe to the Indian subcontinent, as well as some of their opponents situating themselves on the left end of the political spectrum, there is a sense among those studying politics that there are some potential commonalities – yet what these are remains unclear. Sixty years after Gellner and Ionescu put their finger on the problems of studying populism, the questions they posed at the time are no less bewildering. Is populism a form of collective action? Does it refer to an ideology, soft or hard, or a doctrine? Is it a discourse and what are the implications of such a definition? Does it refer to particular types of leadership? And, even when agreement is not forthcoming with regards to these questions, does the implication that Narendra Modi's politics in India today shares commonalities with Recep Tayyip Erdoğan's appeals to the people, or the different proponents of Brexit, or the *gilets jaunes* or movement parties such as Podemos and political organisations such as SYRIZA (Coalition of the Radical Left – Progressive Alliance), the Five Star Movement or the Northern League and the Front National, make sense? What does this proverbial motley crew of contenders for the designation 'populist' have in common, if anything at all, especially as some would fit a top-down and others a grassroots mode of political discourse/action, and, if they do, is the use of the term 'populism' in their cases warranted and useful?

The situation becomes further complicated as the use of the term has now breached the boundaries of academic inquiry and has acquired the status of a catch-all term in political debates and even everyday conversations. Interestingly, an examination of the way the term populism is used in British media suggests that 'any political actor who is in the news frequently for a substantial amount of time probably runs the risk of being labelled "populist" sooner or later' (Bale et al. 2011:121); the list of political actors labelled 'populist' in the British press in 2007 includes politicians as different as Jacob Zuma of South Africa, then-British Prime Minister Gordon Brown, Iranian President Mahmoud Ahmadinejad, former Italian Prime Minister Silvio Berlusconi, Hugo Chavez of Venezuela and the American conservative presidential candidate Mike Huckabee. Apart from usually being iconic and controversial personalities, it is not entirely clear what these politicians have in common. What is more, populism is used as a badge of honour as well as an accusation, an attempt to delegitimise opponents. Echoing the impasses already reached in the field of social sciences, such discussions confuse the meaning of the term by conflating all sorts of popular mobilisations with far-right politics, from the Occupy movement worldwide, to the Arab Spring or the Gezi protests in Turkey and even left-wing challenges to political systems or the forms of governance or the economics underlying neoliberal globalisation.

When our discourse becomes so saturated by references to populism that the polysemy of the term destabilises its heuristic or conceptual usefulness, the term becomes problematic. It lacks some degree of specificity that can allow its demarcation, juxtaposition and location in our conceptual universe and bestow it with a critical edge, and, by extension, utility and efficacy in terms of research but also in terms of its deployment intro the realm of actual politics. Are all evocations of the people in politics tantamount to populist politics? Or do specific types of interpellation of the people qualify as populist? And of course, can populism be politically progressive and at the same time regressive?

Clearly, a critical review of the vast and growing literature on populism is not an easy endeavour. The reference to multiple phenomena is, as already stated, a factor of immense complexity that any review needs to engage with. But even in the case of consensus among researchers over specific phenomena in given social-historical contexts (for instance, European far-right populism), one needs to sift through a plethora of diverse definitions and a variety of disciplinary and theoretical perspectives underlying them. In the following pages I attempt to organise some of the key studies on populism through a categorisation that is based on the distinction between a number of overarching, though often overlapping, approaches, notably, ideological or discursive dimensions of populism; the organisational aspects of populism; political performance aspects of populism; populism as a societal response to a crisis.

Perhaps the most widespread approach to populism revolves around its ideological or discursive dimensions. Nevertheless, there is a significant divergence of opinion as to the meanings of these terms and their relevance to populism, and, therefore, the diversity of the ideological and discursive perspectives is considerable. Perhaps one of the most influential definitions of populism nowadays shares this emphasis. Empirically grounded in studies of European right-wing populist parties, this definition suggests that populism is a 'thin-centred ideology' that considers society to be ultimately separated into two homogeneous and antagonistic groups, 'the pure people' versus 'the corrupt elite', and argues that politics should be an expression of the *volonté générale* (general will) of the people (Mudde 2004:543). Populism here is understood as a set of ideas whereby society is understood as characterised by an antagonism between the people and the elite. In this ideological framework the virtuous general will (the will of the people) is placed in opposition to the moral and political corruption and lack of accountability of elite actors. Because populism is defined by Mudde as a thin-centred ideology, it is malleable and adaptable. As such, it can be fused with left- or right-wing ideologies that are 'thicker': 'Which ideological features attach to populism depend upon the socio-political context within which the populist actors mobilize' (Mudde and Kaltwasser 2011:2).

The 'thick/thin' ideology distinction underlying the ideational approach of Mudde and Kaltwasser draws on Michael Freeden's conceptual analysis of ideologies, particularly his attempt to make sense of ideologies like 'environmentalism', 'feminism', 'nationalism' (Freeden 2003), or, more recently, 'populism' (Freeden 2017), which, from his point of view, like mainstream ones, have an identifiable morphology, yet this morphology is a restricted one in contrast to the former; that is, it revolves around single or limited issues. The implications of this distinction are quite significant and raise a host of methodological and practical/political issues. If populism is seen first and foremost as a thin cluster of ideas, the methodological implication is that research should focus primarily on statements and texts made by political actors and not much more, as this is where, it is argued, its 'essence' lies. And, from a practical point of view, a definition of populism as a thin ideology renders populism nothing more than a skin-deep element of a political phenomenon whose centre of gravity lies elsewhere, in its articulations with other 'thicker' or more complex ideologies. Effectively a little more than Brubaker's understanding of it as discursive and stylistic repertoire (2017), or Weyland's as a political strategy (2001), populism in itself has neither progressive nor regressive qualities, nor does it have the capacity of bringing social and political change as this potential lies in its articulation with 'thick' ideologies that incorporate 'deeper' visualisations of society and provide the direction of social change. Curiously, the thin ideology thesis, or at least its implications, are embraced by another important current in the study of populism epitomised in the work of Chantal Mouffe. Drawing on Laclau's earlier work on populism as well as their own work on radical democracy (see Laclau 1977; Laclau and Mouffe 1985), Mouffe argues in favour of a qualitatively different populism that would be best placed to counter and challenge reactionary, xenophobic versions of populism as well as inherently undemocratic, neoliberal, technocratic political modes of governance. Populism:

> is not an ideology or a political regime, and, as such, cannot be wed to a specific programmatic content. Better seen as a strategy, it is compatible with different forms of mobilization and governance. It is a way of doing politics which can take various forms, depending on period and place. It emerges when one aims at building a new subject of collective action – the people – capable of reconfiguring a social order lived as unfair. (Mouffe 2018)

And in a later article, Mouffe elaborated:

> A left populist strategy acknowledges that politics is a partisan activity in which affects play an important role. Drawing a political frontier between

'us' and 'them', the 'people' and the 'oligarchy', it is able at mobilizing the affective dimension that is at play in the construction of collective forms of identification. (2020)

This particular understanding of populism effectively reduces it to some sort of glorified political rhetoric. If populism can be of the left as well as of the right, one could ask, is it merely a political tool, a means of mobilising citizens? Isn't populist discourse a means of constructing or fashioning the political, and doesn't it have repercussions beyond the original mobilisation? Are there any examples of such mobilisations that can point to particular ways of understanding politics, representation, democracy and, at the end of the day, political, social and human rights?

Despite their differences, the ideational approaches and Mouffe's perspective share an understanding of populism as a political Zeitgeist that is increasingly characteristic of the current sociopolitical conjuncture, a thin ideology, a political or rhetorical style or a strategy characterised by 'people-centrism' and a binary, antagonistic representation of society and politics, that takes the concrete form of 'anti-elitism'.

But populism does at least, as Hawkins (2010) suggests, assign a binary moral dimension to political conflicts with all the implications that such antagonistic moral frameworks have as far as politics is concerned. Indeed, as I argue later, far from focusing on one issue or being an ideology with a limited bandwidth, so to speak, populism, with its binary view of politics and its aversion to pluralism and particularism, has no negligible repercussions on the visualisations of society and politics that it engenders, the notions of rights and their subjects that it supports, and the conceptualisations of democracy it is open to, regardless of its 'left' or 'right', 'authoritarian' or 'progressive', hue.

Another strand of thought suggests that populism is mainly discernible through a repertoire of organisational features. Weyland (2001:14), apart from advancing his 'populism as political strategy' perspective, locates at the centre of populism the predominance of a personalistic leader who enjoys 'direct, unmediated, uninstitutionalized support from large numbers of mostly unorganized followers'. Taggart shares this view and suggests that, as populism, in his opinion, lacks key values, it is 'particularly liable to the politics of personality' (Taggart 2000:101), while Canovan suggests that the charismatic leader adopts an essentially anti-political approach by offering a direct and unmediated form of representation unencumbered by 'institutional niceties' (Canovan 2002:34). Others, such as Roberts (2006), point out to the variety of organisational forms of populist movements and refute such interpretations. Instead of emphasising the charismatic leader, they propose a focus on patterns of political mobilisation. Jansen (2011:82) for instance identifies as populist mobilisation 'any sustained, large-scale political project that mobilises ordinarily marginalised social sectors into publicly visible and contentious political action, while articulating an anti-elite, nationalist rhetoric that valorises ordinary people'. Jansen's definition encompasses a discursive dimension – a particular rhetoric, as he calls it – as otherwise, the choice of mobilisation modes alone affects considerably the eligibility of political parties or movements widely considered as populist to be counted as such. Such an additional element can be a corrective to the tendency of considering charismatic leadership to be sufficient for a movement or organisation to be considered populist, which might lead us to confuse and conflate charisma-led organisations that would not meet other potential criteria with populist ones. Jansen's approach constitutes an attempt to go beyond a simple correlation between particular organisational aspects and populism and to integrate discourse and organisation in the study of the latter. Indeed populism – the visualisations of society upon which it rests and that it propagates – finds expression in particular configurations of mobilisation, representation and leadership, as I argue later.

Others, such as Helström (2013:9), propose an understanding of populism as style, or a way of doing politics. Helström argues that this style usually involves a charismatic leader bypassing conventional politics (party politics for example), and encouraging direct channels for popular participation. This type of perspective focuses on performative aspects of the phenomena that it brands populist, largely neglecting ideology, again not countenancing, or, at least not focusing on the possibility that populism might be central in the construction of particular frames of interpretation/institution of society and politics.

Many of the charisma-centred perspectives – both organisational and performative – also tend to be based on notions of charisma as something that 'precedes' and is external to populist politics, or rather lends itself to it. They thus fail to recognise the social construction of charisma and thus the fact that populism might engender the exceptional conditions for the construction of charisma (see Gurov and Zankina 2013), that might also enrich our understanding of the phenomenon.

Another important aspect of the current debate on populism that needs to be addressed relates to the ways its relationship to some sort of societal upheaval or crisis is theorised. A considerable body of research focuses on populism as a response to social and economic dislocation as a result of modernisation, immigration into Europe or neoliberal policies. Early work, such as that of Germani (1978) and Di Tella (1965), focus on the impact of modernisation in Latin America, while Pappas and Kriesi (2015) demonstrate notable rises in populist vote share in Central and Eastern Europe and the Mediterranean and mixed results in the north as a result of 'crises', as does Botelho (2019) in his correlation between income inequality and populist sentiment in Europe. One cannot deny that constituents of populist movements support them as a response to some external stimulus, usually a crisis. Yet the notion of crisis has remained relatively untheorised in the literature, and is often taken for granted as a 'fact' rather than being scrutinised and integrated into a theory of populism. This 'reification' of crisis underestimates, or overlooks, the possibility that it is often the perception of a crisis, or rather the construction of one, that makes mobilisation possible. Moffitt (2016:113–32) makes this point in remarking that more often than not, political crises are staged/performed by populist entrepreneurs even when such crises are, in reality, non-existent. But the connection of the social construction of crisis with populism as a political phenomenon can be traced back as early as 1978, when Stuart Hall et al., in *Policing The Crisis*, referred to a sequence of 'moral panics' around apparently non-political issues as race, law and order, permissiveness and social anarchy, which 'served to win for the authoritarian closure the gloss of populist consent' (Hall 1985). Although the term 'populism' is not expressly used in *Policing the Crisis*, the book explores the phenomenon that Hall later names 'authoritarian populism' (Hall 1980), and sees is as part of 'a fundamental shift in the modalities through which ruling blocs attempt to construct hegemony in capitalist class democracies' (Hall 1985). Hall's coupling of the concept of 'moral panic' with his notion of authoritarian populism was intended to draw attention to the construction of the crisis that made the ascendance of the New Right in the UK in the late 1970s and 1980s possible. Borrowed from Stanley Cohen's study of the creation of the Mods and Rockers as folk devils and therefore a threat to societal values and interests, moral panic refers not only to the performative, discursive, cognitive and affective modes of the construction of such a threat and of ways of coping with it, but also of the ways in which societies conceive themselves as a result of this process (see Cohen 1972:9; also Sofos 1996c). This particular theorisation of crisis in the context of moral panics casts the construction of social crises as inherent to the very essence of the moral panic, not simply as its cause: the crisis that gives rise to the moral panic and the responses to it should be understood not as distinct stages linked through causality but rather as a single yet multifaceted process.

There are clearly merits in many of the above propositions, and, more interestingly, one can discern some elements of convergence: fertile ground for synthesising elements from a diversity of propositions. Indeed, a robust, rigorous theory of populism will be marked by its multidimensionality and flexibility, and, more specifically, it will rely on identifying not only links between performative, organisational and ideological aspects, but also the ways in which each of these aspects relates to, and affects, others.

In contrast with such understandings of populism, this book will draw on an alternative conceptualisation of it as a political logic. This logic informs 'technologies' that polarise politics sharply, distinguishing between friend and enemy whose difference and interests are irreconcilable (for an outline of this approach, see Sofos 2018b). The central argument in this volume is that, in this context, populist conceptualisations of 'the people' posit it as the sole bearer of rights, at the expense of particularistic or individual rights, and, that, clearly, this has repercussions on the political process. And although I cannot disregard the prevailing argument that the appeal to a sovereign *people* in populism is in essence a democratic one, I would say that populism shares with democratic politics the demand for sovereignty of the citizenry but imagines this citizenry in a fundamentally different way (as an indivisible *people*) and, as I argue in Chapters 6 and 7, 'effectively' displaces sovereignty, or divorces it from its material dimension of empowerment.

Turning to the study of populism in Turkey, the astonishingly preponderant mobilisation of 'the popular' in politics, combined with an apparently institutionalised centre–periphery divide in Turkish political life (Aytaç and Elçi 2019:90), or a low–high divide (Baykan 2018:61–104) in a society that facilitates polarisation (Erdoğan and Uyan-Semerci 2018), has provided the opportunity for insightful work on issues of mobilisation, leadership and discourse. However, the centrality of the notion of the people in politics sometimes leads to a misreading of the ways in which the term 'the people' is deployed as a political category and gives rise to flaws in the analysis of political discourse, action and mobilisation. Following Laclau and Mouffe's (1995) and Mouffe's (2018) analyses, Tekdemir (2018) and Erdoğan et al. (2018) interestingly imply that the leaders of the secular, Islamist and leftist presidential coalitions/parties are all 'in some sense' unequivocally charismatic, or at least 'charming', although they all leave the reader in suspense as to the location and role, if any at all, of charisma in their theoretical toolkit. On the other hand, Aytaç and Elçi (2019) seem to suggest that they can discern populist parties in Turkey dating back to the 1960s largely due to the charismatic character of their leaders, while Tekdemir goes even further and argues that the Gezi urban protests could also be characterised as populist (perhaps because we have grown accustomed to disregard the insights of the literature discussed earlier on plebeian politics, which is possibly more suited to this case).

This ubiquity of populism in studies of the Turkish case brings into sharp relief the problems concerning our theorising of populism. If researchers identify virtually every expression of collective action in Turkish politics as populist, one cannot help but ask; is populism endemic in Turkish politics? Does it constitute a dominant trope of articulating interests, demands, fears and aspirations? As I have argued elsewhere (Sofos 2018b), one could argue both yes and no, depending on one's definition of populism. Turkey is indeed a challenging case that can lure researchers to the appeal of a minimal (as proposed by Mudde and Kaltwasser 2012) understanding of populism, but also to the comfort of a conceptual/terminological laxity, I would argue, that deprives the concept of the critical edge and the political utility that it should, in my opinion, have. If, following Mudde, we accept that populism is in practice a complementary ideology that 'does not so much overlap with, as diffuse itself throughout full [sic] ideologies', we may end up with a theoretical framework that renders any reference to the people as part of a binary understanding of 'the political' sufficient to qualify as populist. Similarly, as already discussed, the major alternative paradigm drawing on the work of Laclau and Mouffe (Laclau 1977; Laclau and Mouffe 1985), despite its post-Marxist psychoanalytical and post-structuralist discourse theory heritage, tends nowadays to converge with the thin ideology perspective for all intents and purposes. With these comments in mind, what would happen if we probed a little more rigorously into the *modalities* of the construction of 'the people', and then discuss which of these may be justifiably labelled 'populist'?

In contrast with such understandings of populism, I draw on an alternative conceptualisation of it as a political logic that permeates relevant technologies of construction in the political field along the lines of a binary divide. This divide is shaped by perceptions of irreconcilable difference and acute antagonism (for an outline of this approach, see Sofos 2018b). Whereas most theoretical approaches to populism tend to understand the binary logic of populism in terms of the oft-cited 'people' versus 'elite' juxtaposition, I would suggest that, although populism is indeed anti-elitist at the level of rhetoric, the true binary it institutes rests on its anti-pluralistic and anti-particularistic emphasis, which is not merely rhetorical but rather inhabits the level of tangible material political action and of governance – the terrain where actual opponents are excluded, silenced or repressed. In fact, I would go as far as to suggest that anti-elitism might often obscure the anti-institutional, anti-particularistic aspects of populism and its inherent aversion to the recognition or assertion of social diversity (see for instance Müller 2014). This distinction is not merely an 'academic' one, but has profound political implications with regards to the conceptualisation of democracy and rights in the populist imaginary.

In this context, populist conceptualisations of 'the people' and their emphasis on the 'general will' effectively posit 'the people' as the sole bearer of rights, at the expense of particularistic or individual rights and often civic liberties, and this clearly has repercussions on the political process. Populist leaderships, despite their appeals to the need to activate democracy and make 'the will of the people' heard and respected, frequently disregard the rights of dissenters – individuals or groups– as well as undermining the legitimacy and efficacy of institutions that may challenge or scrutinise that will, such as courts, other watchdogs, effective pluralistic parliaments and constitutions (see Sofos 2016). Appeals to 'the people', an entity hard to define, let alone to consult, a collectivity that 'speaks' with one voice that is hard to decipher, whose existence defies the complexity of the social and the plurality of the political, leave the door ajar for political entrepreneurs who may want to bypass institutional checks and balances in the name of the vague, as such frankly non-existent, 'popular will'. Populist democracy is averse to the need for interrogation of all groups from others which, as Giddens points out, is the condition of producing mutual respect in a pluralistic society (Giddens 2006).

Turning to the issues of organisation and mobilisation that preoccupy a significant segment of research on populism, it is important to stress that, apart from their practical implications, they have discursive repercussions, that is, they narrate/institute the putative subject that they refer to, which is 'organised' and 'mobilised'. Thus I am proposing to treat them as meaning-production features of populism. Leadership, organisation and modes of mobilisation and political action are more often than not in tune with a 'democratic' system premised on the notion of *one* indivisible 'general will', and are geared towards plebiscitary or extra-institutional forms of popular expression and rapport with the leadership of populist movements. Whereas liberal democracies can be criticised for lacking soft extra-institutional and institutional 'spaces of hearing' for the diverse voices emanating from different segments of society (Sofos and Tsagarousianou 2012:269), populist visualisations of democracy cultivate extra-institutional domains of expression of *one popular will* at the expense of institutions where social pluralism can find expression.

Seen in this context, we cannot disregard the frequent and well-documented coupling of populism with charismatic types of political leadership (see for instance Weyland 2001; Canovan 2002; Helström 2013), as charismatic leadership lends itself to the extra-institutional expression of the logic of the *one popular will* that populism rests on. But charismatic leadership is only part of a broader emphasis on modes of leadership, representation and organisation that reflect and reinforce the putative unity and homogeneity of 'the people': 'unity' of leadership of a 'unitary, indivisible people'. At the level of governance, again, apart from its practical appeal, preference for executive presidential systems or unitary leadership systems should be seen as a rejection of the 'corrupt' and 'divisive' representative character of parliamentary systems, while plebiscitary politics can serve to reduce the complexity of politics to 'us versus them' formulations and the issue of political representation to binary representations with all the homogenising implications these have with regards to 'the people' and their 'enemies'. The extra-institutional space instituted and inhabited by populist movements is one sustained through collective action, mobilisation and performance (in the sense given to the latter by Butler (1993) as the reiterative power of discourse to produce the phenomena that it regulates and constrains. Performativity is largely the avenue through which ambient anxiety mutates into indignation – a staple element of negative affect in populist movements (see Nguyen 2019) – and into a sense of crisis and trauma, and ultimately into injustice, agency and identity.

Although not all populist movements are equally durable, approaching them as thin ideologies disregards the capacity of populism, regardless of left or right hue, to reconfigure a complex social and political domain into a binary field through a multiplicity of 'abstract' yet socially effective and active significations – to draw on Castoriadis's discussion of significations and the social imaginary (1987:362) – particularly with reference to defining friend and foe, notions of rights and their legitimate bearers as well as the meaning of democracy that I discussed earlier.

As I have already hinted, populism, as a term, loses its critical edge by being defined as simply a discourse or style that interpellates the people or pits them against the elite(s), as many attempts to define it contend. Most of the different approaches discussed here, despite their apparently different emphases on discourse, rhetoric, modes of organisation, and leadership, suggest that there is an underlying logic permeating them all that visualises society, actualises democracy and frames political mobilisation in very specific ways, and is not present in all popular mobilisations.

Structure of this Volume

The argument advanced in this book is organised for the most part in chronological order given the social-historical approach adopted, with the exception of Chapter 1, which provides the space to introduce the main questions and objectives of the research and put forward the case for the suitability of Turkey for such an investigation. After a brief critical review of the relevant literature on 'the popular' and 'the populist', as well as work on these with regards to Turkey, the chapter concludes with an outline of a working definition of populism, elements of which will be drawn on during the discussion of the politics of 'the popular' and of populism in Turkey.

The first steps towards constructing a genealogy of the notion of 'the people', as the societies of Anatolia and eastern Rumelia transition from the imperial world to the era of nationalism, are taken in Chapter 2. Sketching the protracted emergence of the republican project out of the interregnum marked by the implosion of the Ottoman Empire, and the anxious search for an alternative political architecture and identity for the post-imperial era, are the main aims here, together with exploring the almost twin notions of 'the people' and 'the nation' emerging simultaneously out of the nationalist struggle and becoming key elements of discursive traditions that inform and circumscribe Turkish politics and its lived experience over the first century of the Republic.

The 'creation' of a new nation out of the Anatolian mosaic relied, for both practical and symbolic reasons, on processes of exclusion and 'othering' as much as on inculcation of the qualities required to be considered 'Turkish people'. Chapter 3 examines the desired qualities of 'the republican people' who, it is argued, far exceeded their ethnic identification and encompassed a particular civic culture that required obedience and deference. The chapter casts a closer look at the processes of legal and symbolic 'externalisation', or mechanisms of abjection, of citizens who lacked such attributes, as well as encounters with the state and its civilising mission upon the 'noble savages' of Anatolia who were deemed in need of tutelage and reform.

Chapter 4 examines the different facets of the state vis-à-vis 'the people' of the Republic and Mustafa Kemal's role in shaping the contours of politics during the one-party period. I discuss the delicate balance between the mistrust of 'the people' and the paternal figure of the state, as concretised in the benevolent, loving persona of Atatürk until his death.

The transition to a multiparty system and republican elite's confrontation with the loss of power are discussed in Chapter 5. The chapter charts how mistrust of 'the sovereign people' materialises through attempts by the armed forces and the republican elite to interrupt multiparty competition by evoking Atatürk's legacy, resulting in the creation of a tutelary democracy and the normalisation of a dual sovereignty system where 'the people' and 'the *abstract* nation', represented by the state elites, compete for primacy. The need to legitimise and normalise subsequent military interventions would eventually compromise the capabilities of the key elements of the tutelary system – the military and the judiciary. Chapter 5 examines the impasses of a system that was geared towards creating a compliant 'people' and the appropriation and transformation of the exclusive divides erected by the Kemalist state into resources for populist forms of mobilisation and politics by the conservative-Islamist counter-elites, what I call 'the populist moment'. The chapter explores the discursive, performative and representation aspects of such populist moments and their implications.

Examining Turkish politics after the 1980 coup, Chapter 6 follows the emergence of the Adalet ve Kalkınma Partisi (Justice and Development Party) under the suspicious gaze of the military and the state elites, and its strategy of neutralising their resistance to an effective outsider claiming the right to govern, but also of connecting with diverse parts of the population using the idiom of the excluded, the repressed and the downtrodden. It finally explores the particular visualisation of the subject/bearer of rights and of the sovereignty inherent in the party's discourse and practice – both cornerstones of its populism, and every populism as I suggest.

The concluding chapter (Chapter 7) identifies the defining elements of Turkey's political culture that have shaped the contours of political action and the ways in which social and political actors experience politics. The chapter explores in some detail the transformations of 'the people' in the course of 100 years of republican politics and assesses the repercussions of the populist turn in Turkish politics.

2

SITUATING 'THE PEOPLE' IN THE FOUNDATIONAL NARRATIVES OF THE EARLY TURKISH REPUBLIC

Introduction: Between Empire and Republic

The transition from the Ottoman state to the new Turkish Republic, between roughly the end of 1919 and the formal establishment of the Turkish state on 29 October 1923, was a complex process of trial and error. The nationalist officers and the bureaucratic middle class that led the process, apart from their overarching agreement on the goal of creating a modern nation state that would be free of the inertia and shortcomings of its Ottoman predecessor, were not unanimous in the detail of their vision. Even the fundamental specificities of what the new nation state would look like in its territory, population composition and identity were not clear – the key actors in the search for a post-imperial order had different views on who the people of this new state would be, and what would be the elements that would bring them together and inspire loyalty and a sense of patriotism. Identification, during this time of transition to political modernity in the former Ottoman sphere, was a fluid and quite often complex process, riddled with contradictions that would ultimately be suppressed with the ascendance of nationalism in general in the territories of the Empire, and the establishment of hegemonic nationalisms including Turkish or Arab ones in particular, in due course.[1]

This is, to be fair, not unique to the post-Ottoman space. As Billig suggests in his discussion of the imagination of nationhood (1995:74–7), contradictory themes, definitions and understandings can coexist within the same

26

experiential framework and context of continuous interaction and negotiation that makes possible, sustains and reproduces social action systems. Some of these key actors remained deliberately vague as to these details as they were aware of the enormity of the task of bringing the pieces of the linguistic, ethnic and religious mosaic of the territories of the Empire that they could salvage, and forging out of them a cohesive nation that would not be susceptible to the pull of centrifugal forces that alternative, competing nationalisms represented and, more importantly, that would be willing to fight for their new motherland. This explains the ambiguity, and even diglossia, of the leadership of the nationalist movement at a time when it seemed that the mobilising force of religion, and of identities other than the Turkish, were greater than an appeal to a clearly defined nation. Turkists were unable to erase alternatives that had preceded their movement, namely Ottomanism and Islamism, which they did not see as necessarily undermining their cause. Turkism often coexisted with them and articulated them in its own discourses. As Özkırımlı and Sofos argue, '[t]he existence of multiple options illustrates the plurality and heterogeneity of the . . . Turkish national movement' (2008:40).

Thus the post-Ottoman future that the National Movement tried to articulate was unavoidably, and often deliberately, open and fluid, with the Second Protocol of Amasya, signed between the National Movement leadership and Ali Rıza Paşa's Istanbul-based government in October 1919, referring to 'the lands inhabited by the Kurds and Turks' (Unat 1961:361). On other occasions though, such as in article 1 of the *Misak ı millî* (National Pact) of 1920, the nation is described as the 'Ottoman Muslim majority' (*Osmanlı İslam ekseriyetiyle*), residing within the Ottoman territories delineated by the Mudros Armistice. Although Turks, Kurds, Laz, Circassians and others are not mentioned explicitly, the diversity characterising this Muslim majority is implicit, as the article refers to its components respecting each other and each other's racial (*ırkiye*) and social conditions (*şerait-i muhittiye*) and status (*vaziyet*) (Yazıcı 2015:35). Far from describing a nation that was in the process of being born as homogeneous, the Pact outlines what united it in its diversity. Similarly, this diversity of the nation is depicted in the Erzurum Congress Declaration, perhaps even more explicitly so, as the Muslim majority is defined as 'all the Islamic elements (*İslami unsurları*) living in this region' connected through mutual respect and genuine 'brotherhood' – the different components of the nation are referred to as *öz kardeştirler* in the text (Yazıcı 2015:23). Such experimentations with pluralism in the definition of the nation and the concomitant references to brotherhood coexisted with timid references to the unity of this multicentric nation, perhaps presaging the future which, as I discuss later, would have little place in notions of brotherhood and mutual respect, as diversity would be deemed a threat and national unity became understood as tantamount to the creation of a monolithic Turkish nation.

The demise of Europe's large empires, including the Ottoman Empire, that had been in progress since the early nineteenth century and accelerated in the course of the Great War, and the parallel encroachment of nationalism as an organising principle not only of statehood, but also of the perception of belonging and of community, rapidly closed off what limited opportunities remained to identify as belonging to a state, religion, locality or tribe. The military and political struggle for the establishment of the Turkish Republic was marked by this transition from an imperial system, where the horizons for imagining one's place in the world were markedly different from the contours of the perception of belonging under the nascent Turkish state. The struggle was also ideological: it was a moment similar to the one that Antonio Gramsci eloquently described, referring to another moment of crisis of hegemony in 1930 in another place, when the masses were no longer firmly attached to their traditional ideologies and identifications: 'The crisis consists precisely in the fact that the old is dying and the new cannot be born; in this inter-regnum [emerge] a great variety of manifestations of anxious excess' (Gramsci 1977:311 – my, admittedly liberal, translation).[2] The interregnum between the collapse of the Ottoman order and the consolidation of the Turkish Republic was indeed a turbulent period when the stage on which the key players of the drama that would unfold 'were supposed to play their part has disinte-grated and metamorphosed into something unrecognisable, surreal, a mobile construction that shifts and changes shape under the players' feet' (Berman 1988:91–2). This was a period of anxiety that required new languages to make sense of the end of the imperial era, and during which a variety of responses were vying to become hegemonic.

In this chapter I discuss the protracted process of emergence and crystalli-sation of the republican project out of this interregnum marked by the death of the Ottoman Empire and the anxious search for an alternative political architecture and identity, and, more importantly, I draw the contours of the notions of 'the people' and 'the nation', which emerge simultaneously out of the nationalist struggle and to a large extent overlap; yet, as I suggest later, this overlap should not be taken as an indication that 'the people' and 'the nation' are identical.

This attempt at constructing a genealogy is intended to identify key elements of these notions, their discursive construction and the political operationalisation, which have become key elements of discursive traditions that inform and circumscribe Turkish politics and its lived experience over the first century of the Republic.

Bringing 'The People' Centre Stage

The army officers and state bureaucrats who undertook the state-building enterprise that culminated in the creation of modern Turkey in the second decade of the twentieth century envisioned a modern state, substantially different from its imperial predecessor that emerged moribund in the aftermath of the First World War – the Ottoman Empire. It was this difference between the *ancien regime* and the New Turkey, and the externalisation of the former – that is, its projection as alien to the experience of the people that the Republic was claiming to express – that was mobilised in the foundational narrative of their project and that informed the binary logic of republican politics, as I try to demonstrate in this chapter.

Atatürk and his associates had realised the limits of attempts by the Young Ottomans in the 1860s to build an Ottoman nationalism (Lewis 1961:152–5), as they were not accompanied by a radical transformation how the subjects of the Empire saw themselves relating to it. Mustafa Kemal and his fellow officers believed that the Ottoman Empire was unable to instil in its subjects a sense of homogeneity and national consciousness as it had lacked the radical reformist zeal of the republican elite. Indeed, as Ahmed Cevdet Paşa a prominent scholar, jurist and reformist of the Tanzimat era, reflected at the end of the nineteenth century, the efforts of a series of moderniser sultans had not gone far enough and had not borne the fruit they should have: 'But among us, if we say the word "vatan", all that will come to the mind of our soldiers is their village squares' (quoted in Lewis 1961:338).

Similarly, attempts to foster a sense of *ittihad-ı Islam* (Islamic unity) from the 1880s onwards under the purview of Abdulhamid II were unsuccessful too, as his investment in the Islamic identity of the Ottoman Empire was rather opportunistic and not matched by a commensurate investment in terms of resources, such as a centralised educational system that could have inculcated a sense of overarching Islamic patriotism among the Muslim subjects of the sultan (Hanioğlu 2002:85–6). The Ottoman nationalist experiment and its Islamic permutation were lacking a centre of gravity, a notion of a motherland (*vatan*) that Ottoman Muslims could identify with, as it had not tried to articulate local (and other particularistic) identities within a meaningful national narrative.

The republican nation-builders[3] were determined not to repeat the mistakes of their Ottoman predecessors and, at the end of the day, they could not afford to. They attributed the Empire's failure to survive to corruption and lack of vision. They dismissed it as an elitist, corrupt state that was alien and unresponsive to the people it was supposed to serve and irrelevant to their lives and aspirations. In contrast, the envisioned republican Turkey, largely inspired by the French model of state building (Mango 2005:10), was supposed to be closer to its citizens – a popular (or 'populist', as Atatürk called it) state, inspired by an emancipatory vision. In a way, while the Ottoman Empire was considered to have been a state run by a small, unaccountable and indifferent coterie of state officials, the Republic that was born out of the rubble of the imperial state was supposed to be the product of a popular revolt and the expression of the will of the people, or so the republican narrative suggested.[4]

In his famous six-day speech (*Nutuk*), which was delivered at the second congress of the Republican People's Party (CHP) in 1927 and set the tone of modern Turkish historiography, Mustafa Kemal articulated the core of this narrative by drawing attention to what he presented as the foundational injustice that fuelled and underpinned his nation-building project in the following words: '[Under Ottoman rule t]he people, left without guidance, waited in the darkness, anticipating an unknown future' (Atatürk 1981:13–14), while, in another point of his address, he reminded his audience that '[t]o silence a guiltless nation that cries out against so much injustice, oppression—even massacres—which it has been called upon to endure is a kind of tyranny to which it is impossible to submit' (Atatürk 1981:333). Overall, his speech encapsulated the trope of the betrayed people, robbed of their own future by the self-driven Ottoman elites. Indeed, one could argue that inherent in the project of republican Turkey was the promise of bringing the repressed, ignored and neglected people to the centre of statecraft, enabling them to gain a sense of direction and introducing a new model of popular governance and accountability.

Anti-colonialism, Injustice and 'The People's' Enemies

At the time when the nation state, as a political project, was taking centre stage in Europe and the rest of the world, the notion of the people as a repressed revolutionary subject was very much present in the ideology of the National Movement in ways reminiscent of the discourses of the anti-colonial struggles that would sweep the globe a little later. The anticlerical and modernising preferences of Atatürk and his entourage that brought them to a collision course with the Porte notwithstanding, a clean break from the imperial past seemed to be the option that had more chance of ensuring the viability of the state that Atatürk and his entourage envisioned. A smaller, weak Ottoman state was likely to inherit the pathologies that had led to the terminal decline of its predecessor, with a faded raison d'être, no sense of identity and little ability to mobilise its subjects to its defence, let alone towards a future course of renewal. The Ottoman Empire was fragmenting into zones under the influence of the British, French, Italians and Greeks, while within various national and ethno-linguistic groups such as the Armenians, the Arabs and even the Kurds, voices demanding a separate future in the form of a nation state, or considerable autonomy, were becoming more audible and, in many cases, more credible among large parts of the population. The struggle to avert the transformation of the Empire into a series of nominal states and protectorates under the tutelage of the victorious forces in the First World War, for the officers and intellectuals engaged in it, had already adopted the idiom of anti-imperialism. Resorting to the use of anti-colonial rhetoric already resonated among some of those whom Mustafa Kemal would later count among 'his people' as they felt neglected, betrayed and abandoned by the Ottoman government, and might overcome the collapse of the empire and endow the ensuing struggle for survival with the dynamism and purpose of a just cause.

To be sure, positing the Ottoman elites and bureaucracy in Istanbul as colonial overlords on the Ottoman periphery was by no means merely a construct of the Turkish nationalist narrative. Notions of 'Ottoman colonialism' (Deringil 2003) and 'Ottoman orientalism' (Herzog and Motika 2000; Makdisi 2002) were articulated and mobilised by the Ottoman elites to formulate a discourse of colonial difference with regard to the inhabitants of the provinces of the Empire, and framed – at least in discursive terms – the relationship between the core and the periphery of the Empire during the second half of the nineteenth century in terms of a binary divide between the civilised (*medenî*, from the Arabic *madinah*, city, and connoting urban sophistication) and the savage (*vahşî*, originally Arabic, meaning wild or savage). That was indeed the case with regards to the Anatolian Turks, to the extent that the word *Türk* (Turk) – which very few people whose language was Turkish would use as an endonym – had a pejorative connotation (Bilmez 2009:352; Kushner 1977:8–9; Lellouch 2013).

Thus, despite the prevalence of Ottoman Turkish as a language of state and of aspects of Turkish culture in Ottoman public life, in the discourse of the founders of the Republic, the fate of the Turkish people was distinct from the fate of the Empire. The Empire became 'externalised' from the Turkish nationalist narrative, relegated to an instance of alien, if not foreign, domination over the Turkish people in a long history of statehood and civilisational achievements of the Turks. The (Turkish) people of Anatolia were indeed considered as the last colonised people of the collapsing Ottoman Empire. Their alleged awakening, after the secession of their Christian counterparts in Rumeli – the European Ottoman lands – and in the wake of the British-instigated Arab revolt in the Empire's Middle Eastern provinces, was considered by the nationalist elite to have been long overdue. The externalisation and transformation in their discourse of the Ottoman Empire into a colonial regime provided a crucial 'Other' and became a pivotal means of conjuring an imagined community[5] made up of the indigenous population of Anatolia,[6] one that eventually culminated in the development of a radically different historical narrative of the Turkish nation's provenance from the one that the Ottoman Empire had been propagating. The mobilisation of localised and more widespread grievances and of the trauma of the humiliating defeat in the Great War fed narratives of political and economic exploitation and cultural

repression, and provided a framework of injustice for the 'colonised' populations to rise against as 'a people'.

In addition, the Ottoman state and its ruling Committee for Union
and Progress (CUP) lacked legitimacy prior to the Ottoman defeat owing
to its pursuit of a disastrous war. It struggled to justify the Empire's war
effort to the Ottoman people. Its legitimacy deficit was only deepened by
the Committee's harsh wartime policies, which had caused the population
hardship and suffering (Akın 2018:11–13). The loss of legitimacy of, or even,
public hostility to an organisation from which many of the nationalist cadres
had originated, and an empire that the Ottoman Turks had lost any moral
and emotional bonds with, made a break with the Ottoman past not only
possible but also desirable for the nationalist movement, as it allowed them
to dissociate themselves from their own past and enabled them to persuade
the population to accept yet another mobilisation, this time for the Turkish
War of Independence.

The republican movement, like the anti-colonial movements that would
soon spread throughout the peripheries of Europe's colonial empires, became
a theatre of nationalism and populism. The proclamation of the Turkish
Republic was thus seen and represented as the moment of the affirmation of
the will of 'the people' to pursue a course to self-determination, and of the
confirmation of its liberation from the Ottoman yoke. The Ottoman rulers,
the republican discourse suggested, had nothing to do with the people of
Anatolia; the elites of Istanbul, with their cosmopolitan attitudes and predispositions, were disingenuous and alien to the simple yet authentic culture
of the decent folk of Asia Minor. This ambient aversion towards the imperial
capital and its cosmopolitan degeneracy is made explicit in Atatürk's *Nutuk*
('speech'), where he goes to great lengths to describe in some detail the city
as a locus of conspiracy, treason and individualistic degeneracy by trying
to link any act of sedition, real or fictitious, by Armenians, Greeks, Kurds
or Muslim 'restorationists', as well as the Ottoman political elite, to the
conduct of illicit activities in Istanbul (Atatürk 1981:4–6). In a way reminiscent of the scepticism that German nationalist, romantic intellectuals
displayed towards the cosmopolitan capital of Berlin (Lees 2002:23–48) and
their juxtaposition to it of the *Völkisch*[7] ideal of the rural homeland, *Heimat*
(Blickle 2004, Eigler 2012), Istanbul was seen as a degenerate, decaying

city, culturally remote from the former provincial town and new republican capital, Ankara, in unpresumptuous Anatolia, which was indeed celebrated as the Turkish homeland. Anatolia, mainly its rural hinterland, was seen, also in ways somewhat similar to the way *Heimat* was looked upon as the locus of cultural authenticity and vibrance that was absent from the imperial urban world and, over the next few decades, it would become the cultural and territorial epicentre of key trends in the debate of how to build the post-imperial order, from the nationalist republican, to the peasantist (*köy-cülük*) (see Köymen 1934; 1939 and the contributions of his collaborators/interlocutors in the peasantist review *Ülkü*) and the Anatolianist one (expressed in contributions to the *Anadolu Mecmuası* review; also see Atabay 2002; Deren 2002 and Özkırımlı and Sofos 2008:134–5), which had a more plebeian orientation.

This juxtaposition of the authenticity of Turkishness with the degeneracy of the Ottoman Empire was rehearsed in several Republic-sanctioned history books, culminating in the four-volume *Tarih* (History), published in 1932 and supported by the Ministry of Culture. The introduction to *Tarih* unambiguously linked the Ottoman narrative with the oppression of the Turkish people and the suppression of its rich heritage. Ottoman historical narratives obliterated the Turks' name from history, the foreword said, ignoring thousands of years of pre-Islamic Turkish history. *Tarih* aimed to break the mould and to challenge the customary association of Turks with the war and destruction by shedding light on their rich history and their accomplishments (Özkırımlı and Sofos 2008:89–98). *Tarih* thus referred to the Ottoman Empire, briefly and in a disinterested way, as the weakest in a series of successful Turkish states, or the 'sick man of Europe', treating it as a foreign empire with minimal relationship to Turkishness (Ersanlı 2003:132–4). *Tarih* was one of the first historiographical resources that was written to support the idea that the Turkish people was a subjugated people, without a stake in the Ottoman Empire, and effectively to turn the gaze of republican Turkish historiography away from the historically and geographically proximate Ottoman state and cognitively and affectively relocate Anatolia to the remote steppes of Central Asia where the Anatolian Turks were told their heritage lay. Apart from the importance of the new nation moving its focus away from a defeated and bankrupt state, it was significant that the Ottoman Empire was cast as a repressive 'other', which, as I argue later, had inflicted untold suffering on the Anatolian people. A similar argument was also made emphatically in *Türk Tarihinin Anahatları*, 'The Outline of Turkish History', prepared by a number of selected members of the Türk Tarihini Tetkik Heyeti (the Society for the Study of Turkish History) in 1929–30 for school use. Although only a shorter version of the book was eventually distributed in Turkey's schools in 1931, it is interesting to note that Türk Tarihini Tetkik Heyeti proposed a distinction between the Turkish elements of the Empire, which were argued to have been a source of vitality in Ottoman history, and its Ottoman elements, which were considered responsible for the Empire's disintegration in the eighteenth and nineteenth centuries.

Part of the broader trend of anti-colonialism becoming 'one of the main forms of nationalism', as Breuilly notes (1982:156), 'anti-colonial' rhetoric was at the centre of the Turkish nationalism of the time. Indeed, the centrality of the often-noted anti-imperialist narrative in it notwithstanding, the Turkish War of Independence was effectively cast as the expression of the Turkish nation/people's anti-colonial struggle against the Empire's foreign cosmopolitan centre. In the nascent republican narrative, Ottoman Anatolia was recast as a territory hitherto dependent on Istanbul (itself cast as the centre of a colonial empire), and the people who called it home were not the dominant ethnoreligious group of the Empire but mere colonial subjects, subjected to the 'rule of colonial difference' (Chatterjee 1993) that sought and deserved emancipation in the form of the Republic. This dual anti-colonial emphasis on national liberation and popular emancipation left its imprint on the institutional architecture of the Republic and on the ideology that underpinned it – Kemalism.

The anti-imperialist/anti-colonial idiom adopted by the republican elite sustained a series of binaries that defined the people, the nation and the Republic in an oppositional relationship against their significant 'others'. Through this idiom, Atatürk and his associates identified three main 'perpetrators of injustice' against the Turkish people: foreign enemies, the (mainly) Christian minorities of the dying Empire and the Ottoman elites. Casting these as the significant 'others' who deprived the Turkish people of its voice, inside and outside the Empire, of its 'rightful' position among modern nations, and, thus, setting them in opposition to the latter, constituted a key building block in the construction of modern Turkey as a nation that had suffered a grave injustice.

The foreign enemies included the allies that emerged victorious at the end of the war and their proxies – namely Greece on the Western Front, and Russian-backed Armenian forces in the eastern part of Anatolia. France and Italy were deploying forces in the south and southwest respectively, and the United Kingdom mainly in the Straits region (Morris and Ze'evi 2019:266), while the latter three entered the imperial capital, Istanbul, on 13 November 1918 and occupied it until 4 October 1923. The occupation of the capital by the European allies had profound repercussions in the collective psyche of the Muslim populations of the Empire as it marked a break in the Ottoman possession of the city after centuries of continuous presence there. The nationalist movement (and, later, the Republic) ensured that the experience took the form of a collective trauma (cf Alexander et al. 2004, Demertzis 2020) and that '[o]ccupied Istanbul functioned as the setting for the emergence of the modern Turkish subject and became a defining crisis' (Göknar 2014:321–2). After the virtual collapse of the Ottoman Empire, they had pursued the dismemberment of its territories. The designs of these forces became a focal point for an array of 'national defence' or 'national rights' committees – comprising CUP branch secretaries, army officers and educators, among others, who eventually joined together under the banner of the Society for the Defense of National Rights and formed the National Movement, which opposed the dismantling of the Empire and the relegation of its Muslim, mainly (though not exclusively) Turkish-speaking populations into the subjects of protectorates, and of occupied and alien territories.

The effective acceptance of the British occupation of Istanbul by the Ottoman government of Damad Ferid Paşa, himself an Anglophile, was cast by the National Movement as an unforgivable act of treason, an alliance with foreign enemies in order to execute a 'death sentence' on the Ottoman state. Nationalist newspapers depicted Damat Ferit as 'the most hated "ominous" figure' and criticised 'his arbitrariness (*keyfiyet*)' and his failure to protect the citizens and the nation (Turnaoğlu 2017:220).

'Already in March 1919, two months before the Greek landing, there was a sense of impending insurrection', say Morris and Ze'evi, adding that '[a]nti-Christian and Nationalist revolutionary propaganda were rampant, and CUP veterans mobilised manpower and amassed weapons' (2019:272). The conditions were in place for the National Movement to designate itself as a struggle against an imperialist intervention. As Morris and Ze'evi point out, as early as in October–November 1918, CUP veterans were preparing for a protracted guerrilla struggle against possible Allied occupation. They amassed ammunition and reconstructed the armed bands that had been active against the Armenian and Greek communities during the war (2019:272).

As Atatürk himself repeatedly reminded interlocutors and audiences, the struggle of the National Movement was a struggle against 'a great injustice' to the Turkish people as these foreign enemies did not acknowledge the Turkish people's right to sovereignty and self-determination as they had done in the case of the Christian populations of the Empire. The victorious European forces, according to this narrative, were unwilling to recognise the nobility and generosity of the Turkish people and their right to statehood and to belonging in the family of modern nations. Fusing economic grievances with ethnic and religious suspicion, nationalist discourse represented the Empire's Christian minorities, especially the Ottoman Greeks and Armenians, as untrustworthy usurers, cheats and exploiters of simple, decent Muslims (Clark 2006:237); linking them with the foreign forces that had designs on Anatolian territory, it represented them as disloyal collaborators. The Empire's Christians were accused by the nationalist and republican elites of having betrayed their Ottoman homeland and their Muslim neighbours and were identified as perpetrators of acts of savagery and injustice against the nation. Given the chaotic and protracted disintegration of the Ottoman Empire, and the unwitting or deliberate collusion of the its Christian communities with the European powers engaged in the division of the Ottoman territories, the republican elite could mobilise the negative feelings of the Ottoman Anatolian Muslims towards non-Muslims in general, and the Christian minorities in particular, where tensions and mistrust had already got hold. Such was the mistrust of the local Muslim population of their Christian neighbours that the American missionary James Barton, after touring Anatolia as early as in 1919, remarked:

Xenophobia burgeoned, mixing hatred for the Allied Powers with hatred for Christians in general. Among most Turks there was no 'spirit of regret, much less of repentance at what had taken place, . . . The spirit of race hatred . . . is everywhere dominant. [The local Christians are] 'in danger of extermination.' (quoted in Morris and Ze'evi 2019:269)

Similarly Kazim Karabekir, commander of the Nationalist forces in Eastern Anatolia, emphasised the importance of anti-minority propaganda by writing in his memoirs that he had 'immunised' the Kurds against Kurdish nationalism by publicising that those advocating Kurdish statehood wanted to 'turn Kurdistan into Armenia' (1990:113), implying that the Armenians had designs on the lands of the Kurds, and suggesting that Kurdish loyalty to the Turkish nationalist project would avert an Armenian takeover of the eastern provinces, as did Mustafa Kemal, in his address to the Sivas Congress in September 1919, where, in order to mobilise the delegates in the face of an imminent and extreme danger, he claimed that the Armenians were 'preparing to expand their borders up to Kızılırmak' and had 'already initiated a massacre policy' (Aşkun 1945:114), thus stressing not only that the Armenians were untrustworthy neighbours, but also that their claims to Anatolian territory were pursued through mass killings of the delegates' co-nationals.

In the few areas where local conditions had not fostered such animosities, such as in the eastern Black Sea region where, as Clark suggests 'intricate, and sometimes hidden forms of symbiosis between Christian and Muslim, Greek and Turk' had a long history (2006:110) and coexistence was more possible, the limits of the injustice rhetoric that had been more easily received elsewhere were tested and had to be overcome with intense propaganda, or, where that failed, the elimination of those who sustained alternative memories and promoted different modes of interaction. The manifesto of the Erzurum Congress of the Vilayets of Eastern Anatolia, convened in August 1919 in order to maximise the support of local Muslims in Eastern Anatolia, alleged that Turks and, more generally, Muslims were the victims of violence perpetrated by Greeks and Armenians and mentioned massacres perpetrated by the latter, inviting the Muslim population to protect the integrity of Turkey, the sultanate and the caliphate (UKNA FO 371 / 4158) Meanwhile Morris and Ze'evi note the intense effort by local nationalists to turn local Muslims against Christian minorities as early as in 1919, before the Turkish nationalist movement had flexed its muscles, and quote a British control officer, based in

Izmit, reporting that CUP agitators 'poison[ed] the minds of a considerable portion of the common people' (2019:272). But these tactics did not always yield the desired results. For instance, the Black Sea coastal city of Trebizond (Trabzon) proved to be resistant to such calls for open animosity against its Christian inhabitants. Far from being tension-free – Trabzon was one of the early Turkish nationalist movement strongholds – the unwillingness of its local representatives 'to bow to Kemal's authority' and the town's residents where discontent with the Kemalist leadership was curbed by a series of disappearances of local notables and murders carried out by Topal Osman, a gang leader loyal to Atatürk (Clark 2006:113).

The Anatolian Christians were not only posited as the new nation's 'other', but also represented as treasonous and ungrateful, and ultimately untrustworthy. During the 1921 constitution debates in the Grand National Assembly, Mahmut Esat (Bozkurt) accused the Christians of being the instruments of foreign powers and effectively excluded them from 'the people' and citizenry:

> They have abdicated from citizenship of this country, . . . due to their betrayal and because they drew a gun [against their Turkish neighbours]. They are the selfish children of Ottoman history and they do not have rights anymore in this country . . . they are the spies of the imperialists and they are the treacherous offspring of this land . . . (TBMMZC, 18.11.1920:437)

The success of the discourse that posited the minorities as perpetrators of injustice and as ungrateful neighbours relied on cases where some of the minority communities had themselves been subjected to acts of violence and savagery being forgotten. It is telling to note instances when local Muslim narratives omitted events such as the Armenian genocide or more localised acts of communal violence that might have countered narratives of disloyalty and ingratitude. Ulgen's examination of Mustafa Kemal's political documents and speeches (2010) documents his systematic effort to reproduce both the myth of 'murderous Armenians' and that of the Turks as an 'oppressed nation' (*mazlum millet*), monumentalising both in official Turkish historiography, notes the stark difference in the rhetoric he deployed in depicting Armenian and Turkish atrocities and hence between Armenians and Turks, and suggests that this discursive regime and its authority in the course of republican history is central to the resilience of Turkish denialism. Interestingly, whereas in 1918, the Ottoman parliament annulled the deportation decree of 27 May 1915 and the confiscation law of 27 September 1915, which had sanctioned the appropriation of Armenian property, the Grand National Assembly of Turkey reinstated both decrees as law on 14 September 1922, thus effectively annulling the small steps taken towards some degree of restitution (Akçam 2006:281) and reinstating measures the CUP had taken to cleanse the territories that experienced the genocide.

Finally, according to the narrative of injustice, the Ottoman elites, blinded by their narrow self-interest, collaborated with foreign forces to partition the Ottoman state and keep the Turkish people politically dispossessed and subjugated. It is in this context that Mustafa Kemal extended an accusation against not only the last sultan, but all Ottoman sultans – 'a bunch of madmen', 'moronic and ignorant' 'animals' (Atatürk 1981:21, 319, 321), whose personal rule (*saltanat- i ferdiye*) served only themselves and was indifferent to the people and the nation, whose right to rule (*saltanat- ı milliye*) they had allegedly usurped.

Most of the disgruntled officers and intellectuals who participated in the National Movement shared a distaste for and mistrust of the sultan's advisors, who alleged that they were keeping him isolated and out of touch, unable to gauge the anxiety, insecurity and anger at the disintegration of the Empire and Anatolia's occupation by foreign forces, while some, including Mustafa Kemal, attributed blame to Sultan Mehmed VI himself for his determination to retain his privileges at any cost. Atatürk repeatedly emphasised the 'unworthiness' of the sultan and his entourage on the grounds of their 'betrayal' and 'lack of loyalty' to the emerging nation. In 1927, as the republican project was gaining international recognition, and as the Turkish army had quashed the Şeyh Said rebellion[8] in the southeast of the country and the ambition to reinstate the caliphate (under Mehmed VI) that it expressed, Atatürk expressly posited the Turkish nation and people in opposition to the former sultan and his entourage in his address at the second congress of the CHP:

If the question should arise as to whether we ought to remain loyal and true to the present Caliph and Sultan – well, this man is a traitor, he is a tool of the enemy employed against our country and our nation. If the nation considers him in the light of Caliph and Sultan, it would be obliged to obey his orders and thereby realize the enemy's plans and designs. Moreover, a personage who would be a traitor and could be prevented from exercising his authority and making use of the power bestowed upon him by his position could not hold the exalted title of Caliph or Sultan . . . How could it be deemed permissible that the crowd of mad men, united by neither a moral nor a spiritual bond to the country or the nation as a whole, could still be trusted to protect the independence and the dignity of the nation and the state. (Atatürk 1981)

This feeling was also echoed by İsmet Paşa (İnönü) in his address at the same congress:

As statesmen, we ought never to forget that the armies of the caliph have laid this country in ruins from one end to the other . . . It is to the army of the caliphate the Turkish nation owes its most cruel sufferings. It will no longer allow this to happen. We shall never forget that it was a Fetva of the Caliph which threw us into the horror of the general war. We shall never forget that when the nation wanted to rise, a Fetva of the Caliph provoked against us a still more terrible assault than that of the enemy. (Atatürk 1981)

The deployment of this divisive discourse between friend and foe was used, not only as a means to legitimise the independence movement and the course of action it chose, but also to delegitimise opponents of the leadership even within the independence camp, as well as to justify punishment of communities and groups that resisted the movement on the ground. Conversely as Turnaoğlu suggests, 'a sharp line was drawn between proponents as friends, patriots, and supporters of the national cause and their good and moral virtues, and opponents as ruthless and cruel enemies' was drawn (2017:208).

Examining such efforts to identify perpetrators of injustice against 'the Turkish people' through the prism of Gamson's work on contentious politics (1992) and, in particular, as an instance of the process he calls framing – a collective process of making sense of particular events deployed by participants in collective action and broader 'audiences', I would argue that locating these significant 'others' and highlighting the ways in which they betrayed and harmed 'the people' of the new Republic constituted effectively a meaning-creation process.[9] The mobilisation of the emotions of those addressed by the republican narrative as 'the people' and the articulation of these emotions into specific cognitive schemata relying on the production of a sense of injustice and moral indignation, was crucial in the formation of a political consciousness that would make possible the engagement of 'this people' in the nationalist struggle and the nation-building effort. It constituted the catalyst that turned a sense of indignation and hurt into a discourse of injustice (cf. Gamson 2011). The sense of injustice and the 'cultural trauma' (cf Alexander et al. 2004) that it entailed drew together the 'multiplex strands of violence, risk and threat afflicting people's everyday lives' that Bowman discusses in his exploration of the role of the experience of violence in identity constitution (2003:320), to mobilise those who perceived themselves as affected. It made possible the imagination of a 'we', of all those who shared its experience, thus giving rise to a sense of agency, which in turn enabled actors to deny the immutability of some undesirable situation (see Gamson 1995:90). The injustice of the war, of the hardship and dislocation it caused – physical as well as emotional – was crucial in setting in motion the processes of reinterpretation of the past and of 'narrating the new foundations' (Hale 1998:6). Mustafa Kemal and his entourage considered reconstituting or reconfiguring 'the Turkish people' as the collective identity of choice as the cornerstone of their project.

As Gamson points out, 'the process of defining this "we", typically in opposition to some "they" who have different interests or values' (1995:99) is a crucial aspect of such framing processes. In a way, the moment when grievances are galvanised into action and eventually translated into identity, and people take it upon themselves to 'transcend the terms and conditions of their daily lives and behave as collective agents who can change them' (Gamson 2011:260), was the moment of the articulation and dissemination of this grave injustice to the Turkish nation by its enemies and of the creation of the National Movement. Framing the localised and diverse feelings of unease in different parts of Anatolia as manifestations of a national existential anxiety, creating the conditions where the experiences of Anatolian Muslim communities could become translatable and resonate with those of other

Muslims in what would become the core of the nation, was crucial in the process of constructing this nation and mobilising (not necessarily and strictly in that order).[10]

It is this framing process and its localisation that can partly elucidate the identity politics inherent in the republican project. The apparent paradox of effectively interpellating a people, or a nation that did not yet quite exist, attempting to make them proud of a national endonym that these people considered pejorative and did not quite identify with, was not a paradox after all.[11] It was the framing as a collective experience the volatility and confusion prevailing in Anatolia at the time, the famine and destruction brought by a long war and the collapse of the state. It was the product of injustice inflicted on Anatolian Muslims, because they were Anatolian and because their Anatolian-ness made them all Turks, that could account for the strategy of the National Movement and its progressive shift in nomenclature and rhetoric, from one that emphasised local rootedness and religious affiliation to one that had Turkishness as its epicentre. What made a Turk precisely a Turk was, in the long term, their acceptance of the republican narrative of the collective trauma and their recognition that their anxiety and suffering at that given time in that given location made them Turks.

Indeed, this combination of a sense of injustice with its localisation in Anatolia were already present years before the proclamation of the Republic, at the time of the articulation of the *Misak ı millî* (National Pact) by nationalist members of the Salvation of the Fatherland (Felâh-ı Vatan) group in the very last session of the Ottoman parliament in 1920, which envisaged the Anatolian peninsula as 'the homeland', the non-negotiable territory of the state – that had not yet come into being – of a people that was still to be named and was designated merely as the indivisible Ottoman-Muslim majority of the land.[12]

To the question 'who are "the people"? or who is a Turk?', the answer was both complex and simple as, apart from the fast dwindling in numbers Christian minorities (whose very religion, however nominal, constituted a prohibitive line that could not be crossed), the people were not 'of this time'; they did not exist but were 'to become'. İsmet İnönü, the first prime minister of the Republic, articulated these essentially binary underpinnings of republican logic, stressing the mix of Turkification and the exclusion of those 'not worthy' that underlay the policies of the Turkish state in the immediate aftermath of the Şeyh Said rebellion of 1925:

> We are openly nationalists . . . and nationalism is our only source of unity. Other elements have no power over the Turkish majority. Our duty is to make Turkish those who are not Turkish in this country. We will get rid of those who challenge the Turks and Turkishness. The first and foremost thing we require in those who will serve this country is Turkishness. (Üstel 1997:173)

This excerpt from İnönü's address to the participants in the second congress of the Turkish Hearths[13] laid out what had been, and would continue being, a key strategy of his government and of the broader nationalist movement of which the Turkish Hearths were a component. The transformation of those citizens of the Republic who were open to being convinced into Turks was essential for their recognition as members of 'the Turkish people'. And those citizens who were reluctant to embrace Turkishness were effectively expendable and certainly undesirable.

Interestingly, in his speech, İnönü relegates the entire 'people' who were supposed to be the source of power and sovereignty of the Republic to an inferior position, as he suggests that they are subservient to country and nation, therefore introducing a further duality in the way of visualising the people and the nation that is worth noting as it goes against the grain of the assumption that the two are coterminous. In contrast with those who were building Turkey, however imperfect they were, the nation was defined as a transcendental subject with its own logic and interests that exceeded those of the actual Turkish people. The latter were imperfect and had to be moulded into the image of the nation. They were expected to serve the Turkish nation, and in order to be worthy of this privilege they were supposed to become Turks.

Six years later, Mustafa Kemal, in a speech he made in 1931, stressed the need for the Turkification process to continue and advocated the conditional inclusion of Turkish citizens in the nation, rationalising it on the grounds of trust:

> If someone who does not speak Turkish claims to belong to Turkish culture and society, it would not be right to believe her/him . . . In the event of a national crisis, these people might cooperate with people who speak other

languages and act against us. The main duty of our Turkish Hearths is to make these people – who are in fact Turkish citizens; our destinies, today and in the future, are the same – real Turks speaking our language (Üstel 1997:366).

'The sovereign people', who would be at the helm of republican Turkey, were imperfect, and this imperfection was a thorn in the eye of the republican elite that needed to be removed in the course of its nation-building project.

A Populist State without 'A People'

In line with the nationalist leadership's assertion that the successor state to the Ottoman Empire would be markedly different from its effectively undemocratic and illegitimate predecessor, the new state was supposed to be republican.[14] This was as much a practical as an ideological choice. The elimination of the monarchy would have a more final character if the new state was premised on a new system of governance that was not associated with the imperial one: no dynasty, but an elected presidency and popular legitimacy that demonstrable by regular approval (at least in principle) of the government by the citizens. Atatürk had made clear his pragmatic reservations to any constitutional arrangement that would imply some sort of continuity with the Ottoman state in his *Nutuk*:

> If you want to say let us depose him [the sultan] and choose someone else in his place, this would not lead to a way out of the difficulty, because the present state of affairs in the conditions prevailing at this hour would not allow of it being done. For the person who must be dethroned is not in the midst of his nation but in the hands of the enemy, and if we intended to ignore his existence and recognise someone in his stead, the present Caliph and Sultan would not surrender his rights, but would retain the seat he occupies today with his Ministry in Istanbul and would continue to carry on his office. Will the nation and the High Assembly in such an event abandon their high aims and throw themselves into a fight for a caliph? (Atatürk 1981:574)

From an ideological perspective, the nationalist movement had already mobilised the principle of self-governance and the sovereignty of 'the people' in its struggle to retain and recapture much of what it considered the Anatolian territory of the nation, and had claimed the moral high ground over the sultan and his government precisely because it was claiming that in a post-imperial future sovereignty should lie with 'the people'. Thus, the state that was to emerge from the independence war aimed to replace the elitist Ottoman social order, which invested power in the sultan and his immediate entourage, with a more broadly based republican system resting on popular sovereignty – deposing the sultan, and later abolishing the caliphate, were not ends in themselves but a means of bringing the people closer to the centres of exercise of power. The principle of republicanism (*cumhuriyetçilik*) provided a vision of a polity that would replace the elitist Ottoman social order.

What is more, the state was supposed to be inspired by what Atatürk later called 'populism' (*halkçılık*) – promising a more egalitarian society attentive to the needs and aspirations of the grassroots. Populism in the republican ideology addressed 'the people' as an active subject that would build the Republic, and recognised it as the locus of legitimacy and sovereignty as well as the focus of the new state's efforts and energies. Atatürk's articulation of the foundational myth of the Turkish Republic, as already seen, partially hinged on an essentially anti-colonial promise: 'the Turkish people' had not been listened to, and had no bonds with the Ottoman political class, which behaved selfishly and with no empathy for the plight of the Anatolian peasant who had to endure war and poverty and was held captive to superstition and backwardness. Thus, the republican project would be based on an antagonistic relationship between 'the (Turkish) people' of the Anatolian homeland and the Ottoman elites that repressed and exploited it. The New Turkey emerging at the end of the First World War was thus one that would draw its legitimacy from 'the people' that had been previously shunned by the imperial elites, and would be premised on its energy, resolve and sacrifices. Indicative of this dimension are Mustafa Kemal's own public statements and speeches. In his Kastamonu speech on 30 August 1925, for example, he delegitimises the sultan's claims to lead the nation, which ultimately, as Atatürk says, belongs to 'the people':

> Would it be permissible to let a Sultan be head of this sovereign nation [*millet*] which belongs to the people? Dear siblings, would it be right for this perceptive nation to give place to those careless, ignorant hypocrites who under the name of the Caliph, claim to be the shadow of Allah and the

representative of the Prophet, in our fatherland or in our conscience, I ask you? (quoted in Nereid 2011:712)

It is true that the principle of *halkçılık* has been insufficiently defined by Mustafa Kemal and his political collaborators and, as a result, it has proved one of the most malleable and vague concepts in the political project encapsulated in the six fundamental pillars of Kemalism (see Akurel 1984; Arar 1963; Tanyol 1984; Tekeli 1978).

Mustafa Kemal stressed the egalitarian spirit of the idea of populism and its political implications:

in our view, farmers, shepherds, workers, merchants, craftsmen, soldiers, doctors; in any social establishment, the rights, interests and liberties of an active citizen are equal. It is possible with the administration of the people's government in the sense that we understand.

Halkçılık, in this instance, has two important dimensions. The first is the essentially democratic promise of a government of the people and by the people, but not necessarily the promise of a formal democracy in the sense of parliamentarianism or some other form of liberal democracy despite the contention of left-wing Kemalists, like Ataöv, that Kemalism's ultimate aim was a democracy with a populist dimension (1981:29–30). The second is the recognition that the people is characterised by a form of radical equality that negates diversity and difference within its ranks. 'The people', therefore, can be a reliable element of the republican political configuration as long as it retains its unity, understood as unity of purpose and lack of particularistic and individualistic considerations and interests.

This duality is evident in the Republican People's Party Programme (1935), where populism is defined in both these senses:

[populism encapsulates] the source of the will and sovereignty is the nation ... It is one of our main principles to consider the people of the Turkish Republic, not as composed of different classes, but as a community divided into various professions according to the requirements of the division of labour for the individual and social life of the Turkish people. The aims of our party (. . .) are to secure social order and solidarity instead of class conflict, and to establish harmony of interests. (CHP 1935:7–9)

Populism, therefore, was democratic to the extent that it encapsulated a solidaristic vision and an egalitarian commitment to the abolition of privilege and status differentials, while more practically, it constituted a means of investing the regime with legitimacy, as I argue in Chapter 5.

Over time, the content of this principle evolved through further clarification by Atatürk himself and his collaborators, and as a result of practical decisions and practice on the ground, and began to acquire a specificity that revealed a number of inherent contradictions in its operationalisation. First, the egalitarianism inherent in the principle of populism was circumscribed and informed by three other key pillars of Kemalism: nationalism, secularism and revolutionism. Nationalism (*milliyetçilik*) put a dent in the egalitarian promises of the founders of the Republic by defining as stakeholders and beneficiaries of the new state only those whom the state itself identified ethnically as Turks. 'The people' was understood restrictively in ethnonational terms, and became coterminous with the Turkish nation, or rather, those who considered themselves to be Turks. Nevertheless, to complicate the situation, not everybody could count themselves among the 'worthy', and the promise of radical equality was restricted to those who were recognised as Turks and, in addition, shared the ideals of the Republic. Mustafa Kemal Atatürk, in *Nutuk*, made it clear that 'the people' whose 'representatives' he was addressing at the General Congress of the Republican People's Party in 1927 had been betrayed by many 'enemies', who had thus forfeited the right to count themselves among the people even though they were formally citizens of the Republic. These included the Christian minorities, who had acted selfishly and brought about the collapse of the (Ottoman) state that they shared with the Turkish people and eventually colluded in the oppression of the latter by foreign forces, but also an assortment of people who would meet the ethnic criteria of Turkishness but would not subscribe to the political tenets of the Republic as outlined in *Nutuk* (Atatürk 1981:7–8) and determined in practice over the past decade.

Even in the early years of the Republic practical steps were taken to demarcate 'worthiness' and ultimately membership of 'the people' that could call the emerging Turkey home. Various researchers suggest that the distinction between 'Turkish citizens' and 'Turks' in the Republic that became evident early on, beyond its descriptive value, acquired more concrete exclusive dimensions. (Aktar 2000:119–24; Çağaptay 2006:69–70; Parla 1995:25–32). Non-Muslims – despite the secular character of republican Turkey, Islam was used as a defining element of Turkishness – were excluded from public service, first de facto, then legally, with the Civil Servant Law of March 1926 stating 'being Turk' (and not 'being Turkish citizen') as one of the preconditions for becoming a civil servant. Another law enacted in July 1932 extended these prohibitions beyond the public realm. The fifth article of this law stipulated that foreigners were obliged to leave a number of designated occupations within six months after the publication of the law in the official gazette (Aktar 2000:119–24; Çağaptay 2006:69–70; Özkırımlı and Sofos 2008:165–6). Similarly the conditions of admission to public schools and state bureaucracy often included references to nationality or race and descent. The last two categories included notices relating to the selection of students for study abroad, recruitment of teachers to secondary schools and admission to military schools and the police force (Aslan 2007:245–72; Bali 1999:410–11; 2008; Özkırımlı and Sofos 2008:166; Yıldız 2001:283–4), while a broader Turkification movement that peaked with the notorious 'Vatandaş, Türkçe Konuş' (Citizen, Speak Turkish) campaign of the 1930s that terrorised bilingual or non-Turkish-speaking citizens into refraining from using languages other than Turkish in public, confirmed the centrality of Turkishness in the republican state- and nation-building project (İnce 2012:59–63).

As the Republic started taking shape, especially after the Şeyh Said rebellion of 1925, which mobilised tribal and Kurdish identity in an attempt to restore the caliphate,[15] the belief among the independence war leadership that Islam could be instrumentalised as a means of overcoming ethnic divides between 'Turks' and 'Kurds' was eroded and Turkishness was transformed from a latent element of the republican vision into its dominant component.

Indeed, the realisation that many Kurds felt alienated from the republican project and had become attracted to an alternative, Kurdish, nationalism was shocking to many in the republican administration and prompted an about-turn. Characteristically, the Minister of Interior Affairs at the time, Şükrü Kaya, expressed this new mood by pointing out the futility

[of] trying to tame this mountainous and virile people by wiping out their leaders, burning their villages and closing the passes leading to their grazing

grounds in the hope that once more the problem of a dissentient minority could be resolved. (UKNA FO 424 / 268 / E129)

This marginalisation of the Kurds in the post-Ottoman nationalist imagination meant that it was going to be a matter of time until the original mentions of the will of the *osmanlı-Islam ekseriyet* – the Ottoman-Muslim majority – in the *Misak ı Millî* (National Pact) of 1920 would be replaced by references, in speeches and documents, to the Turkish nation and its struggle for self-determination. This shift was confirmed in *Nutuk*, where Atatürk recast the character of the National Pact from an attempt to salvage Ottoman territories and preserve the Ottoman state by its Ottoman-Muslim communities, as it was hitherto represented, into an explicitly Turkish struggle by 'the Turkish people' to create the Turkish Republic (Adak 2003:516). There was no discursive space for an alternative way of imagining the emerging nation, especially one where Islam would play the defining role.

Secularism: The Impassable Route from the Anatolian Masses to 'The Sovereign People'

The pillar of secularism constituted a key aspect of the radical overhaul of the Ottoman system, particularly subsuming the power of religion to that of the state and harnessing it to render it an aspect of Turkishness (Özkırımlı and Sofos 2008). At first sight, secularism was the product of the belief of several members of the republican elite that if Turkey aspired to take its place among the modern nations of its time it had to cut its ties with the regressive elements of religion – what they considered to be the superstition and backwardness of the non-rational thinking it promoted. Such an assumption would be incomplete if one did not situate the principle of secularism in the competition between the National Movement and the Istanbul government under the Porte since 1919 and the gradual realisation in that context that religion provided a significant power base for the sultan and could become a source of political capital for potential contenders. On the other hand, Mustafa Kemal and his supporters could not ignore the fact that it was Anatolian Muslims – not Christian minorities – who were most likely to constitute the raw material for the new nation, and thus Islam needed to be mobilised to this end. Echoing the processes of nation building in the Balkan ethno-sectarian states that had seceded from the Empire, where Christian affiliation became a marker of majority ethnic identity, Turkish nationalists made Islam a marker for Turkishness. This contributed to the early National Movement casting itself as a movement of Anatolian and Rumelian Muslims and not as the expression of Turkish national aspirations, which remained implicit, as I argue later – so much so that Atatürk circulated a number of proclamations on 21 April 1920, stating that the Grand National Assembly would open in two days' time and undertake 'such vital duties of the utmost importance as saving the independence of the country and the exalted post of the Caliphate and the Sultanate'; and on 25 April 1920, including the supplication for God's mercy and for success for whoever worked to save the caliph, the sultan, the nation and the country (Satan 1985:115–16). In addition, the Republican People's Party (Yüksek Seçim Kurulu Milletvekili Genel Seçimleri Arşivi, RPP) had adopted a nine-point platform for the electoral campaigns of its members as late as in 1923, a few months prior to the abolition of the caliphate, including a pledge that the Turkish Grand National Assembly would 'support the office of the Caliphate which is an exalted office among Muslims' (in Tunçay 1989:355). This maintenance of a delicate balance between maintaining an Islamic dimension and opting for a secular nationalist course led to the eventual decision to abolish the caliphate, and thus to sever the National Movement's links with traditional Islamic authority. The decision brought considerable anxiety to republican officials and supporters of a Muslim modernist solution – many of whom, as Zürcher points out, saw the office of the Ottoman Caliphate as a possible counterweight to the growing personal power of President Mustafa Kemal (2017:398), and necessitated resorting to pre-emptive measures, such as the passage and execution of the 1923 High Treason Law, as 'a precautionary measure to contain domestic opposition', and managing the flow of news on worldwide Muslim reactions to the abolition (Hassan 2011:157).

But, apart from the rupture signalled by the abolition of the caliphate over the longer term, the distancing of the republican elite from Islam took the form of a gradual shift.

Secularism in this context, and from the mid-1920s onwards, served largely as a boundary-drawing mechanism demarcating Turkishness, giving a specific meaning to the National Movement and excluding alternative interpretations of it. Having said that, secularism still retained its pragmatic utility and continued to serve as a means to both restrict the influence of religion and at the same time harness it and mobilise it. As my earlier discussion of nationalism has suggested, secularism did not eradicate the role that Islam played in conceptualisations of Turkishness; indeed Islam provided a means of integration for Muslims of non-Turkish origin into the Turkish nation and a boundary that excluded non-Muslim citizens from effective membership in it.

Interestingly, the centrality of secularism in the republican ideological and institutional architecture, and its use as a tool for creating 'the sovereign people' of the new state and instilling into it the appropriate national consciousness, had another paradoxical dimension. Whereas secularism was seen as a means of freeing the nation from the irrationality and superstition that the nation-builders deemed to be inherent in religion, it carried with it a mistrust of those the regime would interpellate as 'the people'. Indeed, even after purging 'the people' from ethnic 'others', the population of Anatolia remained, to a large extent, religious, tied to traditional religious authority, and, some at least, maintained affinities with the institution of the Caliphate and Abdülmecid II, the last Ottoman caliph. As Mango points out in his biography of Atatürk, such was the affection for the Caliphate and religious authority at the time of the independence war that many Anatolian Muslims indeed misread Atatürk's ascendance as a development that would restore the Caliphate's authority, and cheered: 'We are returning to the days of the first caliphs' (Mango 1999:394). Whereas this ambiguity was useful to the republican leadership, and was indeed instrumental in securing legitimacy and support during the crucial years when the republican movement and its leadership strove to consolidate their gains, it was ultimately unsustainable in the longer term, as the Şeyh Said revolt of 1925 made clear. Şeyh Said, a supporter of retaining the caliph's religious authority but also a regime opponent with influence in republican Turkey's Kurdish-populated areas (Olson 1989), drew upon a widespread popular bond with the idea of the Caliphate, tribal networks and a nascent Kurdish identity among the local population that appears to have alarmed the republican government and to have given particular shape to the principle of secularism from that moment on. Apart from punitive measures taken to suppress the Kurdish character of the rebellion,[16] the government moved to disband the relatively short-lived Progressive Republican Party (Terakkiperver Cumhuriyet Fırkası, TCF), which had provided a forum for opponents of the abolition of the caliphate. All TCF offices were closed down, and a decree signed by Mustafa Kemal, İsmet İnönü and other cabinet ministers ordered the disbandment of the party on 3 June 1925 (Özoğlu 2009).

According to the decree:

> [A] number of persons holding official functions within the Progressive Republican Party in the Istanbul area have used the principle of respect for religious opinions and beliefs, included in the party's program, as a means to deceive public opinion and to stimulate religious incitement . . . Official representatives of the Progressive Republican Party have used the principle of respect for religious ideas and beliefs, included in the party program, as a means to gain support for the propaganda of reactionaries who pretend to save the country from atheists and that this has led to many serious incidents during the manifestations of the latest [Şeyh Said] insurrection. [. . .] Under these circumstances, it is impossible to allow a movement aimed at the use of religion for political purposes to exist. (Özoğlu 2009:206)

The rationale that the TCF was 'manipulating religion for the purpose of gaining political power and registering members based on the claim that their party respected religion while the government party did not' (Özoğlu 2009:114) reveals the scope and emphasis of republican secularism from that moment on. Atatürk further tightened his grip on power in 1926 when an alleged plot to assassinate him was uncovered in Izmir, leading to a sweeping investigation that not only incriminated former TCF leaders and cadres but was also used to suppress other dissident activists (Zürcher 2004:207).

The realisation that national sovereignty, as expressed in the form of Atatürk's reign and reform blueprint, on the one hand, and Islamic authority on the other, were incongruent prompted a more aggressive attempt to undermine the hold of religion over society through an onslaught on religious institutions, practices and symbols. Islam, seen as a link with the Ottoman past, a past from which the Republican elites were trying to dissociate themselves, had to be symbolically downgraded. More practically, the ulema (Muslim scholars) and the various *tarikat* (sects) provided alternative power bases in society that might in the long term threaten the envisaged reforms. A series of measures abolished the independent religious authority of institutions such as the Caliphate, the role of the deposed sultan as Sheikh-ul-Islam and the Office of the Şeriat (Shari'a law), disbanded the *tarikat* orders and replaced religious law with legal frameworks modelled on Western European civil and penal codes. The resolve shown by the government manifested itself in the adoption of the Gregorian calendar, the introduction of the Latin alphabet and the establishment of Sunday as the weekly holiday. The interventions went even further with the passage of legislation regulating the public attire of the population.

The Hat Law of 1925 required men to wear Western hats and banned the use of any other headgear such as the turban (headgear worn by the Ottoman military and ulema) or the fez (headgear worn by the late Ottoman bureaucrats) (Yilmaz 2013:22–77).[17] To continue wearing the fez would be interpreted as disobedience towards the government, and was punishable by imprisonment. The Hat Law was enacted as the Law on the Restoration of Order of 4 March 1925 was in force in the immediate aftermath of the Sheik Said rebellion indicating the effect the rebellion had in shaping the government's secular agenda and authorising the government:

> [to] prohibit on its own initiative and by administrative measure (subject to the approval of the President) all organizations, provocations, exhortations, initiatives and publications which cause disturbance of the social structures, law and order and safety and incite to commit reactionary acts and subversion. (Özoğlu 2011:100)

The reforms in this domain were completed in 1934 with the introduction of a law relating to the wearing of 'prohibited garments', Bazı Kisvelerin Giyilemeyeceğine Dair Kanunu (2596 / 3.12.1934), which banned garments related to religion outside places of worship, and the campaign against the veil in 1934–5, targeting the more sensitive issue of female dress, especially the *pece* (full facial veil) and the *carsaf* (complete cover of the female body), which, however, did not result in legislation (Yilmaz 2013:78). 'The people' that Atatürk claimed were sovereign were deemed not ready and certainly not dressed for the occasion.

But as the government was taking measures that curbed the hold of religion over the population, it did not lose sight of the parallel recognition of an existential threat to the Republic, now posed not by Christian minorities, which had been depleted, but by the emerging politics of national identity among the country's Muslim communities – especially the Kurds.

Ultimately, despite its apparent incongruence with the building of a secular state of sorts, religion, or rather religious uniformity, was an important resource for the construction of a new state and a new society. Whereas nationalism and Turkishness were self-evident realities for the state-building elite, so was the realisation of the limitations of building a totally brave new world, a secular state, premised on a modern secularised and national(ist) society that had liberated itself from the shackles of tradition and religious belief. The Kemalist elite's revolutionary zeal was tempered by its pragmatism. Despite their embracing of modernity, the exigencies of their nation-building project took priority over all other principles and objectives. Building successfully a modern Turkish nation 'from scratch' against the grain of a pious society that was to a large extent unfamiliar with the notion of Turkishness from which its putative leaders were preaching and drawing legitimacy – short of declaring an all-out war on that society – required drawing on the raw material that was available in the towns and villages of Anatolia. The nation-builders had to realise that future Turks who go on to form 'the sovereign people' of the Republic were whispering prayers to a certain God, that the daily and yearly calendars of their communities were marked by numerous religious occasions that made time meaningful and community and solidarity possible. This pre-existing community of Ottoman Muslims living throughout the Kemalists' sacred land of Anatolia could not be radically erased for a new nationalist Turkish one to be built in its place. Accordingly, the primacy of religion in people's lives was not essentially challenged, although the notion and incumbents of religious authority that could pose a threat to the new state and its nationalising project were severely weakened wherever they could not be eliminated altogether. What is more, upon the social fabric underwritten by a sense of common faith and solidarity, the Kemalists grafted new elements that encouraged, or even forced 'the people' to think about who they were in novel and unfamiliar ways, to render their local identifications or primary affinities with their Islamic faith secondary to an overarching national

Turkish identity – to effectively become Turkish. Reassembling elements of 'the people's' identification with the Republic did not, in principle, challenge the contours of the confessional community that predated its national(ist) identification.

This prompted a parallel strategy under the banner of secularism. Its self-avowed secular commitment notwithstanding, the republican leadership was aware of the strength and potential of religion to cement a sense of national unity among its Muslim population and counter nationalisms that competed with the Turkish one, and, consequently, developed an instrumentalist and accommodationist attitude towards Islam, at least initially. This paradox of rejecting religion in principle as a key societal force in post-Ottoman Turkey yet embracing this very potential in practice has been one that has indelibly marked social and political life.

The solution to this conundrum would place religion under the purview of the state. Although in theory religion – that is, Islam – was defined as a strictly private affair with no place in the public domain, in practice it was transformed into yet another state apparatus dedicated to colonisation by the newly formed state of everyday life and the inculcation of a statist paternalistic logic, as we will see later in more detail. Contrary to the argument that the establishment of the Republic displaced Islam and banished it to the margins of Turkish social and cultural life, it should be remembered that, in Republican nationalism, definitions of Turkishness drew on Sunni Islam, as the first attempts to Turkify the culture and society by the Kemalist elites involved measures that discriminated against non-Muslim minorities and subsequently heterodox Muslim minorities such as the Alevi.

A State in Motion and the Normalisation of Exception

The rapid transition from the Ottoman *ancien regime* to the republican order was underwritten by what has been considered to be the rather unclear principle of revolutionism (*inkılâpçılık*). Akural, himself a victim of Kemalist zealotry, writing in 1984 and maintaining a critical and rather sceptical distance from the excesses of Kemalism, proposes a rather modest interpretation of the principle – which he conflates with reformism – arguing that '[r]evolutionism, devoid of any content of its own, merely refers to Atatürk's methods of implementing secularism and nationalism', although he admits that '[w]hat Atatürk meant by revolutionism (*inkılâpçılık*) has never been sufficiently clarified' (1984:141–2).

According to Ahmad, '[t]he meaning of revolutionism was disputed in the Party [Republican People's Party], the moderates interpreting it as reformism, the radicals as revolutionism' (1993:63). However, in practice, for most of the republican period it could be argued that revolutionism was informed by the exigencies of the enterprise of state building generally. The Republic was supposed to be a distinctive state with the task of rebuilding the basic infrastructure required for the resumption of life and production after a devastating war and the depletion of the country's skilled population. It was required to design and set up political and economic institutions, but also educate, and even, as indicated above, radically transform its citizens, by demanding specific modes of conduct, managing memory and forgetting and implementing a host of radical measures that were required to build a new people and nation, to sever the links of the society with the *ancien regime* and to bring the nation state of Turkey to the level of the advanced states of the time. Although the Turkish Republic was not unique in this respect, the ambition inherent in the project at hand was bold and uncompromising and, as such, the 'republican revolution' became an open-ended process that eluded the prospect of political normalisation. This sense of permanent revolution, as I argue later, shaped considerably the raison d'état of modern Turkey and imprinted on Turkish politics the logic of what the German legal theorist Carl Schmitt called a state of exception (*Ausnahmezustand*) (see Agamben 2005; Hirst 1999; Schmitt 1985, 1988, 1996). This notion of continual exception occasionally took the form of legislation, such as the declaration of martial law to counter the Şeyh Said rebellion as outlined earlier in this chapter, and the promulgation of *Iakrir-i Sükûn Kanunu*, the Law for Maintaining Order on 4 March 1925, which lasted a full four years and essentially put Turkey under long-term martial law (Szurek 2015:75; Zürcher 2017:173), targeting not merely the perpetrators and supporters of the rebellion but also other opponents of the government generally, and of Mustafa Kemal in particular. During this period, public debate and criticism of the government and its reforms were muted, opposition was silenced, and the republican elite, then more than ever wedded to the personality of Atatürk, pursued virtually unimpeded the sweeping modernisation plans proposed by him and his entourage

(Zürcher 1991). However, reducing the state of exception to the introduction of emergency legislation does no justice, as I demonstrate in the next chapter, to the incorporation of the logic of exception to the 'structure of feeling' permeating Turkish society (to draw on the concept developed by Raymond Williams 1954:21; 1977:133):[18] that is, the cognitive and affective element that underwrote a fundamental cultural cohesion and that inflected the living experience of the time. Nor does it take into account the actual understanding of the state of exception by key theorists including Schmitt (1985:5–15) or Agamben (2005:6) as something that lies outside the time and space of the law and is not circumscribed by it. Chapters 4 and 5 explore in more detail the ways in which, in republican Turkey, exception has materialised both within the confines of the legal and, more crucially, been determined outside the law and without need of its sanction, but has also colonised the lived experience of politics.

Inextricably linked with the notion of exception and the principle of revolutionism is the principle of statism (*devletçilik*), the last of the pillars of the Kemalist state-building project. Kemalist ideology put the state in a central position in the building of the Republic, primarily as the state constituted the crystallisation and locus of reproduction of the revolutionary energy and impetus inherent in the republican project. Furthermore, on a more practical and, perhaps, profane level, Kemalism envisaged and relied on an effective state, able to foster the wellbeing and compliance of its citizens internally and fend off threats externally. Statism was inextricably linked, at least ideologically, with the idea that a strong state was indispensable to the survival of 'the people' and 'the nation'. In the eyes of its creators, the republican state was seen, not merely as an administrative, or even redistributive, institutional constellation, but as something much more pervasive and transformative. Its anti-imperialist and anti-colonial self-designation, as well as the revolutionary influences of developments in nearby Russia, and later in interwar Germany, shaped the republican leadership's blueprint of state building, as did their perception of the need to 'catch up' with the modern society of states that I discuss in more detail in the next chapter.

According to Mustafa Kemal, the strength or weakness of the state constitutes a reflection of the homogeneity or fragmentation of its subjects/citizenry – a united people/nation could thrive in a healthy national state, and in turn their unity would ensure the strength and longevity of the state itself. It follows that a strong, cohesive and viable state cannot be other than a nation state in the most literal and strict sense of the term. In his six-day address to Republican People's Party representatives in 1927, Atatürk implicitly compared the Ottoman and the envisaged Turkish state that was still in formation:

> ... the inner structure of the state, including many cultures and national characters, different aspirations, and disharmonious peoples with their contradictory wishes, is undoubtedly without a solid ground and therefore rotten ... Because the inner structure of a state like this is not national, its political system cannot be national. As a result of this, the policies of the Ottoman state were not national, but personal and ephemeral. (Atatürk 1981:344)

As the harmonious and homogeneous people of the republican state was not yet in place but, at best, a work in progress, the state embodied the aspiration, in addition to discharging the functions of administering, redistributing and social reproduction identified in various strands of state theory (cf. Held 1989; Poggi 1978; Poulantzas 1978), to operate as a reticular system of control and regulation of private life, of regimenting and mobilising society and of redefining the values and common sense of 'the people' who were supposed to be sovereign.

Atatürk and his followers favoured the state-led development of the economy and society as opposed to private initiative. On 20 April 1931, he expressed his philosophy on the necessity of state domination of the economy in his manifesto where he outlined the six principles of republicanism:

> Although considering private work and activity a basic idea, it is one of our main principles to interest the State actively in matters where the general and vital interests of the nation are in question, especially in the economic field, in order to lead the nation and the country to prosperity in as short a time as possible. (Lewis 1961:280)

This emphasis on an interventionist and pervasive state was so ingrained in the logic that steered the nationalist project that it extended even to the fields of artistic expression, culture and civil society, where the state took the lead and established cultural institutions, learned societies and even publishing organisations as the nationalist leadership was resolute in shaping identities, ideas, tastes and behaviours.

The state was considered to be pivotal in building the emerging Turkey, at least in its long formative years, partly because of necessity and partly as a result of design. Necessity, because the country that emerged after the War of Independence and the Lausanne Treaty lacked the human capital that could bring the desired economic take-off through private enterprise and, as in most postcolonial states, because private enterprise was considered unreliable and not necessarily geared towards the imperative of state building. Design, in the sense that the state was viewed not as a sedentary organisation, but as the embodiment of a liberation struggle that was far from concluded. Just like other anti-colonial movements, the fine line between the movement and the state was very thin indeed. As Melber points out in his analysis of the transition of Southern African liberation movements into governments, such a shift reveals a feature inherent in the former: they retain a movement character (2018:685) and, quoting Canovan (1999:14), they 'often have more or less charismatic leaders, vivid individuals who can make politics personal and immediate instead of being remote and bureaucratic'. This was true in the case of the transition between the National Movement and republican government, whereby the state, and the ideology that underpinned it, were conceived in terms of a permanent, or at least long-term and extensive, revolution under constant threat and thus marked by almost continual exception; a veritable state in motion. Contrary to the argument prevalent in the literature that the notion of revolutionism, referred to earlier, has been, perhaps, one of the most underdeveloped or vague of the six pillars of Kemalism, I would thus argue that it, and its connotation of incessant motion and activism, constitutes the leitmotif of the Kemalist project, and thus underlies the nature, operation and legitimacy of the state and the content of its secularist strategy, and circumscribes its nationalist mission and populist character.

This broader combination of state paternalism with state activism was inspired by what we can describe as a mistrust of the very people whose sovereignty the Republic was supposed to represent or express. The imperative of building and consolidating a strong modern nation state as well as the disintegrative effect – at least perceived as such by the republican elite – of

Ottoman experiments with parliamentary politics in 1876 and 1908 respectively, meant that modernisation was going to be selective and driven from above. This entailed a state acting not as an arbitrary institution or as an expression of various class interests, but as an active agent that, while purportedly taking its inspiration from the feelings and aspirations of 'the nation' and 'the people', would shape and reshape it to 'elevate' it to the level of contemporary (read Western) civilisation. This envisaged a strenuous process of social engineering, to 'enlighten' 'the people', so to speak, and 'save' them from the clutches of tradition, and the establishment of formally democratic, but in essence authoritarian, political institutions that would safeguard the unity and modernisation of Turkey even after the formal end of the one-party system, effectively in 1950. As I discuss in more detail in Chapter 5, single-party rule did not promote direct democracy despite such suggestions by some commentators (Mango 1999; Ruysdael 2002). One of the main reasons experiments with pluralism failed during this period was arguably that not all groups in the country had agreed to a minimal consensus regarding shared values and rules for regulating these disagreements – mainly with regards to secularism, but also the role of the state – and the ways dissent could be expressed. In response to such criticisms, Atatürk's biographer, Andrew Mango, attempts to contextualise the failure of the republican experiment to foster a pluralistic political system by comparing it with other authoritarian systems of the interwar era:

> between the two wars, democracy could not be sustained in many relatively richer and better-educated societies. Atatürk's enlightened authoritarianism left a reasonable space for free private lives. More could not have been expected in his lifetime.

And others, like Atatürk's adopted daughter, Afet İnan, suggest that although Atatürk sometimes appeared not to be a democrat in his actions, he always supported the idea of building a democratic society. To demonstrate her father's commitment to democratic rules İnan quotes one of his speeches about the importance of democracy in 1933:

> Republic means the democratic administration of the state. We founded the Republic, reaching its tenth year. It should enforce all the requirements of democracy as the time comes. (İnan 1999:260)

Be that as it may, democracy did not seem to be one of the priorities of the Republic as I argue in the next two chapters, despite such pronouncements of enlightenment and democratic vision, and although the authoritarian and non-pluralistic character of the republican state should not be seen in a void but, indeed, as Mango suggests, it must be situated in a comparative international context. Even in the latter case, one should not let this comparison dissimulate other factors related to the particular modalities of imagining the state and 'the not so sovereign people', as well as those of building the institutional framework of the Republic.

Notes

1. Indeed, the fluidity of the contending anchors of identity that were available to different actors is confirmed in recent research. For instance, see Özkırımlı and Sofos (2008), who discuss the Turkists' attempts to synthsise Ottoman and Islamic affinities with a Turkish identity, Provence (2011), who traces the ideological transition of Ottoman army officers from a vague and diffuse post-Ottoman identity and the attraction to the Kemalist struggle to Arab nationalism or, Bilmez (2009), whose study of the contribution of Shemseddin Sami Frashëri to the construction of both Albanian and Turkish identities shows in plain relief not only the oscillation of some members of the Ottoman intelligentsia of the time between Turkish and other national identities (in this case Albanian), but also the lack of any sense of contradiction in such complex identifications.

2. The original sentence 'in questo interregno si verificano i fenomeni morbosi più svariati' has given rise to considerable controversy over the intended meaning of 'fenomeni morbosi' in Gramsci's discussion of the interregnum. Hoare and Nowell-Smith's translation 'in this interregnum a great variety of morbid symptoms appear' (Gramsci 1971:276) is too literal while the translation popularised by Slavoj Žižek 'Now is the time of monsters' (2010) is too liberal, despite its appeal. I would suggest that Gramsci alludes to the ideological excesses taking shape at the crucial juncture of the year 1930 characterised by anxiety and disillusionment, such as the possibility of an uncompromising fascism, a catholic zealotry or an untempered leftism that was already taking hold of the Italian Communist Party. I therefore opted for the use of the, not entirely satisfactory, yet more accurate, expression 'anxious excess' to denote both the ambient anxiety and confusion of the period (discussed in more detail in Chapter 3) and the intransigence and passion of the emerging nationalist ideologies.

3. The relationship between republican nation-builders, the Young Turks and the CUP is a complex one. As Zürcher (1992; 2017) points out, despite the apparent discontinuities, there is a strong element of continuity as many of the republican cadres started their nationalist activism through some form of association with or membership of organisations related to the Young Turk movement, and, in addition, the infrastructure and much of the human capital of the national movement that Mustafa Kemal eventually led, had been the product of the work of Karakol, the CUP clandestine organisation in Anatolia. In view of this continuity, I henceforth refer to both as the nationalists or the nationalist movement. Where there is divergence between the two in terms of philosophy or action, I make the appropriate clarifications with regards to specific actors, their views or actions.

4. However, it is important not to underestimate the class dimension of the republican nation builders' aversion to the Istanbul bureaucratic elite and the court of the sultan. Most of the leaders and cadres of the National Movement were military officers, and therefore part of the very same Ottoman state apparatus that the Istanbul bureaucracy also served. Most officers, having graduated from the military-service academies in Istanbul and elsewhere, served the Ottoman state in its different provinces during the First World War. The free and subsidised late Ottoman military education system had made extensive free education of prospective military officers a priority, and provided an upward social mobility avenue as cadets were customarily drawn from the upper peasantry and the urban lower middle class. Their education had bestowed on them status and respect, and, among other skills, the ability to communicate with and mobilise members of the subaltern classes from which they had emerged (Provence 2011:207). Their distance from the Istanbul elite class and the centres of power in Istanbul, which took decisions that they felt affected their raison d'être, had given rise to widespread resentment among them. In addition, their ability to mobilise and inspire ordinary people made them act as contenders and, therefore, develop views and aspirations that posited them in an antagonistic relationship with the imperial elites.

5. The everyday use of terms such as 'imagined' or 'imagination' often implies an opposition between the 'real' and the 'imagined'. Anderson (1991) stresses that imagining (national) communities is by no means conjuring something artificial, that 'imagining' is a lengthy process:

> forging links between social groups, of inventing community and suppressing differences, of establishing the context in which the members of the community under construction can develop common experiences,

and interpret past experiences in similar ways. It involves the organization of collective memory, and thus, of collective forgetting, and of the rituals and institutions that support such projects (Hobsbawm and Ranger, 1983) . . . nations are imagined but also real, concrete entities. (Sofos 1996a:74)

Indeed, as Laclau and Mouffe (1985), and before them Foucault (1972), have suggested, any manifestation of the 'social' is the product of this process of imagination, or of discursive construction, to use their own terminology. I would thus suggest that imagination involves creating economies of truth, making sense of the raw material of social experience, in fact, creating this very social experience through discursive practices.

6. Although Istanbul and the westernmost European territories of the Ottoman Empire (Eastern Rumelia) were eventually included in republican Turkey, the Anatolian peninsula was more closely associated with the notion of the motherland (*vatan*). It constituted the territory of national resistance *par excellence*, where Mustafa Kemal landed to start the liberation struggle, where Kazim Karabekir defended the eastern borders of the Republic against the Armenian forces and where the curtain of the War of Independence fell with the capture of Smyrna from the Greek forces (*İzmir'in Kurtuluşu*) in September 1922. As I argue, Anatolia had the aura of cultural authenticity that distinguished it in the eyes of the nationalists from 'degenerate', cosmopolitan, 'inauthentic' Istanbul (although the city of Smyrna was also referred to as 'infidel Smyrna' (*gavur İzmir*) due to its large Christian population (see Morgenthau 1918:32). In view of the centrality of Anatolia in the Turkish national(ist) imaginary, the word Anatolia refers henceforth to the locus of the republican *vatan*, and Rumelia will be alluded to when it is mentioned explicitly in the sources used or when it is the location of events discussed.

7. The term 'völkisch' relates to a traditionalist, nationalist movement (*Völkische Bewegung*) that was active from the late nineteenth century until the Nazi era in Germany. Premised on the idea of 'blood and soil', and, although not a homogeneous set of beliefs, but rather a 'variegated sub-culture' opposing the socio-cultural changes of modernity, it was characterised by antisemitic tendencies, an egalitarian–'populist' emphasis, a romantic nationalism inspired by agrarian ideals that romanticised the countryside (Camus and Lebourg 2017:16–18).

As John B. Thompson points out, the term 'völkisch' was used originally as a German translation for 'national', but it gradually became a word of combat which accentuated racial opposition against Jews. It was thus integrated into a tradition of anti-Semitism that reached back into the nineteenth century . . . The crucial transformation underlying these developments is that 'völkisch' became the positive expression for the negative term 'anti-Semite'. As Liebermann von Sonnenberg declared with a chilling sense of foresight in 1881, it is no good being 'purely anti-Semitic, for one must struggle to unify all Germans in a genuine Volksgemeinschaft ("Community of people/race")' (1984:216).

8. The Şeyh Said rebellion constituted the most significant challenge to the nascent Republic. It was organised by Şeyh Said – an influential Naqshbandi sheikh of Kurdish origin – and initiated by the mobilisation of militiamen belonging to the former Hamidiye Light Cavalry Regiment, a mainly Kurdish militia established by Sultan Abdul Hamid II, who in 1923 had formed Azadi (Freedom Society). Şeyh Said, who supported retaining the religious authority of the Caliph but was also a regime opponent with influence in republican Turkey's Kurdish populated areas, had originally envisaged a broader Sunni uprising for the restoration of the Caliphate but, eventually, led a localised rebellion drawing upon a widespread popular bond to the idea of the Caliphate in the Kurdish provinces of the Republic, tribal networks and a nascent Kurdish identity among the local population (Olson 1989). As Zürcher points out, 'While the leadership was undoubtedly motivated by the desire for an autonomous or even independent Kurdistan, the rank and file acted from religious motives, demanding the restoration of the holy law and the caliphate (2017:172). The government in Ankara declared martial law for one month in the east of the country while it amended the High Treason Law to penalise 'the political use of religion' (Zürcher 2017:172). Upon the appointment of İsmet Paşa, a radical Atatürk ally, as Prime Minister in March 1925, the assembly passed the Takrir-i Sükûn Kanunu (Law on the Maintenance of Order) (Zürcher 2017:173), which gave Mustafa Kemal and his supporters the freedom to conduct purges for four years. The rebellion was defeated after the Turkish army resorted to a barrage of aerial bombardments and an extensive mobilisation of its military (Van Bruinessen 1992).

9. While collecting and evaluating material for this project it became evident that reconstructing the lived experience of politics during the period under examination faced a crucial limitation relating to 'the missing voices' of the early republican era. Brockett (1999) emphasises this deficiency in the historiography of early republican Turkey and stresses the need to 'decolonise' the history of the period from the dominance of elite accounts of the way the Anatolian population 'lived' politics, interacted with the state and responded to the challenges of the time. Oral history research on this topic would give us

the opportunity to gauge the 'structure of feeling' of the period (see Williams 1954, 1977), especially its plebeian dimensions. As the individuals who lived during that period are passing away, so are their memories. Invaluable contributions to salvaging their testimonies can be found in the work of Yilmaz (2013), Türkyilmaz (2016), Türköz (2007). See also Özyürek's exploration of individual private memories in the context of public memory and history in late twentieth-century Turkey (2006) and the collection of work in Özyürek (2001). Studying meaning creation and mobilisation processes such as the ones I am referring to here and the rest of this book will draw on these sources, but will also rely on complex methodologies of reconstructing such structures of feeling.

10. Indeed, despite the analytical distinctions made by Gamson (2011) whereby he identifies processes of the production of a sense of injustice, agency and identity, it goes without saying that these are components of collective action that should be seen as threads coming together and giving shape and form to a complex social artefact.

11. As Lewis suggests, to be called a Turk constituted an insult to the Ottomans:

> The people had once called themselves Turks, and the language they spoke was still called Turkish, but in the Imperial society of the Ottomans the ethnic term Turk was little used, and then chiefly in a rather derogatory sense, to designate the Turcoman nomads or, later, the ignorant and uncouth Turkish-speaking peasants of the Anatolian villages. To apply it to an Ottoman gentleman of Constantinople would have been an in insult. (Lewis 1961:1–2)

12. The National Pact (Misak-ı Millî) was a text comprised by six resolutions passed by the Ottoman Parliament during its last session on 28 January 1920. The Pact resolutions were published on 12 February 1920. The Pact, endorsed by the Salvation of the Fatherland (Felâh-ı Vatan) group of parliamentarians supporting Mustafa Kemal's strategy, reflected the views of the nationalist movement, including the positions taken at the Erzurum and the Sivas Congresses. Misak-ı Millî's six resolutions were officially endorsed by Mustafa Kemal Atatürk, who declared: 'It is the nation's iron fist that writes the Nation's Oath which is the main principle of our independence to the annals of history.' According to the resolutions, those areas of the Empire that were within the Mudros Armistice line of 30 October 1918 and 'inhabited by the Ottoman-Muslim majority' were an 'indivisible whole' (Cagaptay 2006:11). The Misak-ı Millî resolutions were

later used as the basis for the claims of the Turkish Grand National Assembly in the Treaty of Kars and of the new Republic of Turkey in the Treaty of Lausanne. (Butler 2011:219–20).

13. Originally established by the Young Turks in 1912, the Turkish Hearths (Türk Ocakları) was an organisation formally intended to raise the social, economic and intellectual level of the Turkish people, and effectively a nationalist movement striving to promote new theories about the Turkish people's history and identity. The activities of the Hearths initially addressed Ottoman Turks, although after the 1917 Russian revolution the organisation also targeted refugees of Turkic origin from Russia (Landau 1995:40–1). With the establishment of the Republic the Turkish Hearths supported the state-building project through training activities for teachers, producing publications, and organising cultural events and national Congresses. In 1927, the Hearths became linked with the Republican People's Party (CHP) and in 1931 merged with the Party (Türk Ocakları 2001) or, rather, were taken over by it (Karpat 1963:59).

14. The principle of republicanism constituted one of what later came to be considered the six pillars of Kemalism (Atatürkçülük or Kemalizm). These were not clearly articulated at the moment of the establishment of the Republic, and were formulated over time, both as included in Mustafa Kemal's vision of what the Republic should be, and also because the principles developed in response to the exigencies of state building and to the challenges the republican project faced. As such, the six pillars did not constitute a coherent ideology and lacked refinement and precision. In the 1930s, when the regime was stable and more confident, Atatürk and the CHP ideologues had the opportunity to articulate and refine them. Atatürk identified republicanism, nationalism, populism, statism, secularism and revolutionism as the guiding forces of his project in a speech on 24 September 1931 (1991:606). CHP political cadres subsequently elaborated on these principles and incorporated them into the party and state ideology (see also Cagaptay 2006:46) after the Republican Party Convention of 1931. These were incorporated in 1937 into the Constitution as the Republic's official ideology.

15. Opposition to the abolition of the Caliphate was considerable (Zürcher 1991), yet muted due to an addition made to the Law of Treason 'making it an offence against the law to criticize the reforms', and the setting up of Independence Tribunals (İstiklâl Mahkemeleri) with the power to inflict the death penalty throughout the Republic without reference to the Assembly (Hassan 2011:158–9) or the right to appeal (Çağaptay 2006:22). Nevertheless, the use of emergency legislation after the Şeyh Said rebellion allowed the İnönü government to shut down several critical newspapers and eventually to close

down the Progressive Republican Party, which had become a gathering place for the Turkish opposition, including some of the key figures of the independence war, a number of Mustafa Kemal's close military and political associates amongst them (Çağaptay 2006:21–2).

16. The Turkish authorities crushed the rebellion with continual aerial bombardments and a massive concentration of forces (Van Bruinessen 1992), while on 23 February 1925, the government declared a month-long state of emergency in the territories affected (Özoğlu 2009) and, as Kastoryano points out, the regime took the opportunity to invoke a state of exception based on the need to preserve the new regime (2013:145). This was prolonged with the promulgation of the Law for Maintaining Order (Takrir-i Sükûn Kanunu) on 4 March 1925. In order to weaken the local communities that supported the rebellion (Gunes and Zeydanlioğlu 2014:10), the government introduced and enacted legislation (such as Law 1204/1927) that allowed it to displace local Kurds who had links to the uprising and resettle them in western Turkey (Casier and Jongerden 2011).

17. The Hat Law was first passed by the Ministerial Council on 2 September 1925, forcing all military, court officers, other civil servants and the clergy to adopt a Western dress code. On 25 November of the same year the Law's scope was expanded to include the entire population (see Türkiye Büyük Millet Meclisi (TBMM), Devre II, 3, Cilt 19, 1925).

18. Williams himself did not give a clear definition of the 'structure of feeling', and over time used it in slightly different ways. For a more detailed discussion of the concept, and for attempts to trace its development in Williams's oeuvre, see Matthews 2001 and Middleton 2019.

3

'THE SOVEREIGN PEOPLE'
IN ANXIOUS TIMES

e canterò di quel secondo regno
dove l'umano spirito si purga
e di salire al ciel diventa degno.

Dante, *Divina Commedia*

'Othering' and Turkishness

As already discussed in the preceding pages, leading nationalist figures, including Mustafa Kemal himself and İsmet Paşa (İnönü), followed the European imagination of modernity in establishing a 'secular' nation state, where the diverse Muslim populations were racialised under the single category, 'Turk'. The founders of the Republic made clear on numerous occasions, especially after the turning point of 1925, that the Republic they envisaged would be a Republic for its Turkish citizens.[1] The annihilation of the Armenian population and forced exchange of Greek Orthodox Christians with Greek Muslims were two critical events that contributed to the 'post-Ottoman' realisation of Turkey's image as an ethno-sectarian state for non-Arabic-speaking Ottoman Muslims.

The tolerance of diversity that was exhibited during the War of Independence, and the references to an (at least internally) diverse Muslim 'people', had run their course and outlived their utility. As the new state had acquired international recognition through the Treaty of Lausanne in July 1923, the republican elites felt that they were given a free hand to work towards the creation of a strong unitary state based on an ethnically homogeneous 'people'. Alternative identities were thus seen as an aberration, with the potential to undermine the unity of the nation they sought to construct. In May 1925, Prime Minister İsmet Paşa, addressing an audience of schoolteachers, expressed clearly the aspiration to create a monolithic (*yekpâre*) state:

> There are Turks who give this land its Turkish character. But this nation does not display the characteristics of the monolithic nation we would like to see. Only if this generation works consciously and seriously, under the guidance of science and life in general, devoting itself to it, can the political Turkish nation become a complete, mature cultural and social nation. In this monolithic nation, all foreign cultures must dissolve. There cannot be different civilizations within this national body. (Kaplan 1999:143–4)

In his address, İsmet Paşa admits that the Turkish nation is in a state of incompleteness and lacks maturity, and suggests that its maturation relies on the eventual prevalence of Turkish culture over all alternatives, which must dissolve as a result of a considerable intellectual and cultural effort. The promise of belonging in the Turkish Republic was extended only to those who would embrace Turkishness as the term was understood by Atatürk and his associates. The Republic, therefore, had no place for those who did not quite fit the image of the ideal Turk. So central was this coupling of Turkishness and the possession of rights in the republican ideology that it would be reiterated time and again, as happened at the Turkish Grand National Assembly in an address by Interior Minister Şükru Kaya, where he reproduced almost verbatim İnönü's words: 'If anybody has any difference inside him, we need to erase it in the schools and in the body politic, so that [every] man will be as Turkish as me and serve the homeland' (TBMM Zabit Ceridesi 1934:249).

This effectively meant the introduction and implementation of a largely unwritten (despite notable exceptions, some of which I discussed in Chapter 2) though not unspoken distinction between undesirable citizens, whose rights were effectively curtailed, and the essentially 'Turkish people'. One of the bluntest articulations of the undesirability of citizens that could not meet this, at first sight, ethnic criterion was made in the autumn of 1930 by Minister of Justice, Mahmut Esat (Bozkurt): 'My opinion, my conviction is that this country is Turkish. Anyone who is not purely Turkish has only one right in the Turkish homeland, s/he is to be a servant, to be a slave' (quoted in Tunçay 1989:301). Five years earlier addressing a nationalist audience at the second congress of the Turkish Hearths, İsmet Paşa starkly cast the relationship between the Turkish majority and the non-Turkish minorities in the country as a binary division between two mutually exclusive and irreconcilable poles; the presence of non-Turks in the country, he argued, 'challenge[s] the Turks and Turkishness' (Üstel 1997:173). This binary representation of Turkish politics drew attention to 'Turkishness' and the 'lack' of it as central elements in determining who has substantive rights and who has not, and left little room for the expression of differentiations or dissent between these two poles: one was a Turk or was not – any deviation from the established definition of Turkishness meant excommunication.

The 'other' citizens, 'lacking' attributes related to Turkishness, were both legally and symbolically externalised and marginalised in a multitude of ways that ranged from administrative and legal restrictions, Turkification (in cases where 'the others' did not display the ethnic markers of Turkishness) and scapegoating campaigns, the exercise of pressure on entire communities, to cultural exclusion and public hostility. Despite the clear ethnic connotations of the references to 'the Turkish people' and to Turkishness in the statements made by republican politicians, I argue in the course of this chapter that 'otherness' extended beyond ethnicity, ethnoreligious or confessional identity and its determination was quite complex, including also features such as discipline, compliance and political identification. As Göçek points out,

> [during the first two decades of the Republic] the secularist premises of the Turkish nation-state precluded the participation of those Turks within the dominant majority who publicly underscored their religious identity. Labelled conservative religious 'Islamists', this segment was initially marginalized and excluded from the Republican order. (2011:5–6)

In this sense, 'the Turkish people', as I contend, were not coextensive to the ensemble of the population that could be counted as part of the Turkish *ethnie*, as Turkishness was intricately woven into what I call republican identity.

But first things first. In the case of non-Muslim citizens, the republican elite was unequivocal in its rejection of their entitlement to substantive citizenship. The non-Muslim communities who had attained economic positions in the Ottoman Empire, despite their constitutional recognition as legally equal to their Muslim fellow citizens in the republican order, and the additional provisions of the Lausanne Treaty guaranteeing their rights were considered an anomaly as they lived in a polity that was inimical to them among a resentful 'people'. Whereas Turkification policies were supposed to ensure conformity on the surface (requiring the use of Turkish as a medium of public interaction, the relegation of religion to the private sphere and the suppression of any performance of alterity), they were largely intended to distinguish, identify difference and ultimately 'prove' the impossibility of assimilating non-Muslim citizens. The rights of non-Muslims were circumscribed by a series of laws and regulations relating to economic Turkification (Aktar 2000:55–6), taxation and property rights (including the notorious *Varlık Vergisi* – 'wealth' or 'capital tax' (Aktar 2000; İnce 2012:74; Turam 2012:43), which led non-Muslim citizens to financial ruin), or employment (Aktar 2000:119–24; Çağaptay 2006:69–70; Parla 1995:25–32), to name but a few of the means the Republic deployed to curtail the scope and effectiveness of their citizenship and excise them from the body politic. Apart from their tangible and material effects, these measures established powerful symbolic boundaries, constant reminders to non-Muslim citizens of the impossibility of belonging to 'the chosen people' of the Republic who were mobilised against the Republic's 'others'.[2]

In the meantime, as the Şeyh Said revolt drew attention to the potential of Kurdish nationalism becoming a contender for the hearts and minds of the Kurdish citizens of the Republic, it caused considerable concern among the nationalist elite, as it challenged the previously held belief that the Kurdish populations of Turkey could be counted on to remain loyal to the Turkish state. As a result, like their non-Muslim fellow citizens, Kurdish citizens living in Turkey's southeastern provinces were viewed with suspicion and would be treated as outsiders to a certain extent. In addition to those involved in the political and military challenge to the Republic (the insurgents and their leadership, whose members were swiftly rounded up and executed), the response of the Republic affected Kurdish communities almost in their entirety. Kurdish language and culture were targeted, as they were deemed to represent visible markers of difference and to have the potential of being politicised if further attempts to mount a revolt took place in the future. Thus, the Kurds had to live under consecutive states of emergency starting from the immediate aftermath of the revolt in 1925 to date, through times of brutal and violent repression, and endure forced internal displacement and a long-term ban on the use of their language alternating with periods of liberalisation. What is more, two years after the revolt, the Turkish Grand National Assembly introduced Law Nr 1164, which paved the way for the establishment of the First Inspectorate-General (Birinci Umumi Müfettişlik) on 1 January 1928. The establishment of Inspectorates-General constituted the vehicle for an effectively localised state of exception, whereby specific territories within the Turkish Republic were administered for a certain period directly by Mustafa Kemal or the head of state after him, through a general inspector (a regional governor) whose authority superseded that of other civilian, military and judicial institutions under their domain (Çağaptay 2006:47–8). The First Inspectorate-General extended to the mainly Kurdish-inhabited provinces of Diyarbakır, Elazığ, Urfa, Bitlis, Van, Hakkâri, Siirt and Mardin (Birinci Genel Müfettişlik 1939:66). Similarly, on 6 June 1936, in response to longstanding concerns regarding the un-Turkish identity and behaviour of the residents of the Dersim region (Beşikçi 1990:29), the Fourth Inspectorate-General (Dördüncü Umumi Müfettişlik) was established, extending to the provinces of Tunceli, Elazığ and Bingöl, which were populated by Zaza- and Kurmanci-speaking Alevis or Kızılbaş (Lundgren 2007:44).[3] The institution of the Inspectorate-General could be likened to a repressive laboratory that aimed unequivocally to assert the authority of the Republic and produce compliant Turkish citizens (Koçak 2003:144), but, more importantly, was one of the institutions that normalised the notion of exception in Turkish politics.

Interestingly, the measures introduced vis-à-vis the Kurdish citizens of the Republic incorporated both carrot and stick – enticements to subscribe to the republican vision and accept their Kurdishness as a regional variation of Turkishness and the exercise of physical and symbolic violence to eliminate the cultural and social buttresses of Kurdish nationalism (see Çağaptay 2006:19–24). Although a large segment of the republican elite perceived the emergence of this competing nationalism as both a betrayal and a threat, the

Kurds were seen as prone to assimilation through pressure and encouragement, even after the insurrections of the 1920s. As a result, the Republic resorted to measures of violent containment of assertive expressions of Kurdish identity, and assimilationist strategies where it deemed that Kurdish populations could be persuaded, through education and military conscription or internal deportation, to adopt Turkish language and embrace Turkish identity.

However, 'the Turkish people' were distinguished, not only from these ethnic 'others', but also from citizens who would otherwise meet the strict ethnic criterion of Turkishness. Already prior to the articulation, in 1931, of the principles of republicanism, nationalism, populism, statism, secularism and revolutionism as the guiding forces of the republican project, it had become clear that those included in 'the people' had to subscribe to a novel political culture, however vaguely defined in the early years of the Turkish state. This republican political culture relied on a radical break with the past and required compliance with particular visualisations of society. Failure to embrace it, or disagreement, not only with the goals of the journey the new state and 'its people' were embarking on, but also their ways of achieving them, were deemed declarations of war on the Republic and were usually met with a response similar to that reserved for non-Muslim and Kurdish citizens.

The Law for the Maintenance of Order, bestowing on the cabinet effectively dictatorial powers ultimately for four years, was complemented by an equally exceptional instrument of implementation, the Independence Tribunals (İstiklâl Mahkemeleri,). The model of the Independence Tribunals, originally established during the Turkish War of Independence to prosecute deserters, was deemed appropriate to prosecute not only those involved with the Şeyh Said rebellion, but also 'dissidents', such as former TCF members (and prominent surviving Unionists), regardless of whether the latter could be proven to have participated in acts against the state (Adak 2003:510). Holding the power to impose the death penalty without reference to the Assembly throughout the territory of the Republic (Hassan 2011:158–9), and denying the right of appeal to those prosecuted (Çağaptay 2006:22), the two tribunals were effectively resuscitated to implement a state of exception and ensure that dissent was quashed without the possibility of due process. The Law also accorded the government the right to ban and suppress organisations, activities or publications that might 'encourage rebellion' (Kinross 1964:400).

In conjunction with the adoption of the Law of Treason and a number of later amendments to it that made it an offence to criticise the republican reforms, the tribunals revealed the lack of tolerance of any deviation from the prescribed path of political behaviour, and the intention to prosecute political deviance. The Law and the tribunals targeted critical voices that might challenge the system of government, the principles of Kemalism or the abolition of the caliphate, and those suspected of holding such positions, thus stifling virtually all opposition to the government. Exceptional powers such as the ones introduced in response to the Şeyh Said rebellion were used, not only to contain the threat of the Kurdish uprising, but also to close down critical newspapers and round up members and sympathisers of the TCF that had become a hub for liberal as well as more moderate reformist dissidents. The array of legal and administrative measures resorted to, as well as intimidation, pressure and public shunning, were some of the earliest instances of the identification of 'others' within 'the people' and of externalising them symbolically but also in tangible ways such as imprisonment, banishment or execution.[4]

Turkishness thus was a shorthand term that referred not only to an ethnic identity but to a set of values and predispositions that the nationalist elite considered to be essential for the success of the republican project as they envisaged it. Dissent and deviation from the prescribed path meant challenging the unity of the nation and questioning the republican leadership. Political divergence was tantamount to not being worthy, setting one apart from the body politic of the Republic. But even after these multiple externalisations, those citizens who were deemed not to belong to 'the other' in terms of ethnicity or religion, or not among 'the dissident other', still fell short of 'the sovereign people' envisaged by Atatürk and his associates. Their putative liberation from the Ottoman Empire did not mean their emancipation as originally promised by the leaders of the independence struggle, as they were imperfect and under probation.

Constantly under suspicion and surveillance, they were subjected to consecutive campaigns to reform them, to teach them the history of the Turkish nation, to suggest to them how to dress and behave, which political choices to make and which to avoid, and, ultimately, think like Turks should and feel happy to 'say I am a Turk', as Mustafa Kemal Atatürk prompted them to do in his speech to commemorate the tenth anniversary of the Turkish Republic.

This lack of trust, and the intolerance of the expression of not only oppositional voices, but also of behaviours and practices deemed inappropriate could, of course, be attributed to the exigencies of building a new state from the foundations, the need for discipline and unity of purpose in the effort to resuscitate and expand the wounded economy of the Republic's territories, to build effective political institutions and disassociate Turkey from the characterisation of its predecessor as the sick man of Europe. These qualifications notwithstanding, as I argue, the elite's mistrust of 'the Turkish people' has constituted a fundamental element of the politics of the Republic over the past century. And, although I have already suggested that 'the people' and 'the nation' partially overlap in the republican narrative, I have also hinted that this partial overlap should not be taken as an indication that 'the people' and 'the nation' are identical. Indeed, in this chapter I build on my earlier discussion of the place of 'the people' in the foundational narratives of the early Turkish Republic and explore in some detail the relationship between 'the people' and 'the nation'. This chapter attempts to unpack the logic of 'othering' inherent in the republican project and explore its manifestations and effects with regards to the ways in which 'the people' and 'the nation' have been imagined, and notions such as those of democracy and exception have been understood and propagated, not only in the early Republic and the one-party state period but beyond it, as competitive elections finally took place in Turkey and their results unfolded and were interrupted during the second part of the twentieth century.

Anxiety, Ontological Insecurity and Nationalist Desire

It is important to note that the project of establishing a sustainable and resilient state, and its implications as far as 'the sovereignty of the people' is concerned, was informed by a sense of ontological insecurity shared by the architects of the state. I use here the term 'ontological insecurity' drawing on a long transdisciplinary tradition informed by the work of Ronald David Laing (1990) in psychology and elaborated on by Anthony Giddens (1991:35–69) in the field of sociology,[5] to describe the ambient anxiety regarding the effectiveness, reliability and survival of the new Turkish state in a rapidly changing world that the nationalist elites experienced as they embarked in the state- and nation-building project that would culminate in modern Turkey.

In order to move from the abstract concept to the particular conditions that prevailed at the end of the First World War, I draw on Kinnvall's approach to ontological insecurity as a broad signifier that brings together and establishes links between 'larger stories or narratives in which security dimensions are embedded, such as narratives of colonialization and globalization', their manifestation 'locally as discursive, institutional and cultural practices that define people's perceptions and thus their different senses of security', and probing its psychological dimension, that is, analysing 'the extent to which individuals become preoccupied with the search for one secure identity, the securitisation of subjectivity, in response to how these individuals are discursively, institutionally and culturally positioned' (Kinnvall 2007:27).

The end of the First World War and the period of the Ottoman Empire's disintegration was a time of instability, of lack of constancy in the social and material environment. The nationalist elite, comprised overwhelmingly by military officers and segments of the Ottoman bureaucracy, felt out of place, humiliated and 'homeless', as did the populace of the rapidly diminishing territories of the Ottoman Empire – the devastation of local economies by the war, the power vacuum that ensued, the emboldened brigands and militias, the breakdown of intercommunal coexistence as a result of the fluctuating power dynamics brought by the war, all undermined a sense of confidence and trust in the way things were, an important element of ontological insecurity (Kinnvall 2004:746). As individuals and communities felt vulnerable and experienced existential anxiety, they sought ways to mitigate this sense of vulnerability. The response of the elite to the new wave of instability and uncertainty, especially the military officers and the state bureaucracy that had experienced defeat during the Balkan wars and whose identities had been shaped under the influence of the Young Turk ideology, was expressed as what Greenfeld calls ressentiment (1992). The status-inconsistency that they experienced as an old world collapsing took the form of securitised subjectivity in the form of a new Turkish nation and the construction of its homeland. At the plebeian level, too, in some quarters, ethnoreligious tensions that had already manifested themselves during the Armenian genocide of 1915 when entire communities were drawn into the spiral of genocidal violence, or after the reckless behaviour of the Greek occupation forces in Western Anatolia, and the revenge-inspired conduct of Armenian militias advancing from the northeast as part of the Russian offensive had created a fertile ground for Turkish nationalist ideology.

The officers and intellectuals who took it upon themselves to create a new state from the rubble of the Ottoman Empire were deeply affected by the collapse of the imperial state. The country that they had sought to reform was no more, its territory coveted by the British, the French, the Italians, and, even more humiliatingly, the Greeks and the Armenians – former subjects of the Empire. The army in which many of them were still serving had been ordered to lay down its arms and remain a mere onlooker to the partitioning of Anatolia, Syria and the Mosul Vilayet – the remaining lands of their country capitulated to the victors of the war. The rapid and radical change affected their status and triggered a broader existential crisis. The imperial vistas that had shaped their identity had been replaced by the much more restricted horizon of the shrinking Anatolian steppe after a series of traumatic defeats in North Africa, the Balkans and finally in the remaining Ottoman territory during the First World War. This sense of loss and humiliation had already been grafted in the experience of the Young Turks and their supporters in the course of the Balkan Wars, which in popular memory registered as the Balkan tragedy (*Balkan Faciası*), when the Ottoman Empire lost most of its European territories to Bulgaria, Greece, Montenegro and Serbia. Such was the sense of loss among the Officers' Corps that the planning and implementation of the notorious Turkification and demographic engineering policies, and the execution of the Armenian genocide, overseen by the Committee of Union and Progress, prompted little protest. What is more, the existential anxiety of the time was still a fresh memory in 1927 when Atatürk delivered his famous six-day speech, *Nutuk* (Atatürk 1981), at the second congress of the CHP; in describing the events between the start of the Turkish War of Independence in 1919 and the foundation of the Republic of Turkey in 1923, he referred no less than 117 times to the threat faced by, and the danger of extinction of, the Turkish state, 'its people' or its army.

The disastrous conclusion of the First World War for the Ottoman Empire delivered another more decisive shock to the officers who had supported the cause of the Young Turks and had sought to further the cause of Turkish nationalism within the Empire. Not only had the homeland they had worked to reform and fought for shrunk to a rump, but also their status among 'the people' they intended to mobilise had plummeted; and so did their cause itself, tainted by the Committee of Union and Progress's advocacy of the war and of the suffering its policies had caused. Yet the implosion of the imperial state gave to the work started by the Young Turks and the Committee of Union and Progress, of which many of the nationalist elite were members or sympathisers, a sense of extreme urgency. As the salvageable territories of the previously multi-confessional and multi-ethnic Ottoman state were limited to the Anatolian peninsula, it was clear to them that Anatolia was going to be where their nation-building work would focus.

The populace of Anatolia, on the other hand, had a different experience of the situation. For the population of the towns and villages throughout the peninsula, the hardships and misery of conscription continued to occupy a place of trauma and horror in popular memory (Provence 2011:17; Zürcher 1996a; 1996b), the devastation of parts of Anatolia and Thrace by the warfare and the extractive policies of the Committee of Union and Progress to support the Ottoman war effort, the famine caused by the international blockade (Fawaz 2014), the mass drafting by the Ottoman army that left families without breadwinners (Webster 1939:58–9) and local economies without workers, the proliferation of irregular armed bands that sustained themselves at the expense of local communities, were key elements of the bitter legacy of the war, long before its conclusion had left indelible marks in the psyche of ordinary people and in their oral culture (Akça 1946; Akın 2018:1–2; Yalgın 1939) and damaged the social fabric of many communities. Introducing his detailed reconstruction of the devastation inflicted on the ordinary people of Anatolia, Akın notes that Yaşar Kemal, who later became a leading literary figure, during an Anatolian village tour in his late teens reciting his poetry and collecting local ballads, found the huge corpus of laments related to the First World War and its ubiquity surprising. These laments served as a repository of the localised memories and experiences of Anatolian peasants during a long conflict that they felt they had no stake in, persisting almost two decades after its end. According to Akın,

> These songs and laments provide an invaluable glimpse into a society at war, illuminating how the Ottomans experienced, perceived, and remembered the conflict. Most important, they offer alternative narratives to official renderings

of the war, which emphasized its political, military, and religious meanings. War is described in these accounts as carnage that includes blood, tears, fear, pain, and sorrow, but not heroism and pride. (2018:1)

Interestingly, the end of the war, the collapse of the Ottoman institutions and the advance on Anatolia by Greek and Armenian as well as the British, French and Italian forces created a moment when what I would call the plebeian (discussed earlier in Chapter 2) experience of the Anatolian populace on the one hand, and that of the nationalist elite on the other, converged and was transmuted into a sense of cultural trauma that has been inextricably linked to the foundational narrative of the Republic.

Although, for the military officers and intellectuals that formed the aspiring elite of the Anatolian 'state in waiting', their ideological affinity and political collusion with the Committee of Union and Progress – whose wartime leadership had fled at the end of the war to avoid war crimes prosecution – constituted a significant liability, it also represented an opportunity. Given the loss of legitimacy of, even public hostility to, the Young Turks, owning up to their legacy would further alienate the rural populace whose recollections of overwhelming devastation and sense of betrayal by the Young Turk leadership and the sultan were recorded by Yaşar Kemal and other folklorists.

Yet paradoxically, the weakening of the moral and emotional bonds between the Anatolian peasants and the Empire that inflicted untold suffering on them provided the nationalist leadership with an opportunity to invest their Turkist project with an oppositional, anti-colonial quality and create the impression of rupture at the level of statehood. This would allow them to continue pursuing their nationalist agenda, the Turkification and population transfer policies that their CUP predecessors had initiated, more or less replicating their authoritarian governance practices while investing them with the stamp of popular vindication. What is more, as the Ottoman Empire, in the eyes of the Anatolian inhabitants, was coterminous with the sultan – the personification of imperial order and power – wresting authority from a monarch whom the nationalist elite considered unpatriotic and preoccupied only with his continued presence on the throne became a rather easy task. Not only did the nationalist elite exploit the conflation of sultan with empire (and its wartime policies) prevalent in the Anatolian plebeian cultures to delegitimise him (as it, itself, was engaged in a power struggle with the Porte), but it also integrated the partial and often fragmented individual or localised ontological narratives/recollections of the hardships of the war in collective public narratives. These public narratives attached to cultural and institutional formations larger than the single individual, to intersubjective networks or to institutions of a national trauma (see Somers 1994:619), provided a basis for building an overarching identity for the Anatolian population, the means of turning 'the populace' into 'the people' and promising to the latter the sovereignty they were putatively denied by the Porte.

As Eyerman points out (2001), trauma lies in the domain, not of experience, but of collective memory, while Alexander also suggests that cultural trauma is the product of a process of 'imagination', of emotional and cognitive processing, and not intrinsic to the actual event associated with it (Alexander et al. 2004:9, alse see Demertzis 2020). Indeed, although the 'reality' behind the trauma would normally implicate the officers that were at the helm of the National Movement in the devastating effects of the war on the Anatolian population, the trauma itself was rather the mediated experience of their suffering. As such it was achieved through the official representations produced by the nationalist elite, a mixture of silences as well as utterances, the product of a process of selection and translation. If the suffering was traumatic for the Anatolian populace, it was so in retrospect (however recent the war might have been), mediated through reminiscence but also cognitive and emotional processing, and, for some, 'tinged with some strategic, practical, and political interest' (see Eyerman 2001:2).

Without intending to underplay the hardships endured by the Anatolian population, the devastated families, the widowed women, the depopulation of erstwhile vibrant villages, I want to focus precisely on these strategic, practical and political dimensions, and argue that the trauma recounted in the addresses made by the nationalist leadership as they visited different parts of Anatolia at the time was not the trauma of individuals or of communities, recounted in the Anatolian plebeian narratives, but the one suffered by 'the people' and 'the nation' that were yet to be born. What is more, not only were the disparate local plebeian vernaculars of suffering, especially, lent a particular historicity and relationality, and became deterritorialised and integrated into narratives of 'the people' but they were also recontextualised, articulated with the anxieties of the nationalist elite and eventually embedded into a broader common stock of experience. This process of creating a 'universal', 'nation-wide' experience out of the multitude of local plebeian lived experiences involved its own particular temporality. The hardship of the Anatolian populace was merged with the existential threat, as perceived and articulated by the nationalist movement; the carving of Anatolia into the protectorates and zones of influence of different foreign powers and the frustration of the sovereignty and self-determination of 'the Anatolian people'. This construction of an accumulated trauma (see Eyerman 2008:166–9) related to events that took place in different moments in time and that hinged on the merging of 'the personal' and 'the local' with 'the political', 'the plebeian' with 'the popular' and 'the national', was at the centre of the telling of the foundational story of the injustice perpetrated against 'the people', briefly referred to in the previous chapter. It is through this public narrative that the populace finally could start seeing itself as 'a people', whose aporia and suffering would eventually be transformed into identity and agency. The war-weary Anatolian population that had lost its appetite for more military adventures for the glory, expansion or even survival of the Empire that by then felt emotionally extremely remote to them, was more likely to accept, and indeed it did so, a mobilisation for survival under a leadership that appeared not only distant from the leadership of the Ottoman state, but also to share in the suffering of 'the people' and to fight under the banner of sovereignty 'for the people'. 'The plebeian' became part of 'the popular', and 'the populace' was transformed into 'the people'.

But, even as the nationalist cadres were, during the War of Independence, working hard to convince the Anatolian population to recognise itself in their agonising call to arms to 'the people' to protect their fatherland (*vatan*), their very reluctance to name this fatherland and 'its people' was indicative of the elite's awareness that the nation-building project they were embarking on was a precarious one and that the uncertainty surrounding it necessitated caution, even to the extent of leaving, on occasion, issues of nomenclature undiscussed and unclarified as suggested earlier.

Thus, despite the proclamations of the nationalist elite to the contrary, the state and 'the people', of whose will the former was supposed to be an expression, could be described as an ongoing project marked by precarity.

Compared to its Ottoman predecessor, the new state in the process of forma-tion had lost fertile lands, urban centres that served as commercial or even industrial hubs, and valuable human capital with the skills to bring about a vital economic take-off. Anatolia was a war-ravaged land and contained some of the most underdeveloped provinces of the former Ottoman space, while the flight of Christian entrepreneurs, which had started in the course of the First World War continued during the independence war, and was formalised and finalised with the Lausanne Treaty, had deprived the country of a mid-dle class with vital know-how and professional networks. Eligür (2019:159) suggests that foreign trade, finance, mechanised transport, export-oriented agriculture and industry were, to a large extent, areas where Christians and Jews predominated in the nineteenth and early twentieth centuries (also see Aktar 2000; Issawi 1982:160). What is more, the non-Muslim minorities that left the country included professionals – doctors, pharmacists, engineers and lawyers (Eligür 2019:159) – as well as an array of skilled workers crucial for the smooth functioning of the economy. If one added to that the failure, resulting from a lack of adequate planning or corruption, of (re)settlement policies for incoming Muslim populations to place the newcomers in locali-ties where they could use their skills (Zürcher 2017:169), the magnitude of the problem was evident.

Equally important to the depleted infrastructure of the emergent Turkey was the state of the nation. Whereas Anatolia and Eastern Thrace contained a much more compact Muslim population than many of the provinces that joined Turkey's Balkan neighbours, they were still home to numerous minorities, even after the population exchange agreed in the Lausanne Convention. Turks, Laz, Cirkassians, Arabs, Albanians lived next to Greeks, Armenians, Jews and Assyrian Christians, although by the 1930s the numbers of non-Muslims in the territory of the Republic had dwindled. Many of the Muslims perceived Islam to be their primary identification, whereas others, less devout, were not convinced by the republican project or did not identify as Turks. The Ottoman Empire might have died in the battlefields and the conference signing ceremonies but was still potent in the minds of many who were supposed to become part of Mustafa Kemal's 'people'. A state had to be created from the rubble of the ruined empire, a nation had to be built out of a cacophony of different voices and identities and become 'the people' of the Republic. What is more, after the Şeyh Said revolt of 1925, the assertion of Kurdish identity added extra complexity to the Anatolian mosaic as their relatively new nationalism turned the Kurdish population from potential Turks to an obstacle to creating a homogeneous nation in the Republic. The challenge of transforming this medley of communities – through persuasion, or, where that did not work, through expulsion and elimination – into a modern nation, where difference was looked upon with suspicion, was the source of considerable trepidation among those tasked with the process of nation building.

To this source of existential anxiety, one should add the dread (in the sense used by Giddens 1991:37) felt by the nationalist elite of lagging behind the Western world, which they had come to see as the locus of progress, development and growth. This is by no means an exclusively Turkish predicament, as Nalçaoğlu points out that the self-concept of societies where modernisation is attempted in a non-Western context is overdetermined by a sense of 'being late' (2002:146). In the case of the Turkish nationalist movement cadres, themselves usually the beneficiaries of education in Germany, France or Britain. or Ottoman education informed by trends in major European countries, as the case of the *mektebli* (graduates of the intensive cadet education of the Military Academy) suggests, late Ottoman modernisation was seen as a largely elite-driven process that took its inspiration almost exclusively from the West. The perception of lag, a projection of an internalised orientalism onto the nationalist discourse, required the deployment of 'corrective' projects both inwards, targeting 'the people', and outwards, convincing the Western nations that the nation led by the nationalist elites had a place amongst them. It is no surprise then that the rejection of their 'modern credentials' by other Europeans affected them deeply and created a sense of urgency for rectifying this 'misconception' or 'misrecognition' of the Turkish nation and its position in the global hierarchy of nations. The exoticisation of the Ottoman Empire and its orientalist invocation as the 'sick man of Europe' reinforced the binary opposition between Western modernity and the 'Orient' that underlay their worldviews and the perceived need among the nationalist elite to catch up with the West, which was seen as the motor of modernisation (Kadıoğlu 1996), informed the normative manual that they employed to understand and address the 'pathologies' of Ottoman society.

Faced with, and having internalised, a Western gaze that exoticised the Ottoman Empire and at the same time ostracised it from what was perceived to be the family of modern nations, and living through the protracted and painful, yet irrevocable implosion of the Empire, the psyche of the first Turkish nationalists was indelibly stamped not only by an obsessive fear of annihilation, but also by an overwhelming anxiety about not 'catching up' with, and being left out, that has often taken the form of a collective angst in the subsequent history of the Republic. Göle (2000:48) has referred to such angst as '[alienation] from their own present which they want to overcome by projecting themselves either to the utopian future or to the golden age of the past'. It is this lack of trust, not in others, as Giddens (1991) suggests, but in the self and its present that gives rise to a sense of an unbearable time-lag, a perception of backwardness (see the relevant discussion of ressentiment in Demertzis 2020), but also a desperate need to refute this feeling categorically, as Reşit Galip, former Minister of Education, exemplifies in his address to the First History Congress in 1932:

> We are the worthy descendants of a prodigious race which carries in its veins treasures of strength and ability, and we must do our utmost to make this truth triumph in the eyes of all humanity, and to disperse the dark clouds which, during long centuries, have been heaped by fanaticism over Turkish history. (Alp 1970:221)

This anxiety is clearly present in numerous speeches of the time, as well as in key texts of the period produced by personalities or organisations tasked with supporting the state and nation-building project. But this sense of angst was shared, apart from those at the helm of the Republic, also among intellectuals and others involved in the state- and nation-building enterprise. In the introduction of *Türk Tarihinin Anahatları* ('The Outline of Turkish History'), prepared by selected members of Türk Tarihini Tetkik Heyeti (the Society for the Study of Turkish History) in 1929–30, this dread takes the form of aporia:[6]

> In most history textbooks published in our country so far, and in their French originals, the role of the Turks in world history has been downgraded consciously or unconsciously. Exposed to false information about their ancestry, the Turks were not able to recognize their true selves, and to flourish. The

aim of this book is to correct these errors which caused so much harm to our nation which finally achieved its rightful place in the world. This is at the same time the first step to writing a history for the Turkish nation. (quoted in Ersanlı 2003:122)

This anxiety caused by the 'misrecognition' of 'the Turkish nation' and 'people' and its conflation with its oriental neighbours takes the form of frustration at the 'hostile narratives' of Turkish history attributed to Ottoman and Western (French, in particular in the text) discursive traditions. The educators who composed *Türk Tarihinin Anahatları* perceived their work as an effort to (re) gain the discursive space that was denied to the Turkish nation by the West and the Ottoman leadership, through imagining (reconstructing) its past. Theirs was a quest for validation of the Turkish nation-building project, and a sense of a robust, communicable, socially recognised, collective biographical continuity (see Croft 2012). More practically, they saw it as a wakeup call for action to reverse this trend of apathy and resignation. Constructing a powerful national story instilling faith in the nation's past was the potential antidote to the existential angst and ontological insecurity generated by a history produced by foreign and Ottoman 'others', where the Turks had virtually no place. By becoming privileged enunciators, endowed with the endorsement and encouragement of the Turkish state, the authors had the ability not only to provide an alternative narrative of the biography of 'the Anatolian people' but also to mobilise the productive (Foucault 1991:194), or formative (Butler 1997:18), dimension of this newly discovered power to contribute, together with politicians, organisations entrusted with the propagation of 'the truth' about 'the Turkish people' (such as the Society for the Study of Turkish History, or the Turkish Hearths) and school teachers in schools throughout the country, to the formation of 'the Turkish people' as a subject.

A similar sense of aporia was expressed by İhsan Şerif, a teacher and delegate at the First Turkish History Congress in 1932:

It is now forty-five years that I have been teaching history. Every year, I went through a period of embarrassment and moral suffering when I had to teach the Turkish portion of history. My words took on a glum and melancholic tone, because I knew very little about what happened in the depths of Central Asia, which, for thousands of years, has been our ancestors' motherland . . .

The history which we taught was not written to inspire in our pupils love for the nation and to rekindle the sacred fire of nationalism. (Birinci Türk Tarih Kongresi 1932:14)

Şerif shares his, and other delegates', feeling, not only of not knowing what to convey to his students about who the Turks are, were and where they came from, but also of shame and pain at this lack of capacity, of knowledge: his is an expression of desperation at being in a non-place (Morton 2011:75), or in the shadows (Spivak 1988:287). He, his colleagues, his students, 'the Turkish people' were people without words, without 'fire', without purpose, at least until the nationalist movement and the historiography it fostered bestowed on them a language in which they could talk about themselves, share the crucial knowledge Şerif yearned for, gave them a past and endowed their lives with a meaning, with subjecthood. This yearning by nationalists, elite and ordinary supporters of the movement alike, to 'discover' their past may have been perceived as a means to empowerment and subjecthood, yet these processes held different meanings and fulfilled different functions for the nation-builders on the one hand, and the ordinary people on the other.

'The Republican People' under the Shadow of 'The Nation'

To Mustafa Kemal and his like-minded nation-builders, the feeling of injustice on the grounds of the 'misrecognition' of the Turkish nation by leaders and citizens of 'modern' nations as essentially backward, superstitious and averse to the enterprising drive that had produced modernity that compounded this angst, was matched by a sense of disappointment: in the villages and towns of Anatolia they could not recognise 'the people' that corresponded to the nation they considered to be superior, or at least equal to its modern Western competitors. To them, Anatolia was marked by the prevalence of a backward Islam, tribalism, ignorance and a lack of willingness to embrace modernity. Identities that privileged family, locality and religion competed with the nation and the cult of its veneration.

This divergence, as I argue in what follows, was at the centre of a binary divide between 'the (imperfect) people' and 'the (idealised) nation', and contributed to the embeddedness of the dread and angst that I discussed in the institutional architecture and political culture of the Turkish Republic.

Faced with this grim reality on the ground, the nationalist movement and its reincarnation in the form of the Republic under Atatürk reacted to the perceived lateness of Turkey by articulating a Turkifying/civilising mission, one that would mould 'the people' who served the Republic and laboured for the achievement of a modern Turkey that could claim its place among other modern nations. It may be argued that such processes of 'nationalisation' of the rural populations by national(ist) elites and the elimination of regional differences and identities were by no means something particular to the Turkish state. Indeed, in France, a prototype nation state under the absolutist monarchy of the seventeenth century, whose revolution launched the very principle of national sovereignty and the ideology of nationalism, the consolidation of the nation entailed the transformation of peasants into Frenchmen (Weber 1976), a process that entailed the use of persuasion, symbolic and even physical violence on occasion; however the people of France did not achieve a real sense of being 'French' until the closing years of the nineteenth century, after a long process of acculturation and inculcation of a sense of national identity (Jenkins and Sofos 1996:10). Similarly, in Italy, a relative latecomer into the club of European nationalisms, Italian rural populations underwent a process that was similar in intensity (de Mauro 1960). Such processes, apart from their occasionally violent aspects, entailed grassroots convergences and interactions and the creation of a sense of affinity similar to the one described by Thompson (1963).

In republican Turkey, the nationalisation of the Anatolian population took place in the context of the binary divide between 'friend' and 'foe' that the independence war and the attempt of European states to partition the Ottoman space had made plausible, and was ascribed a sense of life or death urgency. What is more, the nationalisation of the population was more explicitly and clearly an enterprise designed by the republican elite and the state, and implemented in a systematic way that entailed the suppression, when co-optation was not forthcoming, of local plebeian cultures and identifications, extensive and intrusive social engineering, including resettlement policies, the banning of other languages, campaigns against minorities and even a civilising mission, which I focus on in the next few pages.[7]

In his address to the second congress of the Turkish Hearths in 1927 (an appropriate setting for affirming the nationalist agenda, as the Hearths were positioned at the centre of the constellation of the nationalist organisations co-opted by the republican government to carry forward its Turkification agenda), İsmet İnönü, one of the most uncompromising proponents of the Turkifying mission of the republican order, outlined the expectations under-lying the project:

> We are openly nationalists . . . nationalism is our only source of unity . . . Our duty is to make Turkish those who are not Turkish in this country. We will get rid of those who challenge the Turks and Turkishness. The first and foremost thing we require in those who will serve this country is Turkishness. (Üstel 1997:173)

Those who did not conform to the idea of Turkishness had no place in the Republic as they were in no position to 'serve the country' (incidentally this latter expression is one that has been extensively used by a host of political personalities, providing suggestions as to their understanding of citizenship). But still, 'the Turkish people' needed to be 'made', had to be convinced, to embrace Turkishness, as formulated by the republican leadership, through the missionary work of organisations such as the Turkish Hearths. Through the imagined community of 'the united nation', a discrete type of politics and moral economy was produced, one that automatically prioritised and naturalised one voice and one set of memories and histories at the expense of alternatives. 'To speak the name – and language – of the nation', suggest Corrigan and Sayer (1985:195), 'both denies the particularity of what is being said (and who is saying it) and defines alternatives and challenges as sectional, selfish [and] partial'.

Such interventions could be likened to 'colonisation' as they sought to introduce and impose values and representations alien to those who were expected to uphold them. Through interventions in the areas of socialisation and social reproduction, the republican elite colonised the very fabric of Anatolian society (see Özkırımlı and Sofos 2008:101). This colonisation of 'the people' who were chosen to be part of the republican experiment led many of them to feel out of place, dislocated in their own land, as they were expected to live lives scripted for them but effectively alien to them. To the alienation of the nascent 'people' of the new state from their own present, which had been prescribed for them by their leadership, the Republic responded by investing in a glorious bygone time, and a utopian future they were intent on building. Paraphrasing Leontis, who originally referred to the role of classical heritage in the formation of the modern Greek 'people' (1995:19), this glorious Turkish past was the particular past that haunted the republican present; the citizens of the Republic were essentially expected to live up to the cultural achievements of their putative ancestors in order for the Turkish nation to gain its 'rightful' place among the 'civilised' European nations; their present was effectively colonised through the past.

As I argue, this past and future of perfection (according to the Kemalists) was the privileged locus of 'the nation'. It signified the effective displacement of 'the nation' from the present, the realm of the mundane, to that of the sublime. 'The people' rather resided in the present, precisely in the realm of the mundane, constantly 'reminded' by nationalist intellectuals, political personalities and an array of so-called civil society institutions such as the Turkish Hearths, or the Society for the Study of Turkish History of a bygone glory that they had to work to emulate in order to build an equally bright future. In the nationalist mind's eye, 'the people' remained incomplete, their culture and worldview belated, their political subjectivity considerably circumscribed and ridden with expectations and disappointment. Inhabiting the everyday, they were expected to labour toward reaching this sublime object of the nationalist desire. This function of 'the nation' as an *objet petit a*[8] fuelled the drive of the republican elite to strive to construct 'the people' in the image of 'the nation' and embedded this discrepancy between 'people' and 'nation' in republican ideology and practice. 'The people' of the present did not conform to the idea of Turkishness as a modern, complete and undivided whole with unwavering resolve and purpose and unquestioned commitment, and were thus seen as an anomaly that aroused suspicion and lack of trust, and had, thus, to be monitored, guided and taught in order to become a worthy part of 'the nation', Turkish republican nationalism's object of desire. As Mardin suggests, in Atatürk's thought, the Turkish people would be educated and inculcated with an appropriate civic culture that would allow them eventually to gain full citizenship through an apprenticeship of indefinite duration (Mardin 1997b:121).

Thus in contrast to 'the nation', which constitutes, in republican ideology, a sublime, mystical, atemporal, even transcendental entity, the time of 'the people' is 'now', while their place in the political architecture of the Turkish Republic could be likened to that of the purgatory in Dante's *Divina Commedia* (Alighieri 1966–7).[9] Here, 'the people' are in a state of waiting, of suspension, expected to labour, forsake their vices, disunity, individualism and attachment to particularistic interests, and leave behind the memory of ethnic or religious affinities that challenge Turkishness. They should yearn for the glorious past that, they are told, they have forgotten, they need to embrace the future prescribed for them, to aspire to a reality that is not theirs (yet), in order to become part of the object of republican desire, 'the nation'. In a way uncannily reminiscent of the theology of Dante's *Commedia*, very much like the sinners in purgatory waiting for salvation, 'the people' are to reject the old ways that led them to sin and acquire new ways of thought and action that will enable them to 'grow'; what is more, they are supposed to willingly undergo 'the suffering' prescribed for them.

'Suffering' aside, the gap between the republican leadership and 'the people' remained difficult to bridge as the Republic was built on mistrust and, to a large extent, contempt for the Anatolian population. In speech after speech, politicians stressed the need to ensure the people were reminded of and inculcated with national ideals, learned about its glorious past and became aware of its bright future, while in document after document, report after report, civil servants devised plans of ensuring a compliant and trustworthy populace through schooling and conscription, as well as different degrees of coercion – from intense surveillance, to population displacement and dispersals, to removal of children from their families to residential schools, to detentions. Many such policies focused on areas where ethnic homogeneity was not evident, especially the predominantly Kurdish-inhabited southeast, as Interior Minister Şükru Kaya made clear in parliament in 1934, several years after the consolidation of the Republic:

> Why should we still speak of the Kurd Mehmet, the Circassian Hasan, or the Laz Ali? This would be a proof of the weakness of the dominant element [the Turks] . . . (TBMM Zabit Ceridesi 1934:249)

As already seen, the republican elite saw itself as a 'civilising' and transformative force. Interestingly, the Anatolian people, who had been exalted as the pure raw material upon which the Republic would be built, the moral force underpinning the claims to legitimacy of the republican leadership, were seen by the nationalist elite through the lens with which colonisers used to see the colonised peoples in the new worlds they were encountering.

It is important to point out that the identification of the Anatolian populace as 'the chosen people' rested on a combination of practical and idealistic elements. From a practical or pragmatic point of view, Anatolia was more or less at the centre of the lands of the defeated Ottoman Empire at the end of the First World War. Its heartland was reasonably shielded and more defensible from the forces that participated in the division of the Ottoman territory, in contrast to the Ottoman capital, which was under occupation. In terms of the local population, the peninsula was also home to a large Turkish-speaking population, with an additional high concentration of non-Turkish-speaking Muslims – Kurds, Arabs, Laz, Albanians, Circassians and Bosnians. War, the Armenian genocide, massacres, Muslim refugee arrivals after the Balkan wars and an exodus of Christians after the First World War, which would solidified after the conclusion of the Lausanne Treaty, had altered the demography of the region and brought a sharp reduction of its Christian population and the loss of the peninsula's multi-religious character (for more details on the demographic composition of Anatolia at the time, see Andrews 1989). A significant Kurdish- and Turkish-speaking Alevi religious community constituted an instance of dissonance, yet although not all Muslims and Alevis in Anatolia identified as Turks, or even spoke Turkish, they were nevertheless deemed to be assimilable.

Noble Savages and 'The Infant People'

From an ideological point of view, Anatolia had acquired an aura of the untainted homeland of the new (Turkish) nation among intellectuals of the period. Indeed, late Ottoman Turkist intellectuals, inspired by the romantic nationalist trends of the period and affected by the loss of the Balkan and Middle Eastern territories during the nineteenth and early twentieth centuries, began to look away from the urban centres of the Empire to Anatolia, virtually the last remaining land of the Empire and its people, when trying to define notions such as *vatan* (fatherland), *memleket* (country), and, more importantly, *halk* (people/folk), in the turbulent era of the

Empire's disintegration. Late Ottoman-Turkish and nationalist republican intellectuals saw the Anatolian countryside, its peasant population and later its folk traditions as the source of a cultural revival that would help to construct a new national identity (Karaömerlioğlu 1999:77; Öztürkmen 1992:189–90).

On the other hand, the Anatolian population was still ethnically, linguistically and confessionally diverse. As Aktar points out, in 1927, Anatolia and Thrace, with a combined population of 13,542,795, were far from linguistically homogeneous, with 86.42 per cent of the population speaking Turkish, and 13.58 per cent speaking other languages (1996:263–90). Moreover, a large part of the peninsula comprised pious communities that were wedded to tradition, while, in some parts, especially Eastern Anatolia (formerly the Armenian Plateau), the population organised itself with reference to tribal allegiances and authority structures. Apart from its towns and areas that were more integrated to the international economy, it comprised an array of mostly conservative communities, localised identities and closed systems of subsistence economy, a far cry from 'the people' with a glorious Turkish past who were supposed to build a modern country in accordance to the nationalist leadership's blueprint. The leadership saw in the Anatolian population both the people's potential and a litany of 'deficiencies' related to their envisaged nation-building project. They saw them as naive, immature peasants whose backwardness could be reversed, and with whose help a new modern country could be built if it was colonised, and of course civilised.

In practice, the nationalist elite shared with its Ottoman counterpart their view of the Empire in terms of a binary divide between the civilised population of the major urban centres and the regions that had been incorporated to the international economy (*medenî*), and the savage (*vahşî*) populace of the provinces including most of the Anatolian inhabitants, as discussed earlier. However, the Turkish nationalists were faced with the challenge of building a nation that would legitimately demand its place among the modern – 'civilised' – nations of the time on the strength of the Anatolian human capital available to them. To do so, they had to reverse discursively (though not politically) the 'civilised–savage' binary by debasing Ottoman urbanity as rootless cosmopolitan, pretentious, duplicitous and treacherous, on the one hand, and elevating the Anatolian 'savages' to 'a noble people' with an authentic culture, in need of guidance in order to 'recover' their lost civility and restore their connection with a glorious past and their worthiness to be part of the Turkish nation. The Anatolians would be colonised in order to become civilised, in order to own the designation Turk, rid it from its pejorative connotations (Bilmez 2009:352; Kushner 1977:8–9; Lellouch 2013) and be happy to be Turks, as Atatürk urged them to be just over a decade later at the conclusion of his address on the occasion of the tenth anniversary of the Republic on 29 October 1933: 'Ne mutlu Türküm diyene' (Atatürk 1933).

This 'anthropology of the primitive', implicit in the nationalist imagination, and the transformation of the Ottoman stereotype of the Anatolian population as *vahşî* into 'noble savages' had interesting parallels within eighteenth-century trends of sentimentalism, primitivism and, ultimately, romantic nationalism (see Herzfeld 1986; Hroch 2007; Özkırımlı and Sofos 2008:86–9; Sofos 1996b:237), which idealised the simplicity and lack of urbane refinement of rural populations on the national peripheries or in colonised territories, and located in it noble attributes such as a sense of authenticity, honour and morality, propensity to hard work despite being branded as uncivilised. This fascination of intellectuals with the trope of the 'noble savage' was mobilised not only in discourses seeking to undermine the Western sense of moral superiority underlying colonial expansion, but also in arguments reproducing the 'white man's burden', that is, the drive to bring civilisation to these populations.

Conversely, the 'noble savage' constitutes a discursive construct integral to representing, in turn, its enunciators as civilised. The invention of the Anatolian noble savages was necessary for the validation of the republican drive to build a 'civilised' nation in Anatolia, and the legitimation of its nationalist fantasy at a time when that very fantasy was at its most precarious state. This was precisely because Anatolia's 'savageness', its plebeian character, constituted an invitation to the nationalist elite to lead it and tame it, and to civilise it. In their eyes, the Anatolian plateau figured like an 'open', 'smooth' space, to draw on the terminology of Deleuze and Guattari (1987:xiii–xiv), in the way the colonial peripheries figured in the eyes of the colonists, and markedly different from the 'striated', 'vertical' and 'overcoded' imperial space 'with its centre of resonance and periphery, its State, its pax . . ., its geometry, its camps, its limes (boundary lines)' (Deleuze and

Guattari 1987:222) that the nationalist elite was striving to overwrite. As such, the peninsula held the allure, as well as the promise, of being rewritten, although not quite a tabula rasa, but precisely because its inherent heterogeneity was 'wedded to a very particular type of multiplicity: nonmetric, acentered, rhizomatic multiplicities that occupy space without "counting"' (Deleuze and Guattari 1987:371) – that is, a fluid domain where boundaries were porous and identities not rigid and reified.

Republican desire was nourished by the positing of the Anatolian populace as infants without the capacity of being autonomous, and thus in need of being nurtured, protected, educated and trained – Anatolian society was backward, begging for the nationalists' civilising intervention, and thus set the ground for an internal colonisation of the inhabitants of the peninsula that was unprecedented in scope and intensity (see Habermas 1987:318–25 but also for a more empirically grounded use of the term, Barkan 1948). This 'civilising' project was so far-reaching as to permeate the furthermost aspects of social life that had never been part of the state's jurisdiction, thus impacting on the modes of the cultural reproduction of their societies and their radical transformation.[10]

The expression and communication of this logic of infantilising 'the people' inhabiting the territory of the new state, by leadership and state or party bureaucracy alike, took various forms in discourse and action, ranging from its articulation in paternal(ist) terms to its manifestation in the form of a combination of pedagogical/disciplinary measures. Numerous were the instances when the leader of the nationalist movement and Mustafa Kemal used paternal(ist) expressions to declare his fondness of 'the people', which, at the same time, effectively circumscribed and delimited their agency. Tomlin (1946:9) quotes Atatürk's own description of his relationship with 'the Turkish people', and, by extension his own perception of republican politics, at least in its early years: 'I will lead my people by the hand along the road until their feet are sure and they know the way. Then they may choose for themselves and rule themselves. Then my work will be done.' Atatürk here assumes the role of a father figure, combining allusions to his fondness for 'the infant people' and asserting his parental authority. Notwithstanding his affection for 'the people' of Turkey, frequently emphasised by Atatürk admirers reproducing this quote, the republican leader clearly expresses his lack of confidence in them. The description of 'the people' is akin to that of children, not yet able to stand and walk, in need of support and guidance. They are *his* people as if they were *his* children, for whom he has a lifelong responsibility. This is by no means a solitary, exceptional expression that can be attributed to a linguistic or emotional slip; Atatürk resorts to this paternal, tutelary trope on other occasions. His sense of political hierarchy and the lack of agency of, again, *his* people, is repeated in a conversation he had with English journalist Grace Ellison at some point in 1926 or 1927, when she met Mustafa Kemal:

> My people are going to learn the principles of democracy, the dictates of truth and the teachings of science. Superstition must go. Let them worship as they will; every man can follow his own conscience, provided it does not interfere with sane reason or bid him act against the liberty of his fellow-men. (1928:24)

Underlying Atatürk's discourse is the assertion of his leadership position over 'a people' who depended on his judgement and deferred to his *auctoritas* – his productive and prohibitive capacity as *pater*/father of his people (see Agamben 2005:77–88). His express intention may have been for *his* people to become versed in democratic politics, reason and science, yet this, paradoxically, would not be the result of their own empowerment but of his *auctoritas*, and will. This tutelary attitude to 'the infant people' was laid bare in the course of a Grand National Assembly session on the Şeyh Said rebellion, when Atatürk said, according to Kinross: 'It is necessary to take the nation by the hand. Those who started the Revolution will complete it' (1964:399). And, on the occasion of the passing of the 'Law for the Maintenance of Order' on 3 March 1925 by the Grand National Assembly, allegedly giving dictatorial powers to the government to quash any signs of Kurdish unrest after the Şeyh Said rebellion of that year, Atatürk justified the harshness of the measures taken by arguing that the state needs to have the capacity to suppress swiftly:

> the aggressive actions of drunkards in the streets, bandits in the mountains, rebels who dare oppose the armed forces of the Republic, and those who *create confusion in the innocent mind of the nation*. (Kinross 1964:400–1; added emphasis)

This was yet another of many similar pronouncements whereby Atatürk assumed the role of the father, looming large, overshadowing the people as only he knew how to distinguish right from wrong and was impervious to the corrupting influences of drunkards, bandits and rebels – the revolting abjects of the Republic.[11] As one of Atatürk's most authoritative biographers, Şükrü Hanioğlu, suggests, the republican leader's references to democracy were circumscribed by his radical vision:

> [Atatürk] was struck by this sentence in particular from Du contrat sociale [sic]: 'I therefore give the name "Republic" to every State that is governed by laws, no matter what the form of its administration may be: for only in such a case does the public interest govern, and the res publica rank as a reality. Every legitimate government is republican.' This was, of course, a rather outdated version of republicanism in the 1920s, but it fit the model Mustafa Kemal had in mind: a peculiar sort of republicanism in which he, as supreme leader, would strive to implement a grand program of social engineering. (2011:110–11)

Bearing this in mind, Atatürk's statement was more about the radicalism of his project and his model of governance than the actual promotion of democracy. It was he who would decide that 'the people' would learn and the content and meaning of what they would learn. His decision to adopt the surname Atatürk – the father of the Turks – confirmed his perception of an 'infant people' in need of protection and guidance. This father–infant relationship was further cultivated by the promotion of a personality cult (Mango 1999; Berger 2020), and was symbolically confirmed by the decision of the Turkish Grand National Assembly in November 1934, not only to bestow on him the surname, but also stipulating its uniqueness and forbidding its use by anyone else (Hanioğlu 2011:185).

As the nationalist movement grew roots, the republican leadership felt that the time had come to educate 'the infant people', setting in motion the deployment of an array of 'reforms' that effectively grafted a litany of expectations and desires onto the social fabric of the land. Republican identity embraced Western modernity across the whole spectrum of daily life, from the mundane (such as sanctioning particular dress codes, the introduction of the metric system and the Gregorian calendar, and changing place names) to the official (changes in the legal system, redesignating the relationship between state and religion). These changes were aimed to break the links of Anatolian society with the imperial order and religious authority, and to modernise Turkey. As Mustafa Kemal put it,

> We must liberate our concepts of justice, our laws and our legal institutions from the bonds which, even though they are incompatible with the needs of our century, still hold a tight grip on us. (Atillasoy 2002:13)

Legal reform involved the introduction of a new penal code modelled on the Italian one, and the replacement of religious Şeriat (Shariah) law with a Swiss-inspired civil code. These reforms left their imprint on processes of social reproduction. The new legal system left no space for traditional religious authorities to regulate relationships and transactions, and introduced important changes such as the transformation of inheritance and property regulations, the abrogation of customs and practices perpetuating the subordination of women and undermining the dignity of women, the abolition of forms of inequality between women and men and the introduction of more equitable family and divorce statutes. These changes were complemented with the Law on the Abolition of Religious Orders (Law number 429), which led to the disbanding of the *tarikat* and *cemaat* (religious orders and societies) that were considered to be acting as mediators and 'translators' of Islam to the ordinary people. Eliminating these mediators between the faithful and the holy text was seen by the republican elites as a means of weakening religious authority and relocating Islam to the private realm. Finally, the abolition of the caliphate (Law on the Abolition of the Caliphate – Law number 431) and subsuming all matters pertaining to Islam (and, more generally, religion) to the Directorate for Religious Affairs (Diyanet), gave the final blow to the possibility of religious authority challenging the political power held by the nationalist elite.

At the same time, a multifaceted educational crusade aimed to create a cultural and emotional distance between the Anatolian population and its Muslim neighbours, bolster its identification with 'the Turkish nation', enhance connections with the 'modern nations' of the West and overcome the sense of lagging referred to earlier. To this effect the Republic took measures to Turkify the Ottoman Turkish language by replacing Persian and Arabic vocabulary and expressions with contemporary, archaic or newly minted Turkish alternatives. Language reform was complemented by an ambitious reform abolishing the Ottoman Arabic script and adopting a modified Latin alphabet. The introduction of the Latin alphabet and the literacy campaigns that followed to promote it and teach it simplified the way Turkish was written, and made it easier for ordinary citizens to learn to read and write. Yet this was much more than a mere reform aimed to spread literacy. Indeed, according to İnönü, the reform

> cannot be attributed to the facilitation of reading and writing. That was the motive of Enver Pasha [one of the CUP leaders who had advocated a script modification to facilitate access and increase literacy]. However, the big impact and the benefit of alphabet reform was that it eased the way to cultural change. We inevitably lost our connection with Arabic culture. Younger generations cannot understand the influence Arab culture and the Arabic language had as we can. (İnönü 1998:108–9)

The language reform was a complex intervention. It comprised a revolution similar to the introduction of the printing press in northwestern Europe, which eventually undermined the position of the Catholic Church. The introduction of the Latin alphabet, the literacy campaigns and the printing projects that accompanied them reduced the cultural capital of religious elites, which drew their authority and status from their privileged and almost exclusive access to the holy texts that had remained remote from the ordinary people. The latter, having for the most part considered the Arabic script arcane and inaccessible, eventually found the new alphabet easier to use and, due to the compulsory printing of all books in the new script from 1929, had more direct access to the printed word, including the Qur'an in its Turkish edition.[12] This direct access to 'the sacred', together with the abolition of Arabic in prayers, altered the relationship of pious Turks with the religious authorities and facilitated the subsumption of matters of religion and worship to the state.

At the same time, the change had a deep psychological and practical impact in the cognitive geographies of ordinary citizens, as it set them apart from other Muslims and potentially brought them closer to Western Europe.

The alphabet served as a cultural boundary that fragmented the notion of the *ümmet* (*ummah*) that was central in the Ottoman official topographies as well as those promoted by traditional religious authorities. The systematic purification from the Turkish language of Arabic and Persian loanwords, replacing them with revived early Turkic words, another boundary-drawing mechanism, especially for younger generations who would grow up using a language remote from those of their Arab and Persian neighbours, carried with it connotations of liberation from the cultural yoke of centuries, although it is hard to know how receptive the Anatolian populace was to such a message given the disruption it caused in everyday communication. Other reforms, such as the change of place names, and therefore memories, which undermined the narrative of Anatolia as an exclusive homeland of a homogeneous 'Turkish people', effectively Turkified space and landscape, dissimulating the absence of populations who had been deported, exchanged or fled (cf. Aydın 2005; Öktem 2004). The 1934 Surname Law (Soyadı Kanunu), adopting the anthroponymic system, dominant in Europe, and obliging the Anatolian population to choose surnames from a stock of approved Turkish names, addressed administrative needs and contributed to 'the Turkification of a population whose surnames were drawn from a multitude of geographies, ethnicities and languages' (Türköz 2007:894). Non-Turkish-speaking citizens were required to relinquish surnames that betrayed their ethnicity and adopt alternatives from an approved list, thus disrupting, at least at symbolically, genealogies within particular ethnic groups and erasing from the public domain yet another marker of difference that went against the grain of the narrative of national homogeneity.

The reforms were not merely about the 'now' or the 'from now on', but extended to the past and the way it would be remembered. As the earlier discussion of the introduction to *The Outline of Turkish History* illustrates, the 'misrecognition' of 'the Turkish nation' and 'people' and its conflation with its oriental neighbours, and the unflattering self-image this had created for the Turks of themselves, had prompted nationalist intellectuals as well as politicians to intervene in the production of history. As Atatürk's personal investment and involvement in the production of new history books indicates, rewriting the past and inserting the new nation at the centre of the narration of the history of civilisation, where the Turks should belong, was considered a priority. The trope that underlay this effort was no different from the one employed by other European nationalisms in the course of the nineteenth century to explicate their discovery of long lost ancestral pasts, as Anderson documents – the Turkish nation was thus awakening from a long slumber 'only to return to its aboriginal essence' (Anderson 1991:195–6).

The Republic's ambition in this domain involved rewriting history books, introducing new syllabuses at schools, archaeological, anthropological and historical research aimed at documenting the antiquity and significance of the Turkish presence in Anatolia and a series of history congresses where what Sofos and Tsagarousianou (1992) have termed 'scientific nationalism' – in this case, an ensemble of scientific or quasi-scientific narratives mobilised to legitimise the particular construction of Turkishness favoured by the republican elite – acquired credibility and discursive coherence.

The Turkish History Thesis, as the core of this project was called, was in itself similar to other nation-building efforts throughout the nineteenth and early twentieth centuries that sought to testify to the long and continuous existence of their respective nations, and hence, their rightful sovereignty over contested territories and identities (Aydın 2010; Sofos 1996b:235). The peculiarity of the Thesis lay in its sheer ambition; apart from demonstrating the autochthony of the Turks in Anatolia, it sought to go against the grain of scientific orthodoxy to prove that Western civilisation had Turkish provenance. Leaving aside the contentious supporting evidence, the Thesis itself and the broader historical and educational reforms illuminate the ambition, and confidence of the elite in providing an alternative narrative and historical memory for the new nation, its belief that, however enormous the undertaking, it was nevertheless possible.

An ambitious vision of educational reform became concretised as soon as the Republic was proclaimed. The education of children and young adults became the responsibility of the state and, in the pursuit of the vision of a homogeneous 'people' 'as a first and significant step, the law on the unity of education closed down religious schools and established coeducation and state control over all educational institutions, private and public' (Tahir-Gürçağlar 2008:60). This imperative of achieving national homogeneity was pursued with zeal by the state bureaucracy, which understood homogeneity, as suggested earlier on in this chapter, as not only creating linguistic, or, even ethnic homogeneity, but, as former Minister of Education Esat Sagay characteristically said, 'transform[ing] every Turkish child into an thoroughly useful Turkish citizen who has fully grasped the psychology and ideology of the Republic, the Turkish Nation, and the Turkish Republic' (Sagay 1994:364–5).

The reform had an exceptionally broad scope, extending beyond formal schooling to society at large, providing lifelong learning. Most of the specialist organisations tasked with producing 'science' that backed up the assertions of the government, or with overseeing some of the reforms promoting and implementing the republican reform programme, were elite institutions with very little reach to the public at large, apart from informing the school curricula and school books. Thus, the nominally civil society-based, yet, in actuality, semi-official Türk Tarih Kurumu (the Turkish Historical Society) and the Türk Tarihi Tetkik Cemiyeti (Society for the Study of Turkish History), to name two examples, that were responsible for the development and substantiation of the historical narrative of the genealogy of the Republic and the Turkish nation, and their linguistic counterpart, the Türk Dili Tetkik Cemiyeti (the Turkish Linguistic Society) remained high-brow institutions and had a very limited direct impact on the less educated populations who lived outside Ankara and Istanbul, as they lacked the model and infrastructure to reach the masses.

To bridge the gap between these and 'the ordinary people', the republican leadership, and before it the acting government of the nationalist movement, envisaged significant reforms. Adult education would be provided through evening classes, apprentice schools and publishing activity (TC Kültür Bakanlığı 1990), while an extensive network of specialist institutions provided various types of national formation to people beyond school age. In order to support alphabet reform, familiarise people with the new script and increase literacy, the government established in 1928 the Millet Mektepleri ('nation schools'), which initially embodied the intention of expanding literacy to the entire population of the new state within fifteen years (Tahir-Gürçağlar 2008:60). Schools were established all over the territory, with one of the first symbolically opening its doors in 1929 in Dolmabahçe Palace in Istanbul, built by reformist Sultan Abdülmecid I, to stress the government's populist commitment. In order to reach the numerous villages scattered all over Anatolia, mobile schools scouring the country were created. The original intention, though, was tempered by the harsh reality of the impossibility of achieving such targets in a society where literacy levels were extremely low and where the enthusiasm of those driving and implementing the effort could not make up for the scarcity of resources available to them, especially in the midst of a global economic crisis that challenged the Republic. Eventually, the Millet Mektepleri found these obstacles insurmountable and were closed down eight years after their establishment (Şimşir 1992:244–5). Another new type of institution, the Halkevleri (people's homes), aimed to inculcate the nationalist, republican ideology, generate support for the reforms as well as to 'train' 'the infant people' for the nation-building task in hand, was founded in 1932. Like the Millet Mektepleri – perhaps even more so, as Karpat suggests – the Halkevleri embodied:

> the principle of populism, one of the six principles in the Turkish constitution of 1924. Their purpose was to bridge the gap between the intelligentsia and people by teaching the first of these the national culture which lay among the Anatolian masses and, the second, the rudiments of civilization, and an indoctrination of the nationalist secular ideas of the Republican regime. (Karpat 1963:55)

The idea of building a *populist* society hinged, at least in theory, on the elimination of class divisions and other particularistic outlooks that undermined national unity. Populism, in this respect met another significant trend that had made significant inroads in many of the republican political class as well as the intelligentsia of the country, peasantism (*köycülük*) that informed to some extent the Halkevleri movement (Karaömerlioğlu 1999). Peasantism was premised on the idea that the locus of authentic national culture was situated in rural Anatolia, away from the degenerate urban centres, but also that the countryside needed to be regenerated socially through the inculcation in it of the homogenising spirit of the nationalist ideal (Köymen 1939). By 1939, the rural areas of the Republic were also included in the project through the creation of a smaller version that was deemed more appropriate for the village populations, the 'people's halls (Halkodaları), which were supposed to further penetrate the countryside, co-opt vernacular cultures and traditions and 'nationalise' the rural populations (Köymen 1939).

The mix of 'practical' activities, such as the teaching of reading and writing with activities aimed to cultivate national consciousness in people was not something new. The Turkish Hearths (Türk Ocakları), developed under the Committee for Union and Progress (CUP) at the beginning of the second decade of the century, were in a sense the forerunners of the Halkevleri. Established in response to similar initiatives taken by the national committees of other ethnoreligious communities in the Ottoman Empire, as the Young Turks felt that they needed to 'catch up' and outdo such initiatives by competing communities, the Ocakları combined cultural and political activities (Shissler 2003:159). Their aim, to 'raise the social, economic and intellectual level of the Turkish people for the perfection of the Turkish language and race' (Landau 1995:41), was interpreted as disseminating the ideology of Turkism, albeit a pan-Turkist version of it (see Akçuraoğlu et al. 2009; Karpat 1963), in a broadly understood way, engaging in an array of activities related to culture and education such as lectures, seminars, language and heritage courses, performances, and book and magazine publishing, and also being hubs of political organisation that were ultimately crucial in the organisation of national resistance after the Ottoman defeat and the Allied occupation (Shissler 2003:159–60). Many Turkists who moved to the nationalist, and eventually the republican, movement had either been active in the work of the Ocakları or were aware of their activities and their success and, thus, the organisation provided a model for the organisation and operation of the Halkevleri and the Halkodaları, which combined education, social-cultural functions and inculcation of the republican values and ethos. Compared with the Türk Ocakları, the Halkevleri were supposed to be more explicitly egalitarian reflecting the Republic's populist ethos – 'populism' as a principle of the Republic had recently been articulated by Atatürk in a speech in September 1931 (1991:606) and the CHP had just incorporated it into the party and state ideology after the Republican Party Convention of 1931 (Cagaptay 2006:46; Karpat 1963:58). Although they were instituted as egalitarian spaces, the overall operation of the Halkevleri was subject to a chain of oversight from the top of the Republican People's Party downwards as the populist ethos coexisted with a suspicion of 'the infant people' and their 'naïveté', discussed earlier, which might make them susceptible to subversive forces and undermine their commitment to the republican project.

The Halkevleri were the product of this duality – combining the aspiration to engage 'the people' and the fear that they were not 'ready' to be engaged. The establishment of the Liberal Party in 1930, at the request of Atatürk himself, who wanted the Republic to acquire the veneer of a multiparty political system, and the related short-lived so-called multiparty experiment of 1930, shook the republican leadership and its confidence in the liberalisation of the political system – the widespread discontent with the Republican People's Party that was visibly displayed during a Liberal Party event in Izmir allegedly prompted Atatürk to liken the political situation to a 'powderkeg' (TBMM Tutanak Dergisi 1951:913–58), and undoubtedly informed some of 'the populist' policies that were introduced during the 1930s. In some sense then, the Halkevleri constitute one of the republican elite's responses to the crisis of legitimacy exposed by the Izmir events, and encapsulate the elite's perception of the urgent need to develop novel avenues for investing itself with some sort of popular approval in its own version of 'populism' (understood as *halkçılık*), while maintaining at the same time its hold on the state, as I argue later. Over time, and after an initial period of indifference on the part of the public, the Halkevleri seem to have had some appeal. Their success, in attracting popular interest and engagement, was not uniform and depended on the motivation of local leadership and the extent to which particular Halkevleri were in tune with the interests and expectations of their users.

At the end of the day, the Halkevleri were unable to challenge, if they were ever intended to, the pervasive top-down model of the Republic's engagement with 'the people'. In a speech mentioned in the peasantist review *Ülkü* in March 1938, Şükrü Kaya, then interior minister responsible for the Halkevleri, described the latter as top-down conduits of knowledge. Karaömerlioğlu suggests the activities of the Halkevleri, especially those intended to actively engage the people as an agent of change,

> can hardly be considered a success. This perhaps stemmed from the mentality of 'for the people, despite the people'. According to this mentality which has been quite strong among Ottoman/Turkish politicians and intellectuals, the elites have the right to think and decide instead of the people themselves and implement policies regardless of whether the people would approve or like them. The ordinary people of the cities and peasants of the countryside

never became actively involved in the activities over the people's houses. The members of these institutions were usually officials of the central government intellectuals, landlords and prominent citizens of the region. (1999:83)

Governing the Wilderness

Referring to the violence of the reforms, CHP Secretary General Recep Peker, renowned for his authoritarian reformist zeal (1931–6), stressed that the exercise of physical 'force' was unavoidable in the course of transforming Turkey, as the society was stubbornly attached to 'old habits' (Karpat 1991:42–64). But, even then, some sections of 'the people' were considered to be in need of more intrusive interventions as they were deemed unruly and inherently treacherous. The Şeyh Said rebellion of 1925 had undermined the nationalist leadership's belief that the Kurdish population of Eastern Anatolia would be loyal to the nation-building project. As the various Kurdish revolts before and after the 1925 rebellion suggested, the Turkish nationalist narrative was challenged by an alternative Kurdish nationalist project, especially in some of the Kurdish-populated regions. The republican leadership's response was multifaceted. Explicitly violent measures such as military operations, arrests, incarcerations and executions of those involved or suspected of having been involved in activities against the state were complemented by an array of responses premised on an extension and radicalisation of the notion of the Anatolian populace as savage. Whereas, as suggested earlier, Anatolians who were considered to be assimilable and not to challenge the republican narrative were casted as 'noble savages' whose disconnectedness from the culture and heritage of the Turkish nation was deemed temporary and 'reversible', and who were treated as 'infants' in cultural and political terms, Kurdish citizens were deemed to be veritable savages – *vahşi*, uncivilised barbarians whose cultures were belated, primitive and inferior and who would benefit from the civilising governance of the Republic. The Kurdish-populated areas of the Turkish state represented its 'Orient' (Zeydanlioğlu 2008), a frontierland whose savage inhabitants posed a challenge and were subjected to the nation state's mission of civilisation and progress. Especially during the 1930s, as the Republic focused on the internal consolidation of the regime and the protection of its territorial integrity, the Kemalist regime and its intelligentsia not only cast the Kurdish population in unflattering terms, but also proposed and implemented policies to address this alleged backwardness of Kurdish society by deploying, and effectively reifying, the Republic's civilising mission. Just as, in nineteenth-century Australian fiction, portrayals of the Aborigines represented them mainly as treacherous cannibal marauders, fierce hordes of savages lacking individuality or humanity, with the exception of the occasional concession of glimpses of the noble savage (Alber 2017; Brash 1974; Healy 1972; McQueen 1974; Richardson 1969) in the dominant official discourse, as seen in *Cumhuriyet*, closely affiliated with the Republican People's Party (CHP) and the republican regime:

> [The Kurds] allow their emotions and brains to be led by simple instincts like ordinary animals and therefore can only think crudely and foolishly . . . there is absolutely no difference between African barbarians and cannibals and these creatures who mix raw meat with cracked wheat and eat it just like that. (*Cumhuriyet*, 13 July 1930:4 cited in Üngör 2011:184)

According to the dominant discourse of the time, the Kurdish population of the Republic were barely human and displayed none of the characteristics of the civilised nations of the world, in sharp contrast to the Turks, whose heritage and glorious history and indigeneity in Anatolia was being 'proven' by the Republic-sanctioned Turkish History Thesis. The Kurds were thus treated as the Aborigines of Eastern Anatolia; their presence in the region inconsequential just like that of the Australian Aborigines, whose claim to their land had been systematically denied by the British and Australian authorities on the grounds that land 'devoid of civilized society' was effectively *terra nullius* (Mercer 1993), or rather, land of the Turkish nation, which represented the only civilised society in Anatolia. The dehumanisation of the Kurds exemplified in the brief excerpt from *Cumhuriyet* above, and their representation as uncivilised was used to dispossess them in terms of 'ownership' of their land and 'sovereignty', and to justify the perpetual quarantine of the southeast, and the displacement, suppression and transformation policies that made up the state of exception that, through different guises, has been in force in the region for most of the life of the Republic.

Mustafa Kemal characteristically reflected on the lack of rights of uncivilised people in his speech at the Akhisar Turkish Hearth (*Türk Ocağı*) on 10 October 1925, just a few months after the quashing of the Şeyh Said

Kurdish rebellion, remarking that 'uncivilised people are doomed to be trodden under the feet of civilised people' (Atatürk 1997:668). The Kurds, deemed to be uncivilised, a reversed and inverted image of the way the nationalist elite represented the Turkish nation, were instrumental in situating the latter in the centre vis-à-vis the peripheral Kurdish 'Orient'. As such, they became a people without rights and without land, to be trampled on and subjected to consecutive states of emergency starting from the immediate aftermath of the Şeyh Said revolt in 1925 to date, and had to endure violations of their rights and liberties and systematic attempts to dilute their identity, partly on security grounds, but also partly on the alleged inability of the Kurds to act in a 'civilised manner', that is, to conform. Substantial parts of Anatolia have experienced martial law and state of emergency regulations almost continually since 1928. Since 1978 the region has been under a state of exception, while in the 1980s and 1990s the conflict between the Republic and the Kurdistan Workers' Party (Partiya Karkerên Kurdistanê, PKK) has entailed further restrictions, the razing down of hundreds of villages and the displacement of many Kurdish villagers, the establishment of Village Guards and military zones. Restricted access to parts of the region were relaxed in 2002 when the state of emergency ended and during the brief peace process, only to be reintroduced in 2015 as the peace process collapsed and a cold conflict heated up once more, culminating in confrontations between PKK-affiliated organisations and the Turkish military, which used its full might to suppress the renewed insurgency, destroying towns and villages in the process.

Interestingly, the anti-colonial credentials of the nationalist movement were not applicable in the case of Turkey's Kurdish population as the Republic, according to the proponents of its Kurdish policies, was merely adapting its more general civilising mission to the specific conditions of Eastern Anatolia. The Republic was effectively appropriating European colonial discourse in its drive to pacify and assimilate the population of its far east. What could effectively be described as the colonial administration of Eastern Anatolia by the Republic under the First Inspectorate-General, referred to earlier in this chapter, may have been justified primarily on the grounds of national security at the time of its imposition in January 1928; however it was coupled with disdain for the backwardness of the Kurds and the evocation of the republican duty to civilise them. And a few years later, the republican leadership turned its attention to yet another area where the 'unruly' Kurdish 'other' challenged its logic of national homogeneity, this time the mainly Alevi region of Dersim, mainly inhabited by Zazaki/Kurdish-speaking tribes with strong local identities. As Van Bruinessen suggests,

> Dersim was, by the mid-1930s, the last part of Turkey that had not been effectively brought under central government control. The tribes of Dersim had never been subdued by any previous government . . . Tribal chieftains and religious leaders wielded great authority over the commoners, . . . were not opposed to government as such, as long as it did not interfere too much in their affairs . . . There was a tradition of refusing to pay taxes – but then there was little that could be taxed, as the district was desperately poor. Young men evaded military service when they could, but by 1935 a considerable proportion of them did in fact serve in the Turkish army. (1994:172)

The government commissioned key republican figures to produce reports examining this region that the republican leadership saw as problematic. They were accordingly asked to suggest a plan for subsuming Dersim to the republican civilisational order. One of the officials commissioned, Staff Marshall Fevzi Çakmak, effectively proposed a state of exception as a solution to the 'otherness' of Dersim. To become 'civilized', the region had to be governed as an 'internal colony' (Dahili Koloni) (Turkyilmaz 2016:170), thus presaging the combination of military, demographic and cultural interventions that were undertaken under the Fourth Inspectorate-General (Dördüncü Umumi Müffetişlik), which treated the region as a colony of the Republic quite cut off from the political process, however flawed, that was enjoyed by other citizens.

This civilising mission of the Republic, its commitment and resolve to tame and mould the 'unaware' and the 'unruly' alike, was taken to extremes during the Fourth Inspectorate in response to longstanding concerns regarding the identity and behaviour of the residents of Dersim (Beşikçi 1990:29, Lundgren 2007:44). In an operation hailed by Turkish and foreign newspapers as 'a successful suppression of a tribal rebellion or a battle against the last bastion of resistance to modernization' (Türkyilmaz 2016:165), the republican 'takeover' of Dersim was spearheaded by brutal suppression, using devastating military force that, according to official figures, claimed the lives of 13,806 locals out of a population of around 70,000 (Prime Minister's

Republican Archives (BCA) 1939; and TBMMZC 1935:175). 'Trouble-some' elements of the population were relocated to other parts of the country where they remained under the jurisdiction of the Inspectorate, which had the power to, and did, restrict their movement. The Dersim region, devastated by the military operations, geographically fragmented due to the establishment of military exclusion zones, with its social fabric in shreds due to the killed, missing, deportees and split families, was turned into an exemplary laboratory of the Republic's civilising mission. To this end, the republican leadership deployed human capital, from civil servants to teachers, and created new institutions and mechanisms that were intended to redeem the savages of the Anatolian frontier, instilling in them the intricacies of civilisation and, effectively, turning them into Turks.

Although this is not the place or the time to discuss in more detail the civilising project with regard to Dersim (for this see Çağlayan 2018; Türkyilmaz 2016; Üngör 2011), what is pertinent to the present discussion is how the educational framework set up to achieve these goals was perceived and communicated by government and local officials expressing the republican ideology underlying the project of assimilation/'civilisation'. Whereas, as pointed out earlier, the law on the unity of education established coeducation and state control over all educational institutions in order to achieve national homogeneity, the state established a specific type of school, the Girls' Institute (Kiz Enstitüsü), the product of a compromise between the state and society, allowing female students of high school age to be educated along the lines of their gender roles rather than in a coeducational environment (Toktas and Cindoğlu 2006:739). Republican and patriarchal desire converged in the Girls' Institutes mission to raise 'productive housewives', but also women who adopt 'Turkish nationalism' and 'Western civilisation' (Çağlayan 2018:10). Despite the Republic's modern rhetoric as far as women were concerned, the new state's approach was overall more conciliatory with the patriarchal system prevalent at the time, thus producing a hybrid vision of the modern woman. According to Atatürk:

> The most important duty of woman is motherhood. The importance of this duty is better understood, if one considers that the earliest education takes place on one's mother's lap. Our nation had decided to be a strong nation. Circumstances today require the advancement of our women in all respects. Therefore,

our women, too, will be enlightened and learned and, like men, will go through all educational stages. Then, women and men, walking side by side, will be each other's help and support in social life. (cited in Arat 1994:60)

The Institutes were thus instrumental in articulating a notion of womanhood within the discursive universe of the Republic and of Turkish nationalism. As Akşit (2005; 2013) suggests, the Institutes produced images of Westernised educated women graduates whose public visibility as modern female individuals went hand in hand with their motherhood role as reproducers of the nation.[13]

Under the Fourth Inspector-General, the local Girls' Institute in Elâzığ became one of the most important institutions, at least in symbolic terms, for the realisation of Ankara's civilising mission in an area that, by definition, was considered uncivilised, defying the allure and reality of Turkish nationalism – both key elements of the Girls' Institutes' mission. The Elâzığ Girls' Institute, situated in a liminal zone,[14] a frontline where the battle between savagery and civilisation was waged at that time, acquired a very particular role, in addition to its general remit (to produce Westernised women and future mothers). It was seen as a civilisational outpost where the cultural superiority of the Republic had to be proven. To this end, the school had been expanded and transformed into a boarding institution to enable it to host girls who could stay away from their families to minimise the negative influence of the familiar environment. In 1937, an order was issued by Abdullah Alpdoğan, head of the Tunceli province that had just been established, and of the General Inspectorate, stipulating that every village should bring at least one girl to the gendarmerie stations to be taken to schools in the province (Prime Minister's Republican Archives (BCA) 1937). The girls were picked by the gendarmes (see also Aslan 2011:75–6), taken from their reluctant families, who often experienced the selection of their offspring as a punishment, and transported to the Elâzığ Girls' Institute to embark on a journey of transformation. Muhtar Körükçü, at the time district governor of the small town of Karliova (*Kanîreş* in Kurdish) in the Bingöl province. refers to the role of the Elâzığ Girls' Institute in no uncertain terms:

You know the story of how in America a cow enters [the factory line] at one end and a sausage exits at the other. Here in Elâzığ we have such a factory of 'civilized people'. In the Girls' Institute, the most primitive and savage young girls are taken in from all villages . . . Madame director gathers children like Janissaries . . . foul, ragged, of a wild nature, obstinate and ill-tempered children with no language are going to school now. It is difficult to believe that the good-humoured, civilized child that offers you coffee two or three years later fluent in Turkish is the same girl. You can understand [they are Dersimli girls] only if you are familiar with [Dersimli] facial features. (1950:55)

Although it may be argued that the words of the district governor of a small provincial town might not reflect official policy and attitudes, they nevertheless echo the discourse of other senior republican leaders such as Mustafa Kemal himself, who had called on intellectuals and organisations such as the Turkish Hearths to produce Turks out of the citizens of the Republic, or İsmet İnönü, who, as discussed earlier had been working hard to drive home the message that the mission of the Republic would make Turks of those who were not, and produce (compliant) citizens, in tune with the Republic's objectives and the national interests. The school in the country's 'east' became precisely a veritable mechanism of conversion, where young local women would disavow or even forget their primitive past and embrace republican nationalism. This republican 'civilisation factory', Kemalizm'in 'Medeniyet Fabrikası' (Çağlayan 2018), with its production of civilised Turkish republican citizens out of savages such as the Dersimli girls of whom Körükçü talks, would be governed with the scientific exactitude of the American factory visualised by Taylor in his *Principles of Scientific Management* (1947).

According to the headmistress of the Elâzığ Girls' Institute, Sıdıka Avar, the young women, abruptly severed from family and their social environment, experienced their first taste of the hygiene brought by republican modernity when they had their hair cut short – a measure that, apart from its value in terms of controlling lice infestations, was symbolic of the life-changing experience they would go through over the course of their education. They were also forced to stop using their oriental *jalwar* (baggy trousers), worn in their everyday life in the countryside, and exchange them for 'modern' school uniforms (Avar 1999:389). Moreover, they often had their Kurdish names, reminiscent of their 'savagery', changed to Turkish ones, and found themselves unable to speak in their native languages, as Turkish, which they most often did not speak, was the only language allowed in the Institutes (Yeşil 2003:121–2). These *rites de passage* marked the entry of the pupils of the Elâzığ Girls' Institute, as well as pupils in the broader east, into a life where Turkishness and being modern were valued at the expense of their Kurdishness or of their local or confessional identity, and were lived as discipline, shame and loss.

Avar recalls the way in which, apart from the daily routines and the curriculum of the Girls' Institute, the Republic sought to crash and demean the pupils' identities in her account of a visit to the Institute by Mehmet Rifat Şahinbaş, Governor of Bingöl, who reduced the pupils to tears of humiliation:

> The governor asked, 'Are these the Kurdish girls'? The expression on the faces of the children immediately changed from affection into apprehension. 'These are the Turkish girls of Tunceli, sir'. The governor continued, 'You have seen how your fathers and grandfathers have paid with their lives for their rebelliousness'. I . . . said, 'Please sir, not the fathers of these children, they are honourable . . .'. 'What do you mean? Aren't they all Kurds?' . . . Although I tried to interrupt him again he continued, 'The government is very strong. It will destroy all of you!' (Avar 1999:197–8)

Yet as the Kurdish region's problematic inclusion within the category of Turkishness was coupled with its equally problematic location on the 'margins of modernity' (Bhabha 1990), the state of exception in the southeast of the country, from the time of the Inspectorate onwards, was also invested with the benevolent aura of a civilising mission that would elevate the savage Kurds from their primitive status and expose them to the advances of rationality and science, in other words civilisation – the republican version of *medeniyet* – whose standard-bearer was the Republic and that was intimately bound with Turkishness according to the republican narrative.[15] Indeed, the overwhelming destruction of Sur, the historical district of Diyarbakır during the 2015 clashes between pro-PKK militants and the Turkish military that lasted 100 days, along with the destruction of a host of other cities in the southeast of the country, was hailed by Turkish President Erdoğan as part of a process of rationalising the anarchic urban planning district (Cupolo 2018), and as an opportunity to rebuild the city in line with modern urban planning principles. In the words of Turkey's Prime Minister Ahmet Davutoğlu:

> These cities have faced unplanned and uncontrolled growth since the 1990s, and would need urban renewal even if these events hadn't happened . . . We'll rebuild Sur so that it's like Toledo: everyone will want to come and appreciate its architectural texture. (*The Guardian* 9 February 2016; also *Daily Sabah* 23 June 2018)

Davutoğlu deployed a vocabulary similar to the one used with reference to the Kurdish population almost a century earlier – unplanned, uncontrolled, in need for a civilising touch in the form of urban renewal. Subsequent information from the office of the Diyarbakır governor suggested that the rebuilding of destroyed urban areas would 'respect and restore' historical structures such as churches, mosques and other buildings of cultural significance, but would involve the demolition of slums, shops and various other commercial and residential buildings, opening the way for TOKİ (Turkey's housing development administration) to build luxurious housing, retail and tourist facilities. But, just as in the 1920s, the civilising mission of the Republic in the form of the proposed urban regeneration is intertwined with the objective of maximising state control by redesigning urban areas in ways that facilitate surveillance and enable better crowd control.

Interestingly, the Republic's position towards its 'savage' citizens has been consistently ambivalent. Becoming Turkish did not quite erase the authorities' suspicions of the innate 'wildness' that the republican institutions tried to suppress in Dersim, in the east in general or in Sur in 2015. I would argue that this suspicion was not merely reserved to the savage children of Dersim or even to the population of the east, but was extended, as already seen, to 'the people' in general, whose reliability never ceased to be questioned.

Apart from the obvious practical objectives of the reforms and conversion practices examined in this chapter, a common element in them was the underlying 'formative' logic, a sense of the mission of moulding a new citizen and, at the same time, the conviction that 'the people' of Turkey were malleable, receptive and ready to embrace the changes that would affect their lives and that they would do so uncritically, as 'an infant people' should. At the centre of the republican worldview was the nationalist elites' sense of superiority vis-à-vis 'the people' and a lack of the will on the elites' part to understand them. According to Brockett,

> Implicit in this ideology was the conviction that the Kemalist elite was distinct from the Anatolian 'masses' in terms of national intelligence and adaptability, and was therefore responsible for leading Anatolian townsmen and peasants out of darkness and into light. The Kemalist conception of progress derided institutions and cultural accretions – especially religious beliefs and practices – associated with the Ottoman-Islamic past; it reflected not only the elite's limited understanding of but also its hostility towards the very beliefs and rituals crucial to the definition of Anatolian Muslim identities. (Brockett 1999:45)

This became evident when some of the reforms, especially those that had to do with instituting a break with the Caliphate and the status quo with regards to religious authority, became the object of hesitation,[16] criticism and dissent. which the regime, especially after its consolidation, suppressed swiftly. But, beyond these, the Republic left very little space for criticism of or debate about the monumental changes it was instituting. The model of societal transformation was unequivocally top-down, and many of the changes that were introduced went against the grain of the daily conventions and routines – the habitus – of the Anatolian populace, challenging their religious/moral and cognitive universes. In that context, the principle of popular sovereignty inherent in the tenets of republicanism and populism discussed earlier, which guided republican nation-building and the new state, applied not to the actual people who bore the brunt of the transformations but to 'the ideal people' in the form of the transcendental nation.

'The republican people' would be loyal to the republican ideology and its leadership, disciplined, undistracted by false ideologies and allegiances and dedicated to building and protecting the Republic. As Üngör notes, the military culture of the nationalist elite informed the way they expected 'the people' to conduct themselves:

> Although the Young Turk officers had taken off their uniforms, military ethics were too deeply imbibed to be bothered by liberal ideas on education. In one of his speeches on education Mustafa Kemal declaimed: 'Teachers!

The victory won by our army only laid the groundwork for the victory to be won by your army. The real victory will be achieved by you. I and all my friends will follow you with absolute faith and will crush all the obstacles you may come across in your path' . . . His idea of using army sergeants as village teachers later translated into the idea of the village educators. According to Kemal, 'just as the army is a school, so is the school an army' . . . During this period military training was added to the curriculum of secondary schools. (2011:178)

And in a speech to a group of teachers in 1923, Mustafa Kemal again claimed:

each country has two armies; the military, which protects the homeland, and an educational army which shapes its future; the educational army of teachers is just as important and sacred as the army of soldiers since it teaches the military, who die and kill, why they die and kill. (1997:167–9)

The republican project, devised and largely implemented by former soldiers, was based on the militarisation of 'the people', that would, as İnönü (another former army officer) had said, serve the country. Theweleit's discussion of fascist propaganda in his study of the fantasies of the German Freikorps soldiers who roamed the German lands fighting 'the Bolshevik menace' (1989), roughly at the same time as the time Atatürk made his address to the teachers of the nation, resonates in the way republican ideology incorporated a militarised identity for 'the people' as the building of the Republic was seen largely as a war against the latter's enemies:

[t]he core of all fascist propaganda is a battle against everything that constitutes enjoyment and pleasure. Pleasure, with its hybridizing qualities, has the dissolving effect of a chemical enzyme on the armoured body. Attitudes of asceticism, renunciation, and self-control are effective defenses. (1989:7)

The battles that 'the people' of the Republic were called to fight required qualities similar to these, even if they were not always to be tested on the physical battlefield itself. The revolutionary element of the Republic rested upon 'a people' displaying obedience, expected to 'fix [their] eyes on the Great Chief's . . . finger', as stressed by a textbook from 1941 (Yücel 1993:129), to

renounce identities, pasts and habits that contradicted the republican narrative, to exercise discipline as they laboured to build the nation and the
Republic. The acquisition of these qualities depended on active moral regulation by the state, 'normalizing, rendering natural, taking for granted, in a
word "obvious", what are in fact ontological and epistemological premises of
a particular and historical form of social order' (Corrigan and Sayer 1985:4);
in other words, the identification of legitimate and deviant behaviours and
the creation of what Rojek calls 'moral atmospheres', the products of inculcation through a combination of moral leadership, propaganda, surveillance
and disciplining (1995:19).

As I have already suggested, and discuss further in the next chapters, just
like the students of the Elâzığ Girls' Institute, 'the people' of the Republic
were at best seen as 'an infant people', immature and potentially mischie-
vous, in need of constant supervision and guidance, and a regime of discipline and order. Just as the Elâzığ Girls' Institute cultural re-education
programme was informed by the fear of the students 'slipping up', using
their suppressed, shamed and forbidden mother tongue instead of the 'superior' and 'civilised' Turkish, or responding to names that they had been told
were best forgotten, so 'the people' were expected to condemn to oblivion
alternative pasts, alternative languages, alternative ways of belonging. Tolerance of any deviation of the civilising project planned for them, acceptance
of difference and diversity, were not possible. Unquestioning faith in the
Republic, self-abnegation, self-discipline and renunciation, subsumption of
'the particular' and 'the individual', led to the myth of a socially, ethnically
and ideologically homogeneous state in which 'the people', mistrusted and
under a permanent state of exception, had to strive to live up to their putative immemorial past and a republican utopia of the future. The civilising
mission of the Republic 'had enabled the new Republican state to control
the production and regulation of knowledge through education and of social
behaviour through law' (Göçek 2011:25).

Notes

1. This emphasis on the exclusive 'ownership' of the Republic by its Turkish
   element was not explicit in the early years of the independence war when the
   leadership of the National Movement was trying to avoid alienating Muslims

who did not identify as Turkish. Özkırımlı and Sofos suggest that this was the reason Mustafa Kemal refrained from using the expressions 'Turk' or 'Turkishness' in the circular of Amasya – effectively the first document of the resistance movement – or the decisions of the Erzurum and Sivas Congresses (2008:163).

2. While Turkish nationalism drew upon a historically conditioned antipathy to Greeks and Armenians, the case of the Jews in the Republic was different. Whereas the Greeks and Armenians had largely supported the allied plans to partition the Ottoman Empire and had even joined the occupation regimes or militias, the Jewish citizens of the Republic remained for the most part impartial and occasionally supported the Ottoman cause. Some, like Munis Tekinalp (born Moiz Cohen) or Emanuel Karasu (born Emmanuel Carasso), were prominent Turkists and advocates of the assimilation of the Jews of the Ottoman Empire or of republican Turkey (Baer 2010:94). This stance gained them a more favourable position, at least initially. Yet their lack of fluency in the Turkish language (most spoke Ladino or French) and their markedly distinct religious practices contributed to their eventual scapegoating. For an account of the position of the Jewish minority in republican Turkey see Çağaptay (2006:24–7).

3. The Dersim case is admittedly more complex than subsuming it to yet another instance of repression of Turkey's Kurdish population would suggest. The region itself has been marked by a distinctively local identity, partly because of its relative inaccessibility, partly because of the mosaic of partially overlapping identities that found expression within its confines and partly owing to the persistence of local feudal and tribal affiliations and local resistance to submitting to the central government (be that the Ottoman or the Republican) and complying to its mandates. In addition, although Zazaki is widely, though not unanimously, considered to be a variant of Kurdish, it is also considerably divergent from other Kurdish dialects and has not always functioned as a marker of Kurdishness. To add to the complexity of the situation, the Alevi confessional identity of many of the Dersimli distinguished them from the mainly Sunni Kurdish population of Turkey's south and east. It thus served as a boundary that Kurdish nationalism managed to overcome much later in its development, and is likely also to have affected the Dersimli's self-perception as Kurds. For some of the complexities of the issue see Dinç (2020:7–8).

4. Indicative of the perceived need to 'cleanse' the Republic of 'unworthy' Turkish dissidents was the insistence of İsmet İnönü on the Grand National Assembly founding fourteen Independence Tribunals in 1920 to protect and support the independence war effort. Out of eight eventually authorised, seven were closed

in 1921, leaving only the Ankara State Independence Tribunal to operate until 1927, and the Diyarbakır Tribunal, re-established in 1925, in response to the Şeyh Said rebellion.

5. In *The Divided Self*, Laing (1990) described ontological insecurity as a state of precariousness where a person lacks the basic existential assurances that a healthy individual takes for granted; that is the ability to 'encounter all of the hazards of life, social, ethical, spiritual, biological, from a centrally firm sense of his own and other people's reality and identity' (p. 39). The individual's relation to their world and other people, from which they believe they must protect themselves, is accordingly seen as dangerous and potentially threatening.

6. The concept of aporia was introduced by Spivak (1988 and 1999), and explored in Morris (2010) and Morton (2011). My understanding of its meaning is informed by Morton's reading. I therefore see in aporia the condition of the 'displaced' non-subject, its location in a (non)place and, therefore, not only its voicelessness but also the lack of interlocutors that can recognise and validate it and its experience. '[T]he concept of aporia thus marks the paradoxical (non) place that the subaltern woman occupies' (2011:75). Spivak resorts to a visual metaphor to convey this as she alludes to 'the shadow' as the location of the female subaltern in 'Can the subaltern speak?'. The subaltern woman is 'even more deeply in shadow' (1988:287) compared to her male counterpart. And, the female subaltern is 'doubly in [. . .] shadow' (1988:288) compared to the metropolitan feminist pursuing the obstinate goal of a feminist global alliance.

7. The case of Greece presents more similarities with that of Turkey (see Özkırımlı and Sofos 2008:77–101 and 145–78) although, again, and, without wishing to underplay the violent character of the nationalisation process, it lacked the consistency of the Turkish nation-building agenda.

8. Lacan in his Écrits (1977) discusses the concept of *objet petit a* as central in the desiring subject, denoting the incomplete or partial object with reference to the unattainable object of desire (Fink 1995:61). The concept is premised on Freud's notion of the 'object' and linked to Lacan's discussion of 'otherness'. While the desire of the 'other' always exceeds or escapes the subject, there nevertheless remains something that the subject can recover and thus sustain 'him or herself in being, as a being of desire' (Fink 1995:61), or a desiring subject. That remainder is the *objet petit a*, the 'object-cause of desire'.

9. Contrary to the established understanding of the purgatory in the Catholic Church at the time, in *Commedia*, Dante diverges and, rather than describing it as a place where repentant sinners pay a debt to God, conjures it as a place where individuals are reformed and undergo a moral change.

10. Needless to say, that the nationalist project affected not only the cultural but also the material reproduction of Anatolian society, as Aktar (1996, 2000 and 2004) demonstrates.

11. Tyler (2013:9–10) argues that regimes create 'national abjects' to justify and legitimise punitive measures putatively directed towards them, even when the measures extend beyond the 'abjects' themselves and often impact the freedoms of all citizens. Beresford et al. (2018) denote with 'political abjection' a sustained political strategy wherein opponents of post-colonial parties/regimes are discursively ejected from the 'acceptable' sphere of politics, and stigmatised. This creates an 'us versus them' dichotomy where opposition to, or defection from, the liberation movement is characterised as unpatriotic treachery and/or evidence of collusion with dangerous others. The republican leadership often designated as 'abjects' those who deviated from expected behaviours and expressed criticism, and established a powerful trope that has been resorted to repeatedly to date.

12. It should be noted that, given that the majority of the Anatolian population were effectively illiterate, the Latin alphabet was the first they (primarily the young) ever learned to use.

13. The new woman in republican ideology derived her individuality and emancipation from her citizenship; in other words, her civic membership of the Republic, 'on a par' with that of her male counterparts, was deemed sufficient to bring about equality. At the same time, while women were held as the guardians of the reforms and of republican modernity and became a potent symbol of a break with the past (Kandiyoti 1991:41) – the unveiled woman, often photographed next to men as a peer, was a favourite visual trope in the republican narrative, and was expected to be socially and professionally active – they were also associated with motherhood (Arat 1994 and Durakbaşa 1998). The female students of the Institutes were broadly envisaged to fulfil these highly symbolic and crucial reproductive roles.

14. Liminality, according to Turner (1974:332), constitutes the state of being 'betwixt and between', where social norms and meaning defy fixity. The eastern provinces, for which the republican intellectuals of the time used the term Şark (East, the Orient) to denote not only their geographical location relative to the rest of the country, but also the ambiguity and fluidity of their identity and their 'incomplete' incorporation in the authority structures of the nation state, were considered by the republican leadership and intelligentsia as liminal spaces. Such a frontier did not conform to the neat ethnic, confessional, linguistic categories associated with political modernity.

15. This sense of a civilising mission has been a staple feature of the republican narrative as Yilmaz is suggesting in her examination of the way a series of (Kurdish) women's suicides (2004) in the Batman region were treated by the state and Turkish intellectuals. According to Yilmaz, women's oppression in the region, cited as the foremost cause of suicides, activates the civilising mission discourse among intellectuals as the liberation of women has been regarded as the first and foremost responsibility of the modern Turkish state since the foundation of the Republic in late 1920s.

16. Disagreements were expressed even in the inner circle of the nationalist elite. Musa Kâzım Karabekir, commander of the Ottoman Eastern Army and later co-founder of the Progressive Republican Party (Terakkiperver Cumhuriyet Fırkası) as a vehicle for an alternative reform agenda, opposed the first official proposal for the adoption of the Latin alphabet on the grounds that it would detach the Turks from the Islamic world and that books written in the Ottoman script would no longer be accessible to Turkish readers (Karabekir, originally in Hâkimiyet-i Milliye, 5 March 1923, from Levend 1949:367) and out of concern that the measures would weaken the republic's claims to Kirkuk that were being negotiated at the time. He was subsequently arrested and imprisoned with many of his party cadres and members.

4

SOVEREIGNTY, LEGITIMACY AND THE VOICE OF 'THE PEOPLE'

'The People' as an Empty Signifier

As the Ottoman Empire was about to capitulate at the end of the First World War, the forces that would eventually form the National Movement represented themselves as campaigning against and making up for the Empire's legitimacy deficit. Having their intellectual and many of their activist roots in the Young Turk movement, they were motivated by the same drive to 'empower' the Turkish national community in an empire that had granted constitutional equality to other ethnic groups and enabled them to pursue their own national goals at the expense of the Turkish nation. In this context, the National Movement, just like its contemporary movements, did indeed challenge the traditional foundations of authority that underpinned the ancient regime, and invested itself with the aura of popular consent (see Jenkins and Sofos 1996:10–11).

What can be said about the National Movement in particular, and Turkish nationalism at the end of the First World War in general, was that its ideology and politics were characterised by fluidity and ambiguity. As I argued in Chapter 3, leaving aside the underlying, yet widely shared, foundational belief that the Christian population of the territories that were included in the National Pact (Misak-ı Millî) and, eventually the territories that were ceded to the Turkish state in the treaties of Lausanne and Kars, were at best 'minorities' and, at worst, unworthy of citizenship, the political project of privileging

Turkishness and subsuming in it all other alternative and potentially competing identities coexisted with a more open conception of the nation that acknowledged, and on occasion formally recognised. diversity among the Muslim peoples of the emergent Republic, their cultures and the ways they were organised. The various disagreements in the National Assembly over the nomenclature that would apply to 'the people' of the Republic were indicative of both the nationalist project's not yet closed character and also the precariousness of its legitimacy, and where that rested.

These ambiguities notwithstanding, the National Movement claimed to be expressing the will of 'the people' of the defeated Ottoman Empire, and eventually of the territories of Anatolia and Thrace, that would become republican Turkey. Long before Mustafa Kemal described the Turkish state as 'populist' in 1931, in an effort to afford it legitimacy, the National Movement was claiming to be acting in the name of 'the people'. Key to this effort were the negotiations that led to the Amasya Circular, which claimed to articulate the desire of 'the people' for justice and stressed the need to hold a representative Congress to this end, where each Ottoman province should dispatch three elected representatives. Furthermore, the Erzurum and Sivas Congresses, held in August and September 1919 respectively, although effectively occasions for the leadership of the disparate nationalist organisations to come together and negotiate a modus vivendi, donned a vestige of democratic representation and of defending the rights of the people of the rump Ottoman territories, as indicated by the name of the Society to Defend the Rights and Interests of the Provinces of Anatolia and Rumeli. But, more importantly, it was the foundation of the Grand National Assembly in Ankara on 23 April 1920, as the War of Independence was raging and Ottoman statehood had all but dissolved, that was intended to convey a powerful symbolic message. According to the National Movement, the convening of the Assembly provided evidence that 'the sovereign people' of Anatolia and Rumelia had a democratic voice that could not be discounted, while, in addition, the Movement itself drew much-needed legitimacy from the Assembly's existence. As Allied forces moved to occupy Istanbul on 16 March, leading to the arrest and deportation of several nationalist deputies of the Ottoman parliament and thus to its effective prorogation, the National Movement seized the opportunity to represent itself to the international community and the local population alike as the only legitimate voice of the Anatolian and Rumelian Muslims. Three days after the occupation of Istanbul by the French, British and Italian forces on 19 March 1920, Mustafa Kemal announced the election of an Assembly with extraordinary powers to sit in Ankara adding – in an attempt to establish also a sense of democratic continuity with the defunct Ottoman parliament, which was eventually dissolved by Sultan Mehmed VI on 11 April 1920 – an enhanced legitimacy: that the Ottoman parliament deputies could be included among its members (Weiner and Özbudun 1987:336). In enacting the 1921 constitution, the Grand National Assembly pronounced itself the 'only and true representative of *the nation*' (emphasis mine), vested with both legislative and executive powers (Özbudun and Genckaya 2009:9–10).

Additionally, the Movement had vested itself with the banner of anti-colonial struggle and, inherent in it, the ideology of popular sovereignty. As already discussed in Chapter 3, when the officers and state officials established the National Movement and proclaimed the beginning of the independence drive, positing the sultan and the imperial court as a defining 'other' in their struggle, they sought legitimacy in 'the people' on whose behalf they argued they were acting, and whose right to self-determination they claimed to be asserting. The centrality of the notion of self-determination in their anti-colonial rhetoric and the demand for emancipation from the imperial order rendered it the dominant principle of political legitimacy and thus set in motion a dual process of delegitimation: that of empire as a political form, and of monarchy as a principle of legitimacy. The anti-colonial hue of the emerging nationalism put on centre stage the notion of 'the people' as a repressed subject and bore in it the kernel of popular sovereignty.

Hanioğlu draws attention to the symbolic politics underlying the emphasis that the National Movement placed on its search for popularity and legitimacy when he points out that Mustafa Kemal deliberately chose names for the official newspapers of the National Movement – *Hakimiyet-i Milliye* ('National Sovereignty') and *İrade-i Milliye* ('National Will') – that suggested that the papers themselves, as well as the broader movement, expressed the will of the people and embraced 'populism' (2011:112). This is, indeed, one of the many instances when the nationalist elite mobilised symbolism in order to create a semblance of democratic governance and demonstrate, and, at the same time, extract legitimacy from a population who needed to be convinced that they shared a vision for the future and that they belonged to the nation in whose name the independence war was being waged and the Republic was later built. This chapter attempts to highlight some of the strategies that were deployed to build a sense of popular legitimacy and their legacy in the latter part of the twentieth century and into the twenty-first.

However, despite its claims to be acting on behalf of 'the sovereign people', the nationalist leadership maintained tight control of the levers of power and tolerated dissent only when that was unavoidable or expedient. The reasons for this are complex and cannot be exhaustively identified and analysed here. I have already discussed some of the dimensions of the nationalist and republican project leaders' aversion to popular democratic governance in the preceding chapters, so here, I attempt to sketch and bring together some of the key practical, psychological and intellectual parameters that played a role in the nationalist leadership's resistance to the building of democratic institutions, and to enabling and encouraging the strengthening and further development of a democratic political culture.

For one thing, if one looks into the particular circumstances of the independence war and the establishment of the new state, it could be argued that the nationalist leadership made strategic decisions that impacted on the shape of the politics of the struggle for independence and of the Republic, driven by a profound sense of what I have called 'ontological insecurity'. This feeling of insecurity was in turn prompted by the existential anxiety discussed in Chapter 3 and played an important role in shaping the attitudes of the nationalist elite to the balance between representation and accountability on one hand and authoritarianism on the other, in the form and content of the politics of both the Movement and the state that sprung out of it. The collapse of the Empire, as already suggested, had been perceived by the nationalist leadership as the collapse of the territorial and institutional framework within which they, and their predecessors in the CUP, had found fertile ground for the development of their political project of constructing a hegemonic Turkish identity, as well as a role and social recognition within it. At the end of the First World War, the Empire barely existed anymore; the sultan exercised only nominal control over the Empire even before the occupation of Istanbul and seemed to have markedly different concerns to those of the Ottoman military officer corps and state bureaucracy. Anatolia and the remainder of Rumelia were being carved up both in the diplomatic conference halls and on the ground, as Greek, French and Armenian military forces were advancing and usurping, in the eyes of the nationalist elite, the rump of the Empire's territory, which was supposed to remain out of the reach of the Allies. Every small tract of territory claimed by the advancing enemy forces was contributing to the rapid demise of these significant frameworks within which the members of the elite had built their social and personal identity, and thus accentuated the need for the officers and state bureaucrats who formed the bulk of the nationalist elite and cadres to assert, securitise and protect their Turkishness, and therefore prioritise the nation and state-building projects at the expense of developing democratic institutions, which they perceived as luxuries, that had the potential to undermine these projects. So, the collapse of the old order, which had served the nationalists to a certain extent, and the urgency of building a new state, and, more importantly, a new nation from unconvinced and unsuspecting human 'raw material' engendered powerful psychological and related practical disincentives for the nationalist leadership to move beyond the abstract notions of national and popular sovereignty and embrace a genuinely democratic system of governance.

In the context of the drive to independence, but also after it was formally secured, the state remained a state in motion, which Mustafa Kemal later described as his notion of revolutionism (*inkılâpçılık*), a state of continual motion, of introducing and implementing change informed by the exigencies of the enterprise of state building in general as well as by the nationalist leadership's perceived need to catch up with the 'modern nations' of the period. The Republic embodied the radical and uncompromising ambition of its leadership to rebuild what was destroyed by the war, but also to educate and even radically transform its citizens by sanctioning specific modes of conduct, managing memory and forgetting and implementing a host of radical measures that were required to build a new people and nation, to sever the links of the society with the *ancien regime*. The perceived incompatibility of the exigencies of nation and state building and the revolutionist drive of the regime on the one hand, and democratic governance on the other, rested to a considerable extent on the already discussed mistrust of the diverse Muslim populations whom the nationalists tended to racialise under the single category 'Turk', that is, 'the people' whom they were seeking to engage, convince and mobilise in the pursuit of their nation- and state-building project. This mistrust was embedded in 'the mentality of "for the people, despite the people" which [was] quite strong among Ottoman/Turkish politicians and intellectuals' as Karaömerlioğlu points out in his discussion of the failure of 'the populist' institution of the Halkevleri briefly discussed in the previous chapter (Karaömerlioğlu 1999:83). This mentality was reinforced by the infantilisation of 'the people' of Anatolia and Rumelia and their perception as unrefined and thus short-sighted, unable to discern the lofty goals of the nationalist movement and unwilling to make sacrifices for them. As such, it diluted, or rather cancelled, the operationalisation of the Kemalist principle of 'populism' that underlay the republican project and was eventually fully articulated in the 1930s; the republican elite acted without consideration of popular concerns and opinions, as it considered that it, not the people themselves, had the right to decide.

To the elite preference for a top-down approach that bypassed 'the people' and their concerns, one could add the intellectual and political environment of the period and the ways that had affected the nationalist leadership and the National Movement activists. Despite the more extensive attention in the literature being paid to the Russian Narodnik movement's impact on Lenin's theory of the relationship between the people and the Communist Party as the vanguard of the revolution (Hobsbawm 1959:173), there is evidence that the ideology of the Young Turks, and later of the National Movement's leadership, were also influenced by the ideology of the Russian Narodniki movement of the 1860s and 1870s (Toprak 1984). Indeed, the Narodniki was a movement of the intelligentsia that sought extensive social reforms and the undermining of another imperial system – the Russian Empire. Their ideology, a type of agrarian socialism, but more particularly the interesting mix of elitism and 'populism from above' developed by Narodnik intellectuals such as Vasily Vorontsov, saw in the Russian peasantry (that is, 'the common people' according to the Narodniki) a potentially revolutionary force, but also placed particular emphasis on the importance of an elite vanguard that would provide the necessary leadership to transform the peasantry, otherwise held captive to tradition and authority, into an agent of radical change (Von Laue 1954). This was echoed in the work of Ziya Gökalp (Toprak 1984). Indeed, the ideology of the National Movement, shaped considerably by Gökalp's ideas, also reserved a central place for 'the people'; 'the people' would fight to achieve the liberation and glory of the nation, yet, as they were not deemed to be 'mature' enough to share the vision of the nationalist elite, they needed to be guided by it, as it constituted a vanguard that could see clearly the direction of the struggle and ensure that the national revolution did not lose its momentum and aim.

The Narodniki's potential influence on the National Movement notwithstanding, in his intellectual biography of Atatürk, Hanioğlu identifies a further, more direct influence that had informed the predilections of the republican leadership. In his intellectual biography of Atatürk, Hanioğlu examines the various intellectual trends that influenced Mustafa Kemal's thought and his decisions that shaped his leadership of the nationalist cause and the Republic. He argues that Atatürk himself, not unlike other officers in the Ottoman army, was acquainted with the work of Gustave Le Bon (1997), whose views on the crowd had made an impression on him. 'As an elitist sympathiser of Gustave Le Bon', Mustafa Kemal, Hanioğlu argues:

> never desired a government of the people or sought to promote genuine grassroots populism. Like many intellectual members of his generation, he ignored Le Bon's mortal antipathy for revolutions in general and the French Revolution of 1789, in particular, and thought that this pseudosociologist's elitism and the ideas of the Revolution could be reconciled. (2011:113)

Accordingly, the notion of a national/popular revolution as envisaged by the republican leadership was informed by a profound mistrust of 'the very people' in whose name the revolution was supposed to unfold. 'The people' of Anatolia and Eastern Thrace were considered to be immature and to lack the vision that was required to see the nation- and state-building project through. Sovereignty could not thus be exercised by 'that people' until they became worthy of membership of the nation and trustworthy custodians of the national culture, heritage and vision. The nationalist elite reacted to the perceived lateness of Turkey, by articulating a Turkifying mission, coupled with a 'civilising' drive for those of those of the population whose Turkishness was not evident, as Turkishness was not merely restricted to ethnic criteria, but encompassed a political culture and a 'modern' way of life. As suggested earlier, until the Anatolian populace was turned into 'proper' Turks, sovereignty of 'the nation' did not mean sovereignty of 'the people', who had very little space to select their representatives and to express their own opinions or to dissent against the priorities, policies and actions of the nationalist leadership.

Clashing Sovereignties, Conflicting Legitimacies

Although all collective decision-making bodies, from the Congresses of Erzurum and Sivas to the Grand National Assembly, were formally constituted through popular suffrage, a number of limitations to 'the sovereignty of the people' were in place and set in motion as soon as the latter expressed their already limited choices. The most important of these, I argue, was 'the sovereignty of the nation', which often superseded and circumscribed that 'of the people'. In the official discourse of the National Movement and the Republic, 'the nation' and 'the people' are routinely conflated, and, therefore, the distinction between them, as well as between national and popular sovereignty, is rather complicated. I have already discussed the distinction between the two earlier: that republican leaders and cadres often emphasised that 'the people' were expected to 'serve the country', to labour to build the nation and the Republic and to speak, as one, the name – and language – of the nation, as defined by the republican leadership. They were expected to display obedience and exercise discipline, to renounce identities, pasts and habits that contradicted the republican narrative; they were supposed to disavow individuality or particularism, whose expression was condemned and sanctioned as divisive, sectional, selfish and partial. The citizens who inhabited the territory of the new state were effectively colonised in the name of 'the nation', whose 'consciousness' (*millî şuuru*) hardly coincided with theirs; whereas 'the nation' was located away from the realm of the mundane, in that of the sublime, the elusive locus of desire, 'the people' resided in the present, precisely in the realm of the mundane, in a different territory and time.

This distinction is implicit, yet was subtly articulated and embellished with patriotic rhetoric in Atatürk's six-day speech at the second congress of the Republican People's Party (CHP) in 1927, which has been described in the literature as a personal development novel (*Bildungsroman*) in which

Atatürk was the narrator and author of the nation's story (Parla 1994:30), or as a foundational narrative of the Turkish nation (Adak 2003; Alaranta 2008; Morin and Lee 2010).

There has been considerable interest in the systematic recontextualisation in *Nutuk* of acts that took place at a time when the National Movement barely existed, from the point of view of the Republic, which was firmly established at the time of the delivery of the speech – and rightly so. Indeed as noted by Adak (2003), Alaranta (2008), Parla (1994), and Morin and Lee (2010), to mention but a few of the researchers that focused on the discourse and rhetoric of *Nutuk*, Atatürk attempts, through his narration, to Turkify the National Movement and the Republic in retrospect, and to reify the Turkish nation, representing it as a given, a homogeneous entity with its own consciousness and will from the outset of the nation-building project, although even at the time of his speech, the Republic was still largely a work in progress. Building on these arguments, I suggest that it is interesting to add another layer to the analysis of the text that, on a closer look, points to a duality inherent in Atatürk's prolific use of the term 'nation'. In his addresses, he often addresses the nation in the sense of a group of people. He talks about the nation 'revolting' against the 'usurpers' of its sovereignty, and regaining it (Atatürk 1981:577). He repeatedly describes the nation's contemporaneity and agency:

> Today the Turkish Nation has reclaimed that sovereignty for itself. This is an accomplished fact. There is no need to discuss this further. It is quite desirable that those present here can accept this truth. Otherwise some heads will roll during this process. (1981:529–30)

And in other instances, such as his address from the Ankara Hippodrome on 29 October 1933, on the occasion of the tenth anniversary of the Republic's foundation, he addresses the people of the Republic as follows:

> Turkish nation, my citizens
>   Today, I repeat with the same faith and determination that it will soon be acknowledged once again by the entire civilised world that the Turkish nation, which has been progressing towards the national ideal in exact unison, is a great nation. (Atatürk's 10th Anniversary Speech 1933)

In such instances, 'the nation' is posited as more or less a group, a contemporary actor with a consciousness and a will. It wants, it aspires, it progresses in exact unison, it is robbed of its sovereignty and regains it, it is invited to act, to labour, to be vigilant, to fight, to safeguard. As such, I would argue that 'the nation' is coterminous with 'the people' (*halk*). Indeed, one can see similarities in the mode of address or of reference to 'the people' on specific occasions regardless whether the term 'nation' (*milliyet* or *ulus*) or 'people' (*halk*) is used. On the other hand, the will and the autonomy of the contemporary 'nation' as 'people' is in other instances externalised in Atatürk's discourse, as well as that of other republican leaders. On such occasions, 'the nation' extends beyond the present time, to the past, or/and the future, which is perhaps coterminous with 'the national ideal' referred to above. A telling example can be seen in a telegram sent to the spokesman of the Ottoman parliament in Istanbul before its dissolution, which Atatürk quotes in *Nutuk*:

> There is no power, no authority that could prevent our nation doing this obligation ordered by history . . . In the eyes of history and fatherland, while the whole world is watching you carrying the burden of heavy responsibility, let it be known to you, gentlemen, that if you base your decisions on the sacrificial determination of the nation, and work patriotically, the whole nation stands beside and supports you. (Atatürk 1981:312–13)

The abstract references to history, which 'orders' and compels the 'nation' (as 'people') fulfilling its 'obligation'; or in 'the eyes of history', this time coupled with those of the 'fatherland'; or, elsewhere, to the 'sacred duty' or to the fact that the Turkish nation was deprived of its sovereignty 'for more than six centuries' by 'violence' (Atatürk 1981:577), suggest a second understanding of 'the nation' as a transcendental entity, removed from the present, which binds 'the people' of *the now* and compels them to act in specific ways. 'This nation' writ large and its earthly essence, the 'fatherland', circumscribe and delimit the will of 'the people'. Indeed, as I have pointed out, 'the people' (or 'the nation' as 'people') in the republican discourse are not free to make choices but feel the weight of the National Will (*millî iradesi*) upon them, as they are ordered, charged with, compelled, watched and expected to obey and live up to it, and to renounce identities and memories and to exercise discipline, all while pursuing the national cause. *Nutuk* is indeed replete with such ambiguous references to the nation and to execution of the National Will, as are other addresses and texts by Atatürk and other republican officials.

Indeed, it could be argued that the republican vision was premised on what one could call a 'creative ambiguity', whereby 'the nation' and 'the people' were strategically conflated in certain contexts and distinguished in others. According to the republican narrative, therefore, the national War of Independence was thus the moment where 'the nation' arose (as 'people') to evict the imperialist forces from its ancestral and present homeland. However, the very same 'people' did not always enjoy the trust of the regime, and the expression of their will, both during the one-party period and the subsequent period of multiparty democracy was often moderated or mitigated by recourse to the other dimension of sovereignty, that of 'the nation'. Thus, as I discuss in the rest of this chapter, in the early republican period the notion of multiparty competition was considered to constitute a fundamental challenge to the notion of the indivisibility and unity of purpose and determination of 'the people' upon which the republican social and political imaginary rested, and was therefore deemed undesirable. Indeed 'the national interest' acquired priority and superiority over the popular will and was used to justify the almost uninterrupted one-party-state period that lasted between 1923 and 1945, despite Mustafa Kemal's repeated expression of the wish that opposition parties should be established and the brief and ill-fated experiments with multiparty democracy during his lifetime.

But, even after the end of the one-party period, multiparty competition sat uneasily with the Republic's political architecture and, more importantly, its political culture, as this was shaped during its formative years, especially in instances where democracy was considered to be testing the boundaries of acceptable political deviation by the Republic's elites or 'guardians'. The coexistence of this duality of sovereignty and, by extension of legitimate political action, as well as the hierarchical ordering of the two have been embedded in the discourse of politics, elite and plebeian alike, and has been mobilised time and again to justify actions or delegitimise opponents, as I discuss in some more detail when I explore the frequent lapses and interventions in the democratic process of what has been called Turkey's tutelary democracy (see Przeworski 1988:61).

The development of the institutions and the political system of the Turkish Republic in its early years provides glimpses at the repercussions of such a duality. Despite the identification of the Republic as a democratic system whereby the voice of 'the people' was heard and listened to, the elements of a democracy, in the form of multiparty democracy whose permutations were adopted by some of the established states of the time, were not in place. During the one-party period the People's Party (later Republican People's Party, CHP) was the only party until 1945, when the National Development Party was established. Despite Atatürk's repeated expression of the wish for, and requests for, other parties to be established to run against the Republican People's Party (Ruysdael 2002:214), democratic pluralism experiments would not take root.

Even before the articulation of 'populism' (*halkçılık*) as one of the Republic's underlying principles, as already argued in Chapter 3, the republican elite mostly recognised that 'the people' was characterised by a form of radical equality that negated diversity and difference within its ranks. In accordance with this understanding, a political process that challenges 'popular unity', in the form of unity of purpose and lack of particularistic and individualistic considerations and interests, was going against the grain of the new state. This became clear in the mid-1930s when the Republican People's Party defined populism as considering 'the people of the Turkish Republic, not as composed of different classes', but merely as a 'community divided into various professions according to the requirements of the division of labour for the individual and social life of the Turkish people' and asserted the party's commitment 'to secure social order and solidarity instead of class conflict, and to establish harmony of interests' (CHP 1935:7–9). This coupling of an egalitarian commitment with a distaste for the expression of social and ideological diversity and difference in the body politic was interpreted and operationalised as a political aversion to overt political competition, especially in the form of multiparty electoral contestation and competition.

Accordingly, the first elections for the Grand National Assembly, held in 1923 were 'contested' by the Association for the Defence of National Rights (Müdâfaa-i hukuk cemiyetleri) that had been established just before the Sivas Congress of 1919, after the merging of several more local Ottoman organisations opposing the partition of the rump Ottoman Empire. This was later refashioned as the People's Party (Halk Partisi, HP), and subsequently Republican People's Party (CHP), the only officially recognised party in the country (Weiner and Özbudun 1987:334–7). Indeed, the establishment of the HP had been announced by Mustafa Kemal in December 1922, when he effectively said that the time had come for the transition from movement to party, and hinted that he would he would establish a new organisation following the signing of the peace accords. Despite Atatürk's decision to mark a transition from the era of the independence war, of 'a state in motion', so to speak, to that of a more normalised politics, his ambition regarding the new party indicated that the logic of exception that had guided the politics of the War of Independence was not coming to an end. As Hanioğlu points out, Mustafa Kemal promised that the party 'would encompass all social classes, including farmers, workers, capitalists, industrialists, and intellectuals, and would serve as a vehicle for the implementation of a major program of transformation' (2011:143). At first sight such a party would have borne significant similarities, in terms of aspiration at least, to what Kirchheimer, identified as catch-all parties in the post-Second World War period (Kirchheimer 1966) were it not for the particular social-historical circumstances of its coming into being.

The CHP was indeed a large elite-driven party, with an aspiration to gain popular approval in the form of popular votes, but unlike catch-all parties, it was operating until 1945 as a political monopoly, in a non-competitive political arena and with no competition countenanced, let alone welcomed, by its masterminds and leadership. What is more, in the absence of a vehicle of contestation, the party did not feel compelled to moderate its stance and occupy the centre space of politics through the promotion of an ambiguous and inconsistent platform, both characteristics of Kircheimer's catch-all parties. In contrast, the conclusion of the peace treaties provided an opportunity for the party to abandon, progressively yet decisively, the ambiguous strategy of the Association for the Defence of National Rights from which it sprang, and to flesh out the ambitious, controversial agenda of its leadership and founder and its uncompromising republican ideology and its corporatist underpinnings. I would thus argue that the ambition of the HP/CHP to 'represent' the entire society was not a naïve democratic ambition but a reflection of the view, predominant within its leadership, of society as a homogeneous and undifferentiated whole, and of 'the political' as devoid of disagreement and contestation. If representation is the applicable term in depicting the party's relation to society, it is not the one that developed in the context of liberal, or, more generally, representative democracy, but the one that developed in the field of aesthetics: the party sought to represent (depict) 'the people' in ways befitting 'the nation' as constructed in the context of republican ideology.[1]

Fresh memories of the independence war, the influx of refugees from Greece and other war zones and the pressing need to resettle them; the overarching need to rebuild an economy devasted by the war and the lack of skilled employees and entrepreneurs in most sectors of production, finance and commerce as the Armenians and Greeks holding such positions had fled the country; and the realisation of the extent of the social transformations entailed in the republican leadership's blueprint of the emergent Turkey, enabled the latter to continue perceiving its role as one of leading a state in motion at an exceptional time. This notion of continuing exception was translated in the political field as the need to prevent contestation and political competition. This impacted on the physiognomy of the HP/CHP and allowed it to enjoy the monopoly of the political arena and remain uncontested, despite the formation, on 17 November 1924, of the Progressive Republican Party. Effectively a splinter of the People's Party, the TCF was created by a circle of politicians from its moderate wing whose position in the Party had become untenable as a result of attempts to silence them by its radical wing, led by Mustafa Kemal and İsmet (İnönü). Critical of the lack of transparency in the way in which the Republic had been proclaimed and of the pace and intensity of reforms, Rauf (Orbay) Bey Ali Fuat (Cebesoy) Pasha, Musa Kâzım Karabekir, Refet (Bele) Pasha, and Adnan (Adıvar) Bey (some of them major figures of the independence war), led a group of deputies out of the CHP and established a new party, whose mention of the Republic in its title symbolically claiming 'ownership' of the Turkish state caused widespread concern in the leadership of the People's Party (HP), as the CHP was known at the time. And although the HP rushed to change its name to the Republican People's Party in order to maintain its symbolic association with, even though no longer its monopoly over, the Republic, the concerns extended far beyond the realm of symbolism. The new party did not dispute the tenets of the HP's secular and nationalist agenda but opposed its radical, authoritarian character, advocating a more gradual and democratic transition. This more moderate approach to social change created a positive response; the TCF quickly drew support in Istanbul, which was still ambivalent about the revolution, and in the east of the country, which was sidelined after Ankara was chosen as the Republic's capital, the conservative values of many of the inhabitants and local leaders had made the government and the HP unpopular and thus prompted the CHP take measures to neutralise the threat of this political newcomer. A more moderate government under Fethi Bey (Okyar) replaced the hardliner-dominated one led by İsmet Paşa (İnönü) to create a more benevolent image for the party, although hardliners continued being present, enforcing party discipline among the CHP delegates in the Assembly and pressuring Fethi Bey to take measures against Party defectors (see Zürcher 1991:169–70). Indeed, the TCF leadership members were approached by Fethi Bey and asked to disband their party voluntarily, without success. The opportunity arose when the 1925 Şeyh Said rebellion in the east and southeast of the country resulted in an overwhelming response by the republican government, not only in the military field but also in the domains of politics and civil society.

The government's declaration of martial law on 25 February 1925 covering the eastern provinces of the Republic, and the amendment of the High Treason Law rendering 'the political use of religion' a treasonable offence, marked a prelude to the end of the short and timid experiment in creating spaces detached from the asphyxiating embrace of the government and the one-party system. Fethi Bey's government, deemed weak by the hardliners of his own party and by Atatürk himself, was forced to resign and İsmet Paşa returned to office intent on bringing an end, not only to the rebellion and the ambition of those who instigated and carried it out, but also to any alternative voices to those of the CHP hardliners. İsmet Paşa immediately put before the Grand National Assembly the Law on the Maintenance of Order (Takrir-I Sükün Kanunu), which gave exceptional powers to the government for a period of two years, effectively enabling it to ban any organisation or publication it considered might disrupt public order, not merely in the east but in the entire territory of the Republic.

The establishment of Independence Tribunals (İstiklâl Mahkemeleri) with the power to impose the death penalty without accountability to the Assembly

(Hassan 2011:158–9) or the right to appeal (Çağaptay 2006:22) led to the imprisonment and execution of many of those involved in the Şeyh Said rebellion, but also 'dissidents' such as former TCF members even without proof that they had participated in acts against the state (Adak 2003:510). A number of later amendments to the Law on the Maintenance of Order made it an offence to criticise the reforms. The casualties of the clampdown extended beyond the 'obvious suspects' of the TCF; the crackdown reinforced by the additional measures taken after an assassination plot against Mustafa Kemal was uncovered in Izmir in June 1926 gave the republican leadership the opportunity to eliminate dissidents and extend its control over information and debate in addition to what had already been in place since the War of Independence (Turnaoğlu 2017:208). Zürcher provides an account of the dramatic onslaught against freedom of expression and the intensification of the grip of the CHP and the government over free speech and its impact on the opposition:

> of the eight of the most important newspapers and periodicals (conservative, liberal and even Marxist) in Istanbul were closed down, as were several provincial papers, leaving the government organs *Hâkimiyet-i Milliye* (National Sovereignty) in Ankara and *Cumhuriyet* (Republic) in Istanbul as the only national papers. All the leading journalists from Istanbul were arrested and brought before the Independence Tribunal in the east. Eventually they were released, but they were not allowed to resume their work. With the press out of the way, on the advice of the Independence Tribunal the government closed down the Progressive Republican Party on 3 June. (Zürcher 2017:173)

The array of legal and administrative measures deployed – under the Law on the Maintenance of Order nearly 7,500 people were arrested and 660 were executed (Zürcher 2017:173) – combined with the orchestration of intimidation, pressure and public shunning were central to the identification and ostracising of 'others' within 'the people' and to their being externalised symbolically but also in tangible ways such as imprisonment, banishment or execution.

The consolidation of the hardliners in the republican leadership and their total domination over the CHP emboldened their ambition. Waves of reforms and campaigns forced the citizens of the Republic to abandon old habits, tastes and practices, adopt surnames and, where they already had done so, often change them to Turkish-sounding ones. Those who were literate – admittedly a small minority – were rendered illiterate virtually overnight as the government introduced a modified version of the Latin alphabet, coupled with a language cleansing campaign. In the east, the use of Kurdish was suppressed, and populations were forcefully displaced after the Şeyh Said rebellion as the Republic was keeping the reigns on information tight.

As the cycle of reforms was reaching its conclusion, Mustafa Kemal, aware that the Republic represented a very different political system than the representative democracies of the West that Turkey aspired to be compared with, and realising the need to create more flexible institutional frameworks that would provide the state and party the ability to withstand and deflect criticism over their policies and reforms, decided to embark on an experiment with party competition. The precedent of the challenge posed to the republican project by the TCF and the prospect of yet another party with an alternative agenda emerging in the process prompted Atatürk to opt for a 'controlled experiment' solution at a time when the hardline-dominated İnönü government and its heavy-handed policies was causing widespread discontent in the country. Thus, in August 1930, the Free Republican Party (Serbest Cumhuriyet Fırkası, SCF) was established by a republican leadership insider, Fethi Bey (Okyar), second prime minister of the Republic (1924–5) and former speaker of the Grand National Assembly, after a request by Atatürk, while Fethi Bey was serving as ambassador in Paris (Tunçay 1989:245–72). Cagaptay argues that the new party was the product of such detailed design that Atatürk's 'childhood companion, Mehmet Nuri (Conker) (1881–1937), a compatriot Salonikan and an indispensable regular at his rakı parties' was appointed SCF Secretary General. Furthermore he notes that '[t]he SCF was orchestrated to such an extent that, before its establishment, Atatürk, İnönü, and Okyar met to decide how many MPs it would have' (Cagaptay 2006:41).

Despite Okyar's impeccable republican credentials, the party was embraced by opponents of the reforms, as well as by other dissidents. Meetings and public events organised by the new party became focal points of popular discontent. A party event in Izmir where Okyar was met by thousands of demonstrators who then directed their rage to the CHP offices, which they attacked with stones (Tunçay 1989:268; Weiker 1973), was the prelude to a SCF rally on 7 September 1930 that attracted over 100,000 people in Izmir

(Mango 1999:472). The coexistence of the new, albeit 'loyal', party with the CHP was not easy and the latter followed the increasing popularity of the SCF closely (BCA 1930a; 1930b). The expression of popular discontent and the relative success of the SCF in the municipal elections (Tunçay 1989:271–5) sealed the fate of the so-called political liberalisation experiment. Atatürk distanced himself from the party, while Okyar and his associates, weary of the possibility of the party becoming a vehicle for opposition to the republican project, decided to dissolve SCF in November 1930 (Tunçay 1989:275; also see Baban 2007:97; Zürcher 1991). The transmutation of discontent into support for the SCF shook the republican leadership as it exposed the lack of legitimacy of its political project, thus fatally wounding its confidence in the 'liberalisation' of the political system, and putting an end to efforts to repeat the experiment. In the early Republic, imagining a space for legitimate criticism was a near-impossible feat.

It is worth noting that, although the literature refers to the establishment of the SCF as a 'political democratic experiment' (Karpat 1959:69), such interpretations are rather superficial. At a closer look, as already suggested earlier, the idea of substantive political competition was something the republican elite was loath to countenance. The reactions of Atatürk and his party to the creation of the TCF, a credible opposition force led by personalities who had earned recognition among the population of the Republic and within the nationalist movement during the War of Independence, indicate their unwillingness to engage with potential public criticism, as did the closures of newspapers and magazines critical of the republican leadership and its project. The popular reaction, a few years later, to the creation of the SCF and its eventual closure confirms this interpretation.

The chance for 'the people', in whose name the republican project was built, to have a voice through electoral competition was aborted before it was even given a chance. Despite the dominant narrative that insisted on Mustafa Kemal's commitment to parliamentary democracy and elections, the fact remains that the opposition that Atatürk envisaged was cosmetic and never 'structural' or 'fundamental' (in the sense of challenging the direction that he had set for the country). Instead, political groups and parties that were seen as detrimental to the republican project as envisaged by Mustafa Kemal were banned or forced to disband.

Furthermore, the establishment in October 1920, on the orders of Mustafa Kemal of the 'official' Turkish communist party, the Communist Party of Turkey (Türkiye Komünist Partisi, TKP), in order to harness the Soviet revolution's appeal among the population of the territories claimed in the National Pact and to counter the influence of the pro-Soviet Union Turkish Communist Party (Türk Komünist Partisi), and its closure soon after (Busky 2002:84; Ciddi 2008:19), together with Atatürk's personal request to Fethi Bey, one of his trusted associates, to establish the SCF, suggest a rather instrumental approach to a multiparty system. Parties that were the product of social and political convergences, such as the TCF, were considered to represent a threat to the Republic as defined by Atatürk and his associates, and thus were suppressed. But parties that were established on the orders, or upon the request, of Atatürk were also short-lived as they had to maintain precarious balances between supporting the agenda of the republican leadership and appearing to oppose the CHP. The closure of such parties as soon as they were of no utility in the case of the 'official' Communists, or when their largely cosmetic, non-threatening role could no longer be guaranteed, indicate that the main interest on the part of the republican leadership lay in the creation of a semblance of political competition with the ruling Republican People's Party (CHP), thus securing a democratic façade for a system that was not open to contestation.

Mustafa Kemal's negative evaluation of party politics in the Ottoman context coupled with his elitism had led him to believe that political parties are detrimental and divisive institutions that undermine the unity of 'the nation' and 'the people' and, by extension, the stability of a new state. His sceptical, or even, inimical view of representative democracy was expressed in a speech in Balıkesir in 1923 in which he also attempts to justify his view of the exceptionalism of Turkish society:

> This nation has suffered much from political parties. Let me acknowledge that in other countries, parties are certainly based on economic interests. The reason is that in those countries there are classes. In opposition to a party that represents the interests of one class, another party is formed to protect the interests of another. This is natural. The consequences we have suffered from the multiplicity of parties, as if there were classes in our country are well

known. However we say that the People's Party, included in it, is not only a part of the nation, but its whole. (Atatürk 1997:101–2)

Mustafa Kemal thus considered the possibility of other parties competing with the CHP a bit of an oddity as, in contrast to the latter and the 'universalist nationalist aspiration' that it embodied, other political parties were seen as lacking the CHP's national mission, indeed hampering it, as they behaved like 'factions' pursuing particularistic interests. Therefore, according to this logic, a political party focusing on sectional interests operates against those of 'the nation and the country when it takes one, or two or three of the nation's various classes in society and occupies itself with assuring only their advancement at the expense of others' (Dodd 1991:28).

Accordingly, Atatürk and his associates maintained a very formalistic view of democracy that privileged form at the expense of the actual content of political processes. The short-lived political parties established in that period were projects that completed an image of democracy that was not democratic. Replicas of the CHP catering to what one could call niche publics, they were established, not to deepen democracy, but with the intention of colonising and neutralising oppositional spaces or serving as a safety valve in a rigid political system.

Thus, to analyse the place of the Republican People's Party in the institutional architecture of the early Republic, the tools developed to study Western political parties are definitely insufficient and would conjure misleading conclusions. Indeed, the party was more akin to anti-colonial independence movements-turned-into-parties of the global south (see Young 2012:16; Zölberg 1966). As mentioned earlier, the CHP emerged as the reincarnation of the resistance movement, and indeed fought its first election under its independence movement name, the Association for the Defence of National Rights. Indeed, the independence movement and the eventual predominance of Atatürk, at the expense of its other leaders, had structured the pathway to the formation of the Party in a variety of ways. For a start, the CHP represented itself as the inheritor of the struggle for independence and the architect of Turkish statehood, and by extension, as its guarantor and, ultimately, owner, very much like the African movements-turned-parties analysed by Young (2012:16). This emphasis on continuity made it very difficult for other parties to emerge as competitors of what was effectively the independence movement, and encouraged those within the nationalist camp who had alternative visions to Atatürk's visualisation of the Republic to remain in the CHP instead of disavowing their own political roots and heritage. The CHP thus, far from being a monolithic organisation, became an arena for exchange of views and often for political confrontations, as the profound disagreements between the hardline and moderate wings of the party, discussed earlier, suggest. However, this apparent internal 'pluralism' of the party was not a principled one as a commitment to the expression of a diversity of opinions was simply not evident. Paradoxically, the presence of dissenting voices in the CHP was instrumental to stifling and controlling public deliberation as it enabled the party to largely contain debates within its confines that should have taken place throughout the society. This was in line with the centrality of the axiom of popular and national unity in republican ideology that rendered political debate and the public expression of dissenting opinion an essentially subversive act, questioning this very unity and, by default, turned dissenters into what Tyler calls 'national abjects' (Tyler 2013). Drawing on the discussions by Lynch, as well as Beresford et al., of the role of anti-colonial national liberation movements – political parties that came to power as 'heroic' liberation movements – installing democratic transitions in sub-Saharan Africa (Beresford et al. 2018; Lynch 2015), it could be argued that as the CHP placed itself at the core of the republican project and identified with the entire nation's prosperity and security (like most of the anti-colonial, nationalist parties in sub-Saharan African countries and elsewhere), it was entangled in a perpetual binary understanding of politics whereby opposition to, or defection from, the republican movement and its particular national liberation narrative was necessarily seen as unpatriotic treachery, as a betrayal of the people and the nation. Beresford et al. argue that anti-colonial parties:

> thus play an extended role of ideological gatekeeping: striving as best they can to control access to the legitimate political marketplace, mediating which groups can legitimately contend for power and which are to be considered politically abject. Though to varied degrees and with differing tactics, these parties discursively legitimate illiberal means to police 'exceptional' threats. (2018:1240)

With the leadership's appetite for multiparty contests lost after the suppression of the first attempt to subject the republican project to meaningful scrutiny as a result of the creation of the TCF as a critical competitor of the CHP in the mid-1920s, and the hastily aborted experiment of the creation of a loyal and, largely cosmetic, opposition in the SCF in the beginning of the 1930s, the road was opened for the articulation of the particular character of the CHP and its symbiotic relationship with the state in more explicit terms, as well as the formalisation and deepening of their symbiosis. This resulted in the osmosis of the two. Güneş-Ayata refers to a memorandum penned in 1935 by then Prime Minister İsmet İnönü, addressed to party cadres and announcing that the Secretary General of the party would also occupy the position of the Minister of the Interior and that provincial governors would also be heads of the CHP organisation in the provinces under their jurisdiction (Güneş-Ayata 1992:74). The concentration of state power of those at the top of the hierarchy of the only party in the Republic and the merging of regional administrative functions with the regional party organisation intensified over the remainder of the decade. The constitutional change of 1937 provided state sanctioning of the CHP guiding ideals by enshrining them in the constitution (Koçak 2013:65), while, following the death of Mustafa Kemal in 1938, the party–state merger found its ultimate expression in the proclamation of Atatürk's successor, İsmet İnönü, as Permanent Leader of the CHP (a title that, until then, was held by Atatürk) and National Chief (Milli Şef), a term popularised by the press at the expense of İnönü's title of President of the Republic or Permanent Leader of the CHP (Van der Lippe 2005:34). This novel element in the republican institutional order not only constituted an attempt to symbolically consolidate the inextricable links between party and state at the very highest level but was also intended to invest İnönü with power over both institutions.

Perhaps more crucially, as Koçak suggests, the use of the title National Chief was deployed to make up for the leadership void caused by the death of Atatürk in 1938, which İnönü's ascendance to the presidency of the Republic alone could not fill. Thus the use of such honorary titles was intended to bolster İnönü's hold on power (Koçak 1986:171). Indeed, the bestowal upon İnönü of the title National Chief could be visualised as the erection of 'scaffolding' around the edifice of Atatürk's charisma, or *auctoritas*, that was rapidly waning after his death, in order to shore up İnönü's *potestas*, both within the party and the nation, to use the conceptual binary employed by Agamben (2005:75–88). At this liminal moment, when the death of Atatürk had deprived the Republic of his *auctoritas* – his personal authority and capacity to stand outside the institutional and legal order (the locus of *potestas*, of power, derived from the constitution and the institutional order of the Republic) as the father of 'the nation' and 'the people' – the title Milli Şef was effectively a means of simultaneously dissimulating that loss and investing the president of the Republic with an approximation of *auctoritas*, endowing the person of İnönü with some of the aura and performative quality of Atatürk's leadership.

Love, Fear and Legitimacy: 'The Infant People' and the Father

Atatürk's death at 09:05 local time on 10 November 1938 in the state residence of Dolmabahçe Palace in Istanbul came as a shock to the citizens of Turkey. The clocks of the building were stopped at 09:05 to mark the time of his death (the clock in his bedroom still does so even today), in a gesture that sought to capture his monumental importance. Symbolism aside, the stopping of the clocks marked, not only Atatürk's passing, but also the end of a particular moment in the history of the Republic and the beginning of another, markedly different, period. The next day, the Republic and 'its people' found themselves 'fatherless' and tried to make sense of what the absence of the Gazi meant, and how they could come to terms with it. The country's leadership devised a programme of ceremonies befitting Atatürk's role over the Republic's formative years, partly to honour him, but partly, in order to endow itself, the party and the institutions of the Republic with the *auctoritas* of the late president. The country's press tried to bring together elements of the official discourse that sought to project a sense of unity in the experience of loss, and the plebeian experience of the loss of the Republic's founder and first leader who, even after his death, loomed larger than life over the stunned citizens. *Cumhuriyet*, one of the closest to the CHP newspapers, led, addressing the mourning Turkish nation on its front page: 'Your immense national mourning', as did *Akşam* and *Ulus* – 'Turkish Nation. You have lost your saviour and your eldest son', with *Ulus* adding, 'The Turkish nation expresses its gratitude to you (sen sağ ol)'. *Tan* referred to the deceased leader, using terms with gravity and interesting connotations, as 'our beloved chief' (*Aziz Başbuğumuzun*, with *Aziz* having religious connotations and *Başbuğ* referring to the ancient Turkic past). Outside the capital, the relatively high-circulation Adana-based *Türk Sözü* opted for a more emotional and intimate headline: 'A sun was extinguished. He was our father (*Babamız*). But he will live forever in seventeen million [of us]' and 'Our Atatürk's eyes were closed to life yesterday morning' [Our Atatürk died yesterday morning]. The headlines expressing the sense of loss kept on featuring on Turkey's newspapers until another solemn moment, the transfer of Atatürk's body from Istanbul to the nation's capital, Ankara. On 22 November, *Ulus* used the new title posthumously bestowed on Atatürk – *Ebendi Şef* (Eternal Chief): 'The Eternal Chief is in Ankara.' *Cumhuriyet* used the 'father' metaphor that was employed a few days earlier by *Türk Sözü*. The headline read, 'Our father is in the heart of the motherland' (referring to Ankara), using the more archaic and less intimate, yet still emotional, expression for 'our father', *Atamız*. Atatürk was represented as the saviour of 'the people', the eldest son of 'the Turkish nation', while a sense of consanguinity, of a familial relationship between the late leader and 'the people' was evoked by expressions such as 'our father' (*Babamız*, a term that children would use to refer to their father, or *Atamız*, a more literary word befitting a less familial context) or 'our Atatürk' (*Atatürkümüz*).

Clearly, not all citizens of the Republic felt the same sense of loss. For many of those who bore the brunt of the violent aspects of the civilising mission he led, who were displaced in the name of national security and Turkification, those who fell victims of political intrigues and vendettas, Atatürk's passing cannot have represented a loss, although it had certainly signalled change. For many others, the shock was tantamount to an experience of sudden loss of someone who had fought to give them a future as everything they had taken for granted was collapsing at the end of the First World War. For those who had accepted the Republic as a civilising force, a force of stability and security in their lives, the death of the military and political mastermind of independence, and the founder and leader of the state of fifteen years represented a loss and, perhaps a source of anxiety about the future. For many amongst those who had come from lands lost by the imploding Empire and sought to build their homes and lives in the Republic – the refugees from Russia, from the Balkans, the exchangees from

Greece – Atatürk was seen as the guarantor of their safety and equality in their new motherland. For people like İhsan Şerif, the teacher encountered earlier in Chapter 3 addressing the First Turkish History Congress in 1932, Atatürk was a man who gave meaning and pride to his Turkishness and represented a guarantor of his identity, as he probably did for the thousands who took to the villages of Anatolia to implement the literacy campaign, or to staff the Halkevleri and Halkodaları and propagate the republican ideology. To those who had worked with him and participated in the republican project from a position of authority, Mustafa Kemal's passing represented much more than the loss of a leader. More significantly, Atatürk's reputation and history were conducive to the cultivation of his personal charisma and *auctoritas*, which placed him simultaneously outside the legal and institutional order of the Republic and at the centre of it, but, as far the state was concerned, these attributes were also a source of much-needed legitimacy.

As argued earlier, the institutional arrangements of the Republic, with the CHP as effectively the only functioning party that was permitted to operate and the one that was inextricably linked to the state and its apparatuses, combined with the republican leadership's aversion to multiparty competition, had contributed to a deficit of political representation, if not of legitimacy. The TCF's unexpected popular appeal, soon after its establishment in 1924, had provided a warning sign for the republican elite that its uncompromising agenda and the pace and intensity of its reform programme were becoming unpopular in parts of the country, especially as instances of corruption were further tarnishing the republican project. What is more, the effective split in the CHP that saw some of the prominent political figures in its fold leaving to form an opposition party had provided more evidence that the republican project was creating considerable unease even within its party ranks. If more proof was needed, it was provided in 1930 with the brief 'pluralist' experiment and its abrupt demise discussed earlier.

As I have argued, the elite's fundamental mistrust of those whom the regime would interpellate as 'the people', who were supposed to be sovereign, combined with their intolerance of the expression of oppositional voices, of dissent, but also of behaviours and practices deemed inappropriate, has constituted a fundamental element of the Republic's politics. As İnce points out,

> In terms of the public rights of citizens, the CHP programmes during the single-party period were not very promising. Article 4 of the 1931 programme listed freedom, equality, inviolability and the right to own property as citizens' public rights, yet said nothing about the protection of these rights by the state. Parallel to this, the duties of citizens were more emphasised than citizenship rights. Democracy was not among the CHP's six principles (generally called as 'Six Arrows') – republicanism (*cumhuriyetçilik*), nationalism (*milliyetçilik*), populism (*halkçılık*), statism (*devletçilik*), secularism (*laiklik*), and revolutionism (*inkılâpçılık*) – which represented the ideals of the party, and were added into the Constitution in 1937. (2012:43)

Even the 1924 constitution (Teşkilat-I Esasiye Kanunu), which was considered to have been premised on liberal principles and which refrained from delimiting individual liberties on account of other notions (for instance, the public good), or bodies such as the state (Tanör 2001:308) did so without specifying particular provisions for the protection and actualisation of individual rights (TC Anayasa Mahkemesi 1924). The rights of the citizen as a social individual were from early on to take second place to the unity of 'the people'. Accordingly, for most of the early Republic, elections meant little more than rubber-stamping the Grand National Assembly candidates fielded by the CHP, as there was no space for contestation and electoral competition. In the polarised political arena, critique of, or even misgivings about, the course of the Republic were often considered to be acts challenging the Republic. Even nationalism, the *point de capiton* of the republican political imaginary, could be considered subversive if it did not conform to its republican variant.

The notion of citizen choice was at odds with the republican emphasis on 'the nation' (as an ideal transcendental community) and 'the people' (as a united, homogeneous imagined community). It comes as no surprise therefore that the choice available to the citizenry during elections was circumscribed by this binary conception of politics and, of course, the one-party system, and are therefore severely limited. As suggested earlier, 'representation' in republican practice did not signify the expression of social and political diversity of the type one would encounter in representative political systems of the time, but rather the reinforcement of a particular visualisation of republican society as homogeneous, in the form of 'the people'. In the republican political imaginary, the CHP and the Republic constituted the institutional manifestations and expressions of 'the people' and their unity, and their unanimous will and resolve. Voting for the delegates of the single party, as much as an act of limited choice, also entailed an inversion of the flow of the conventional process of representation: it functioned as a 'confirmation' or, at least, tactical acceptance of this imaginary unity proposed from the party to 'the people'. The reasons for this were many, but were largely rationalised in specific ways that left their imprint on society and the politics of the Republic for generations to come. The exigencies of building a new viable state from the rubble of the Empire, the need for discipline and unity of purpose in the effort to resuscitate and expand the wounded economy of the Republic's territories, to build effective political institutions and to disassociate Turkey from its predecessor's characterisation as the sick man of Europe, were some of the excuses used to effectively defer the sovereignty of 'the people' to a later time.

This reminder that the War of Independence may have been formally won but the tasks that it entailed were still outstanding was issued on the tenth anniversary of the Republic, when Mustafa Kemal, addressing 'the Turkish people' from the Ankara hippodrome, characteristically said:

> We have accomplished many and great tasks in a short time. The greatest of these is the Turkish Republic, the basis of which is the Turkish heroism and the great Turkish culture. We owe this success to the cooperative progress of the Turkish nation and its valuable army. However we can never consider what we have achieved to be sufficient, because we must, and are determined to accomplish even more and greater tasks. We shall raise our country to the level of the most prosperous and civilized nations of the world. We shall endow our nation with the broadest means and sources of welfare. We shall raise our national culture above the contemporary level of civilization. Therefore, we should judge 'the measure of time not according to the lax mentality of past centuries, but in terms of the concepts of speed and movement of our century. Compared to the past, we shall work harder. We shall perform greater tasks in a shorter time.' (Atatürk 1997)

This impatience, largely fuelled by a discourse of lack, of not having yet achieved, of needing to do even more, faster, tirelessly and incessantly, was coupled with a discourse of ontological insecurity, a discourse of the fear of lagging behind (discussed in Chapter 3). Thus, as the Republic was consolidating itself, the threat of mutiny and secession in the east, the existence of 'treacherous' dissidents, such as those who conspired to murder Atatürk in Izmir,[2] or of those who wanted to use religion as a political instrument, or those who 'refused to assimilate to "the nation"' and to 'internalise the republican narrative', were interpreted, or rather used, by the republican leadership as indications that the state should resist the pause that consolidation entailed, that it had no choice but to move and keep on moving, had to push its reforms and its cultural revolution forward, to keep on civilising the east and the west of the country alike, secularising the entire Republic, teaching citizens how, as well as what, to read and write, and thus required not only to not allow the divisive effect of multiparty competition to poison the body politic of the Republic but also to turn the informal 'state in motion' and its underlying 'state of exception' to a formal, legal one, severely constraining democratic dialogue and contestation throughout the territory of the Republic and violating even the most fundamental human rights of some of the population. Thus, the state resisted attempts at consolidation and continued to define politics as a struggle of *them* versus *us*, in the process othering populations, cultures, political views and their proponents. This state in continual motion, motivated by never waning suspicion and vigilance, was inimical to the luxury of divisive experiments such as elections. In such visualisations of the Republic under threat and in perpetual motion, there was very little, if any, space for particularistic concerns, class-based demands or views premised on cultural difference as these were considered aberrant and selfish challenges to the edifice of the homogeneity and unity of 'the people'. Whereas the Republic denied the need for competitive elections, it had not instituted adequate avenues through which the will of its citizens could be 'read' and be seen to be taken into account. As the one-party election cycles were not the optimum means of concretising sovereignty and the legitimacy of institutions, it followed that other, less politically risky avenues needed to be explored. In other words, if the material content of the sovereignty of 'the people' could not be determined through elections, it should be gauged in other ways. 'The people' needed to be included somehow, yet the response to how this would happen was complex and some of its elements have already been discussed in the preceding pages.

I have argued that a formal political field structured along the lines of liberal democracy was not considered suitable for 'the people' of the Republic by the republican leadership, as such a framework that was putatively unnatural and irrelevant to the particularities of the Turkish society served to (re) produce a fragmented voice, or rather, many voices, especially as 'the infant people' were not equipped to express themselves as one. More than requiring the right to vote, 'the infant people' were deemed to be easily confused, in Atatürk's own words (Kinross 1964:401), to be easily distracted from working faster, tirelessly and incessantly to reduce the gap between 'the idealised nation' and the existing 'nation as people'. They were thus in need of tutoring/tutelage 'for they knew not what they wanted', in contrast to their leadership, who could see undistracted ahead and plot the path to be followed.

It is in this particular context that the leader of the republican project found a perfect fit. Atatürk was charismatic leader who had managed, during the War of Independence, to articulate the disparate plebeian voices, anxieties and suffering in a nationalist vision, and, later in the republican project, had developed a unique rapport with 'the people' that most other republican leaders had not. The Gazi (a term meaning 'conquering hero', used to denote his bravery in the wars), as he was widely known before he was offered the surname Atatürk, had acquired widespread popularity among the Anatolian population for his defence of the Anafarta front in the Gallipoli campaign and by claiming credit for the Ottoman victory at the Battle of Gallipoli in 1915 (Zürcher 2017:415). His role in the War of Independence, especially the victory over the Greeks in the battle of Sakarya in September 1921 and Izmir's capture in 1922, which sealed the outcome of the independence war had created an aura of valiance, bravery and commitment. The Grand National Assembly's recognition of his qualities as a military leader through the award of ranks and titles such Commander in Chief of the nationalist forces, Army Field Marshal and 'Gazi' (Shaw and Shaw 1977:357; Zürcher 2017:160, 415) had positioned him at the centre of the nationalist mythology and helped him to overshadow other leaders of the movement and thwart their leadership aspirations. More importantly, the Gazi had become a household name in Anatolia's towns and villages and identified as a saviour and a paternal figure. As Yilmaz aptly points out, '[i]n the popular imagination, Mustafa Kemal, as the hero of the War of Liberation and saviour of the nation, appears to have firmly taken the place of the Ottoman Sultan' (2013:73). Discussing a local commemoration of Ertuğrul Gazi in the north-western Anatolian town of Söğüt, Yilmaz argues:

> a vast majority of Turkey's population the slogan 'Long Live the Sultan' ('Padişahım Çok Yaşa') successfully transformed into 'Long Live the Gazi' ('Yaşasın Gazi/Yaşasın Mustafa Kemal Paşa') and 'Long Live the Republic' ('Yaşasın Cumhuriyet' and 'Yaşasın Türk Milleti') as the figure of Atatürk effectively replaced the figure of the Sultan as the symbol of the idealised form of the state in the popular imagination. (2013:213–14)

Or perhaps, even more than that. Unlike the sultan, whose remoteness from Anatolia's daily life made him an abstract figure of authority, Mustafa Kemal, especially in Republic's earlier years, invested in contact with 'the people'. Whenever he travelled through Anatolia to deliver addresses in support of the republican reforms or on inspection tours, his appearances became local events. Local residents would cherish a mere glimpse of Atatürk and his companions, even if he was passing by: 'a quick glance at Mustafa Kemal and Latife Hanım when they got off the boat in Trabzon, a quick glance during his visit to a school in Mersin, a quick glimpse of Mustafa Kemal and Reza Shah in Bankalar Street in Istanbul, a brief conversation during his visit to an elementary school in Bursa' (Yilmaz 2013:221–2). What is more, these memories would become part of personal and family narratives, in which details of encounters with Atatürk would be vividly imparted, as indicated in conversations I had with interlocutors who had this type of 'indirect contact' with Mustafa Kemal. It is this politics of immediacy that made more inroads into the lives of ordinary citizens and made Atatürk an object of affection.

As Zürcher points out, as the Republic had consolidated its control over both the press and the educational institutions through the education reforms, it had a powerful means of communication at its disposal, which it mobilised to spread the republican message (1992:189). This message included the cultivation of the persona and mythology surrounding Mustafa Kemal, the benevolent and just saviour of 'the Turkish nation'. Numerous stories of encounters of Atatürk with ordinary people, conversations with children and adults from all walks of life were recounted in the press, while his role in the crucial years of the independence war, and even earlier, with some of his former associates who became contenders for the leadership of the nationalist project airbrushed out of the picture, was propagated in the teaching of history in schools (the history of the Turkish revolution became a compulsory subject in 1934). The figure of Gazi, remote yet omnipresent, became a staple element of the Anatolian townscapes soon after the proclamation of the Republic, statues of him were erected in town squares and other public spaces. The narratives of his human, intimate encounters, his passionate, paternal addresses to the nation, combined with his ubiquitous presence in public spaces, and the official exaltation of his valiance, foresight and fairness were crucial ingredients in the development of a personality cult. Atatürk, himself aware of the importance of his public image, made a conscious effort to project himself in ways that confirmed his central role in the nation-building project. As opponents were eliminated, the history of the Republic was eventually depicted as the single-handed achievement of one man. Zürcher 2017:185–6). *Nutuk*, his six-day speech to the CHP congress, apart from being a narrative of the nationalist project in ways that would influence Turkish historiography for decades to come, also provided an opportunity for Kemal to project a public image of himself as an unwavering, proud, committed, selfless person possessing political acumen and the ability to make strategic and effective political interventions. His ability to remain aloof from daily politics, or rather to appear to do so while keeping a tight grip over decision making and participating often in debates, allowed him to present himself as having long-term vision, standing above political arguments, disagreements, the corruption and the intrigue that made up the dailiness of politics. This contributed greatly to his dissociation from the oppressive, arbitrary and violent manifestations of the state in the everyday life of the population of the Republic and enabled him to establish a semblance of intimate connection with the individual citizen.

His addresses to the nation were emotional, inspirational and encompassed an element of intimacy as he interpellated the citizens as '*his* citizens', '*his* nation', '*his* people'. It is this affectionate side of Atatürk, who, during his Anatolian tours would grant 'his people' glimpses, or brief encounters, would roll up his sleeves to support the Republic's literacy campaign by teaching in person, the paternal *Atatürkümüz*, the *Babamız* or the *Atamız* whose passing was mourned on the front pages of the nation's newspapers in November 1938, and whom the public affectionately looked to and later recalled. Yilmaz remarks that it appeared that the myth of the Gazi as a benevolent saviour had taken root among the Anatolian population since even the authors of oppositional propaganda leaflets could not ignore his popularity, having to refer to Mustafa Kemal as 'the man you call the Great Liberator' (2013:258–9), alluding to the fact that the audience they were addressing needed to be swayed from their acceptance of Atatürk's importance, authority or charisma.

Such was the appeal of Mustafa Kemal's personality that

> the public generally maintained a careful distinction between the benevolent state epitomized by Mustafa Kemal and the local practices [of state repression and violence]. Physical violence and other injustices committed at the local level were seen as excesses that Atatürk and the others at the head of the state did not authorize or condone. (Yilmaz 2013:73)

This affectionate identification of Atatürk as a father figure for the Republic's citizens was instrumental in structuring the particular ways in which they experienced the state, but also how they perceived themselves in relation to politics, during his life but also later, after his death. His paternal interpellations became a route for them to identify with him through fantasies that idealised him, and posited him as a protective father figure, and an object of love and admiration (Freud 1923; 1955; 1961; 1964a; 1964b), as ethnographic studies focusing on memories of the period suggest. Mustafa Kemal was the face of the ideal state, the one promised and juxtaposed to the impersonal, imperial order that Atatürk had liberated them from. Atatürk's fairness and benevolence constituted qualities of the ideal 'populist' republican state, which was supposed to serve them, 'the sovereign people'. Even when 'the paternal' turned to 'paternalist', when the Gazi encouraged them to wear hats in his speech in Kastamonu (see Nereid 2011), chastised them for their unwillingness to abandon their old ways and habits, or visited them to teach them the new alien script imposed by his own reforms, many of the citizens recognised the mainly enabling and 'enlightening' dimensions of his presence. After all, he was the saviour, the man who had believed in them and had fought the invading armies to protect them.

To be sure, Mustafa Kemal's 'charisma' was not the product of his own individual personality traits – at least not of these traits in themselves; Marsden and Snow warn against such facile explanations, and remind that charisma is the product of a relationship and a social context. Indeed, it is, as they say,

> an influence relationship marked by asymmetry, directness and, for the follower, great passion. Asymmetry means that the leader has profound influence on attitudes and behavior of the following but that the opposite is not true; the following does provide the all-important empowering responses, to use Laswell's terminology, but its other influence on the leader is muted. Directness means the absence of significant mediation of the relationship, by either formal structures or informal networks. Great passion . . . means intense devotion to and extraordinary reverence for the leader. (Marsden and Snow 1991:5)

In the eyes of the citizens who looked up to him and idolised him, Atatürk symbolised, or represented, the part of the state that extended its reassuring hand to guide and nurture those who accepted more or less willingly the designation of 'infant people' mentioned earlier. But, for the same citizens, the state also had another less agreeable, more pervasive and persecuting and punitive facet, one that caused anxiety and fear. The republican state was visible and ubiquitous, as the Republic had extended its presence in the Anatolian countryside considerably. It manifested itself in the form of its bureaucracy, of its more effective control over the countryside, its expectations of compliance, its drive to 'civilise', and the threat of the exercise of violence through the deployment of its repressive apparatus in case of deviation from expected behaviour. As Zürcher notes, in the early Republic:

> The gendarme and tax collector became more hated and feared than ever. Resentment against the state, in itself a traditional feature of country life, became more acute because the state became more effective and visible. It was also exacerbated because the state's secularist policies, especially the suppression of expressions of popular faith, severed the most important ideological bond between state and subject. (Zürcher 2017:208)

Encounters of 'the people' with government officials represented the authoritarian and repressive aspects of state power, what Lacan describes as the 'name-of-the-father', with all its prohibitive and restrictive dimensions (1977:67). As Yilmaz suggests, drawing on her ethnographic research, encounters with this repressive dimension included not only having to comply with the new laws of the much more present state, or even with the sanctions stipulated in the legislation, but also with the exercise of violence by the state's representatives embedded in daily life, as well as in its more exceptional manifestations:

> As such, it was a more effective deterrent in shaping citizens' actions than the punishments prescribed by the legal system (or the knowledge and memory of the sentences passed by the Independence Tribunals after the hat riots in 1925). This fear, especially of physical violence, was implicit in the personal memories of my elderly informants of rural origins, as an important factor in the adoption of the hat. (2013:73)

In this situation the state was experienced in the form of a duality, or a split. The fantasy of the benevolent Gazi was a locus of idealisation and projection (see Klein 1975:6–7), a refuge from the anxiety and fear generated by the violent facet of the state, which was not a welcome force. What is more, the largely imagined, direct and unmediated relationship of 'the people' with the paternal figure of Atatürk, made it easier for them to recognise themselves as, and identify with, the united and homogeneous 'people' he addressed them as. Their common bond in the person of 'father' Atatürk makes it possible for those comprising 'the people' to think of themselves, to draw on Anderson, as in 'a deep horizontal comradeship', setting aside the 'actual inequality and exploitation' that may have prevailed at the time (Anderson 1991:7). As Atatürk was addressing 'his children', despite the asymmetry of his relationship with them, he was making good the promise of radical equality, inherent in his notion of 'populism' (*halkçılık*), which negated diversity and difference within its ranks at least at the symbolic level, as discussed earlier; they were all his children. To his direct approaches to 'his people', they returned, as empowering responses, their gratitude, affection and allegiance. The early republican political culture could be described, in Burghart's terms, as 'lordly' in the sense that the state was personally represented by Atatürk, whose will expressed the common good of an indivisible body politic (see 1996:302–3).

This brief detour into sketching the contours of the lived and imaginary experience of the republican state through the idiom of fantasy and projection aimed to throw some light on the way in which, republican propaganda and violence aside, Mustafa Kemal's unmediated rapport with 'his people', his perceived benevolence and care for them, constituted a means of making bearable the state in its entirety, and of facilitating the eventual success of the republican reforms. Interestingly, in the context of the single party state and the republican aversion to multiparty politics, this asymmetrical rapport featured in the imagination of individual citizens as the 'democratic' element of an otherwise undemocratic state. It is important to note that, regardless Atatürk's official position as President of the Republic and chair of the CHP, this rapport was not of a formally political nature, at least it was not perceived as such by the citizens. As my earlier references to ethnographic research among citizens of the period suggest, Atatürk was not only venerated but also seen as a person who could hear and connect with the ordinariness of the lives of 'his people'. The relationship was cast by both leader and his following as one that unfolded outside the arena of formal politics; unlike the relationship these citizens had with their 'representatives' in the Grand National Assembly, their bond with Atatürk was voluntary and extra-institutional. This extra-institutional dimension of politics and its legitimacy in Turkish political life is something we will return to as it is crucial in our understanding of how 'the political' is structured. This 'duality' of the state, was reflected in the development of a 'duality' of sovereignty and, by extension of legitimate political action (referred to earlier), has been central in shaping the political imaginary and the political culture of the Republic.

Indeed, Zürcher and others have suggested that the institutionalisation of the regime through the strong links between the CHP and the administration of the Republic and their spread into the most remote corners of Anatolia, the military and the legal and educational system, were crucial to the survival of the Republican nationalist project after 1938, when Atatürk died, and after 1945, when the CHP reluctantly opened up to multiparty politics. I would suggest that this institutionalisation was partial as it did not enjoy the confidence of the citizenry and did not have time to establish firm roots in the body politic of the Republic. 'The people', treated as infants, relied on the imaginary figure and later the myth of Mustafa Kemal, to which they felt emotionally attached. The distinction citizens frequently made between the benevolent state represented by Atatürk and the coercive local application of state power facilitated continued allegiance to the nation state, despite these local excesses of the exercise of state power and the arrogance of the republican elite (including Atatürk himself), which considered that popular assent to its plans was unnecessary and unimportant. Yet this reliance on the imaginary father figure represented by Atatürk for the legitimation of the largely undemocratic Republic also represented a precarious balancing act that the death of Atatürk was going to put to the test.

Notes

1. It should be noted that this is by no means a unique element of the early republican political imagination. Raymond Williams argues that 'represent', in its earliest uses in the fourteenth century, has an aesthetic connotation, as it means 'making present' in likenesses in paintings or plays, before it acquired a slightly different meaning denoting 'standing for' or 'symbolising'. In their modern political sense, especially in the context of representative democracy, the terms 'represent', and 'representation' carries with it the tension between 'making present' the views of an absent person or persons, and 'standing for' or 'symbolising' the persons themselves (Williams 1983:266–9).

2. Although most of the opposition to Mustafa Kemal had been neutralised in 1925 after the quashing of the Kurdish rebel political opposition, he, well aware of the capabilities of his opponents from the CUP and the CHP, still felt insecure. In May and June 1926, while on an extended inspection tour of the south and west of the country, just as he was about to arrive in Izmir, a plot to assassinate him, also known as the Menemen conspiracy, was uncovered. The plotters were arrested and turned out to be a small band of professional gunmen led by a former representative in the national assembly (and secretary of the Defence of Rights Group), Ziya Hurşit. The Ankara Independence Tribunal ordered waves of arrests that included almost all the surviving prominent Unionists, as well as the former PRP members of the assembly, on the grounds of having supported the assassination plot and of having planned a coup d'état. Of the accused, sixteen were condemned to death. A second trial opened in Ankara in August of more than fifty important former Unionists. Even more than the first, this was a show trial in which the policies of the CUP leaders when in power and their opposition to Mustafa Kemal were the real themes and the conspiracy of June 1926 was a side issue. Four of the accused were hanged, while a number of others received prison sentences (Zürcher 2017:174–5).

5

THE POLITICS OF THE REPRESSED

'Rekindling' a Flame Long Gone

The death of the Eternal Chief, as Atatürk was posthumously designated, as already pointed out, created a gap in the Republic's political system, as it removed one of the pillars that bestowed on it the effects of his *auctoritas*, derived from his charisma and his privileged relationship with 'the people', within the political elite and in the country at large. The republican elite, partly in order to endow itself, the party and the Republic's institutions with the *auctoritas* of the late president, planned the transition in ways that would allow it to emphasise the inextricable links connecting Atatürk, the state and the CHP. In strictly ritualistic terms, Atatürk was celebrated and commemorated, not only as the deceased President of the Republic, but also as the lost father of 'the people'. The mourning mood of the sober ceremonies was reflected in the press coverage of Gazi's passing and the popular reaction to it. Atatürk's body lay in state in Dolmabahçe Palace flanked by three high torches at each side symbolising the six pillars of Kemalist ideology. There, over three days, thousands of mourners paid their respects (*Hürriyet*, 10 November 1998) and, after a religious funeral closed to the public, Atatürk's body was transferred with military honours to a special funeral train awaiting it at İzmit, whence it completed its land trip to Ankara, where it was greeted by his successor, İsmet İnönü, and other high-ranking government officials amid widespread demonstrations of grief and mourning (Zürcher 2017:185).

İsmet İnönü, elected as president the day after Atatürk's death thanks to support from CHP hardliners and the Turkish military, and as CHP leader at an extraordinary party congress in December 1938, was designated Permanent Party Chairman and, to ensure that the continuity of leadership of the party and the state became visible to the public, he was proclaimed National Chief (Millî Şef), a title used for Atatürk in the 1930s. In that congress, Mustafa Kemal was designated the 'eternal party chairman', in an attempt to stress that his legacy was being kept alive in the CHP. İnönü made clear that his predecessor's basic policies would be left intact, as would the guiding principles of Kemalism. The Republic claimed the unbroken continuity between the Atatürk era and the uncertain times whose arrival had been marked by his death. Yet the elaborate and solemn rituals and the ample use of honorific titles were pasted over tensions that existed within the republican leadership. Mustafa Kemal, semi-retired in his presidential residence over his last few years, had often interfered in government business without prior coordination; even when he was remote from day-to-day politics, and despite İnönü's dominance in the Grand National Assembly had maintained his authority and overruled several of İnönü's cabinet decisions, creating considerable tension and eventually forcing him to resign in 1937, and replacing him with his rival, Mahmut Celâl Bayar (Zürcher 2017:183–4). Despite their rivalry, İnönü kept Bayar as prime minister after Atatürk's death in order to reinforce the impression of continuity and unity in a government that he considered of paramount importance in Atatürk's absence. A few months later though, Bayar tended his resignation due to difference of opinion with regards to the economy, but also as he was being undermined by the new president, thus returning complete control of the state to him.

However, the void in terms of the *auctoritas* that Atatürk could so easily deploy, and his disappearance from the political scene as an arbiter between contending factions in his party and the republican elite as perhaps the only one who could maintain the semblance of unity and purpose of the Republic, had already undermined the legitimacy of the republican institutions. The deceased president easily projected an image of a national leader rather than the head of a faction in a divided political elite; his 'ownership' of the republican project in the eyes of the public made it easier to ostracise and symbolically annihilate other political adversaries leaving the body politic of the Republic intact. However, for İnönü, the brave new world of post-Atatürk politics was different. Despite the deification of Atatürk through his memorialisation in public spaces, in the school curricula, press and public life, although the CHP turned his legacy into immutable principles that could not be amended or revised in time, İnönü had a hard act to follow and, despite his political acumen and popularity within his party, he could not be much more than the leader of an elite faction, albeit a dominant one in the late 1930s and 1940s. By the end of the Second World War, İnönü had lost the authority that his association with Atatürk had endowed him with. In addition, the war had damaged the economy and alienated the government from the public and from segments of the republican elite within the CHP (Zürcher 2017:208–10). Inflation had hit hard the rural populations, who had seen no improvement in their living conditions while the high cost of living combined with increased taxation had demoralised the civil servants who were crucial to the maintenance of the republican order and undermined their support for the party of the Republic. Inönü attempted to reverse popular anger by vaguely promising to address the Republic's legitimacy deficit and by introducing the Land Distribution Law (Çiftçiyi Topraklandırma Kanunu) in January 1945, which prompted the already existing fissures within the CHP to manifest themselves and eventually led to the emergence of political opposition. The critics of the Land Distribution Law, Adnan Menderes and three other deputies, former Prime Minister Celâl Bayar, Refik Koraltan and Fuat Köprülü, extended their criticism to the government's authoritarian style and demanded the full implementation of the democratic promise of the constitution. Whereas their criticisms targeted the republican and party leadership, they were very careful to ensure that their opposition was firmly grounded, in terms of argumentation, on their belief in the republican project and the legacy of Mustafa Kemal. The 'father' of the Republic and of 'the people' had become the battleground upon which the major political battles in the life of the Republic would be fought and key contenders for power would rely on his legacy as their main source of legitimacy.

İnönü, unable to maintain tight control of the state and CHP apparatus, but also taking into account the international configuration in which Turkey was taking its position after the end of the war, decided to go the way that his predecessor had taken with the SCF and the so-called liberalisation experiment fifteen years earlier. He hoped that he could replicate 'the junior partner of the CHP' formula that Atatürk had envisaged for the SCF. Once more, the usual lack of commitment to democratic principles underlay the move toward multiparty politics: the opposition that İnönü and his associates envisaged would be cosmetic, sufficient to stem public dissatisfaction and 'tick' the 'democratic regime' boxes enabling Turkey's admission to the emerging transatlantic political architecture under the aegis of the United States – a new parameter in the government's thinking.

The 1960 Coup: Kemalism Resurrected or Reinterpreted?

On 7 January 1946, Menderes, Bayar, Koraltan and Köprülü founded the Demokrat Parti (Democratic Party, DP). The popular reactions wherever the party opened local offices suggested that the 'junior partner scenario' envisaged by the CHP leadership underestimated the intensity of public discontent. The CHP, intent on maintaining its dominance in politics, left very little time for the DP to prepare for the first 'democratic' elections, as it brought them forward to 1946. The DP reluctantly contested the vote, which was marred by vote tampering and intimidation by the authorities and ended up with 62 of the 465 seats in the Assembly (Erogul 1970). As Zürcher points out:

> there was no guarantee of secrecy during the actual voting; there was no impartial supervision of the elections and, as soon as the results were declared, the actual ballots were destroyed, making any check impossible. It has to be remembered that at this time all local and provincial administrators were RPP party members, who had great difficulty in discriminating between political opposition and high treason. (2017:214)

İnönü's selection for the post of prime minister, Recep Peker, a prominent hardline supporter of the one-party state, was heavily involved in an unsuccessful attempt to intimidate the DP into conducting itself as a junior partner in the government (2017:214). It soon became evident that history would not repeat itself and that the DP would not be intimidated or close down. Four years later, the one-party regime was dealt a deadly blow as the electorate returned the DP to office with 408 seats and 53.4 per cent of the vote against a mere 69 seats and 39.8 per cent of the vote for the CHP. The DP, distancing itself from the CHP and its authoritarian legacy and exploiting the widespread disaffection with the government's pervasiveness, undertook to protect the citizens from the state, thus pitting itself against the state bureaucracy (Ahmad 1993:105), and aimed at decreasing the influence of the military (Göçek 2011:27). Just as in the case of the ill-fated multiparty experiments of the 1920s and 1930s when religious conservatives effectively colonised the oppositional parties, Islam was politicised and became one of the key issues around which the DP mobilised (Karpat 1959:271–92). Whereas the DP leadership went to great lengths to express its commitment to the principles of Kemalism, albeit Kemalism without the CHP, the army and civil bureaucracy perceived the ascendance of the DP as a counter-revolution that threatened the ideology of Kemalism and of their privileged position derived from their self-designation as its guardians. On top of ideology and status issues, inflationary pressures had decreased the real value of their salaries, intensifying their disgruntlement with the Democrats (Ahmad 1993:121–2; Aydemir 1973:264–70). The polarisation of Turkish society and the Turkish political and bureaucratic elites, kindled by 'the return of the repressed', the conservative, religious part of the population and segments of the rural populations that felt they had been excluded and suppressed by the republican state, and the CHP's reaction to what its leadership saw as the unravelling of the Kemalist state, as well as increased tensions between the DP and the state bureaucracy, led to a hardening of the positions of the opposing parties and increased violence, especially against those who dared criticise the existing political system (Göçek 2011:27). In Vaner's words, '[this] change in ruling elites, which derived from important social transformations and reflected a shift in political structures, was perceived by the army as the degradation of its own institutional prestige and a challenge to its image within society' (Vaner 1987:237–8).

Thus, on 27 May 1960 a military coup planned by a group of young officers under Alparslan Türkeş and eventually led by General Cemal Gürsel, ended the DP-led multiparty experiment. As Hale points out the designation of the army as a guarantor of the Republic did not entail such action:

Atatürk's revolution had left the Turkish army as the ultimate guardian of the republic, but effectively separated it from ultimate responsibility for government. In 1960, this tradition was dramatically broken when the army intervened to overthrow an elected civilian administration. (Hale 1993:88)

Nevertheless, the army coup culminated in the suppression of the DP and its cadres, and the trial and hanging of senior DP leaders. On the day of the coup, Türkeş, in a radio broadcast, made a statement that paid lip service to the junta's commitment to democracy and to the cooperation of the citizens and the armed forces;

> Great Turkish Nation; Starting at 3:00 am on the 27th of May, the Turkish armed forces have taken over administration throughout the entire country. This operation, thanks to the close cooperation of all our citizens and security forces, has succeeded without incurring loss of life . . . We ask our citizens to facilitate the work of our armed forces, and assist in re-establishing the nationally desired democratic regime. (Dilipak 1991:70)

More illuminating as to the idiom of the new regime was the first report of the Constitution Commission established by the military junta, which found the Menderes government 'antagonistic to the army, courts, university and Atatürk's reforms' (Ataöv 1960:20). Although the reasons for the coup were complex and touched upon not only ideology or the status of the Officers' Corps, but also economics and international realignments, the mention of the DP policies being antagonistic to Atatürk's reforms is significant as it reveals a continuity in the tendency of drawing on the founder of the Republic's *auctoritas* in order to legitimise political choices and action. During the preceding decade both main parties had also opted to evoke Atatürk's legacy, trying to outbid each other in terms of their commitment to the principles of Kemalism, turning them into a malleable set of ideas, an ideological battleground, an empty signifier to be colonised. The particularity of the armed intervention lies in its extra-institutional character, its claim to operate outside politics just as the Gazi did, talking his language, addressing his people not from the space of politics, the locus of *potestas* corrupted by short-sighted politicians, but from the locus of *auctoritas* that Atatürk inhabited.

The 27 May military intervention used the idiom of 'exception' that was also deployed during the early Republic. The military junta defined the political process that they violently interrupted as a crisis of political division and fragmentation, and decided on instituting a state of exception (Schmitt 1985:13). They identified the enemies of 'the nation' (Schmitt 2007:26), some of whom they executed, imprisoned or purged from their positions. They did this in the name not of a law but of Atatürk's *auctoritas* and legacy, in their capacity as custodians and their ability to define what is best for 'the people' against their expressed choice. The dual sovereignty that I identified earlier when discussing the analytical distinction between 'the transcendental nation' on the one hand, and 'the nation as people' on the other was evoked as the armed forces deposed the elected government in the name of 'the nation' and its interests. Notwithstanding the military takeover of power (*potestas*) by the National Union Committee (Millî Birlik Komitesi, MBK) – bringing together the coup instigators – it is worth noting that its most radical members spent considerable time in the countryside (until November 1960 when they were all removed from their posts), spreading their interpretation of Kemalism, social justice and national independence (describing post-war Turkey as a colony of the USA), and even symbolically keeping under house arrest fifty-five landowners in Western Anatolia, attempting to restore/construct the *auctoritas* of their 'own' Atatürk, which had been wounded by the corrupt politicians (Kitsikis 1981:257–8).

The 1960 coup can be seen as a reaction to the waning appeal of Kemalism in a number of ways. The inability of the Kemalist elites, state bureaucracy and the army to reproduce Mustafa Kemal' authority after his death and therefore maintain the ability to control the crucial state and social institutions that this authority afforded them, had already dented the statist ethos associated with the CHP and its founder. The inclination of politicians, especially those of emerging parties such as the DP or its successors, broadly understood, to abandon the heritage of *inkilapcılık* (understood as state-driven continuous revolution), and the rise of new elites not drawing their dynamism and appeal from their association with the state, undermined Mustafa Kemal's vision of the direction of the Turkey that he and his associates had built. Equally important was the entry of 'the infant people' int the political arena after Inönü's reluctant consent to ending the one-party system. The 1960 coup put in sharp relief the tensions between multiparty competition and the conviction held by some quarters of the state, the political establishment and society that 'the people' and their choices could not be trusted and should not be respected.

In a period of eighteen months, the military junta introduced a number of reforms aimed at resetting politics which, however, reflected the divisions between the coup protagonists (see Zürcher 2017:254–6). The most radical measures included the setting up of a set of revolutionary courts intended to 'cleanse' Turkey of opponents of the military intervention, the outlawing of the DP, the dismantling of its leadership, the prosecution and imprisonment of most of its leaders and activists and the creation of the National Security Council, chaired by the President of the Republic and composed of an equal number of members of the civilian government and the armed forces to putatively assist the Council of Ministers and facilitate coordination on issues of national security, broadly defined as 'the protection of the constitutional order of the state, its national existence' (Özbudun 2000:107–8). This definition of national security opened the way to the military, whose presence in the National Security Council was decisive, to focus not only on defending the country against external and internal threats, but also to act as an arbiter in political life whenever it deemed that politicians were disregarding the constitutional order, or internal threats were jeopardising the state.

Adnan Menderes – the first elected prime minister deposed by the coup – and his close associates, Hasan Polatkan and Fatin Rüştü Zorlu, were executed in September 1961. A new constitution was introduced, aimed putatively at introducing checks and balances and keeping political parties under the scrutiny of the military. But the eventual marginalisation of the radical officers of the MBK who, by November 1960 were purged from the MBK and of their revolutionary fervour, opened the way for a gradual restoration of the politics that the former had seen as the reason for their intervention. A general election scheduled for the fall of 1961 returned politicians to the helm. The vote produced a fragile coalition government bringing together Inönü's CHP and the Justice Party (Adalet Partisi, AP, an organisation widely recognised as the political heir of the outlawed Democrat Partisi), each of which took just over one-third of the vote. The product of a hesitant compromise between the two rival parties, especially as factions within the army considered the poll results disappointing, the coalition collapsed in May 1962 over its inability to offer amnesty to the imprisoned DP politicians. This was the herald of a series of weak coalitions until the ascendance of Süleiman Demirel, a former engineer, to the leadership of AP in 1964, and the party's landslide victory a year later. Two earlier coup attempts were unsuccessful as the officer corps considered that the 1960 military intervention had limited the ability of civilian governments to undermine the delicate balance of power that the coup had established.

Despite the fact that the AP was seen as the reincarnation of the disbanded DP, Demirel was able to remain in office due to the complex compromises inherent in the 1961 constitution that constrained the Defence Minister's ability to exert control over the armed forces and subjected the government to an array of checks and balances, such as an independent justice system that vigilantly scrutinised the executive. At the same time, he expertly cultivated his own and his party's popularity by mobilising Islam and traditional values in his discourse and resorting to anti-communist rhetoric, which often made inroads into the AP's public order policies and made possible convergences between the National Intelligence Organisation (*Milli İstihbarat Teşkilât*, MIT) and the armed forces, whose integration in NATO had allowed communism to be identified as a potential security threat.

Having said that, the AP of the mid-1960s was a fragile organisation as, at the level of national politics, it was the product of a difficult coexistence and compromise, often marred by infighting, between Demirel's more liberal faction on the one hand, and a conservative elite made up of affluent landowners and nationalists on the other (Zürcher 2017; Sezgin 2013). A further complicating factor was the centralisation of the party administration, which not only put at a disadvantage Demirel's party rivals, but also alienated and kept distant grassroots activists at the level of the neighbourhood or town as well as local conservative, nationalist and Islamist networks and organisations, which were not integrated into the party but operated on its periphery and often lobbied its leadership. Several mediating levels between the grassroots and the party administration and a clientelist structure distorted local and peripheral voices and reinforced the fragility of the leading party of the period (see Sezgin 2013), as I argue later.

Kemalism and Its Challengers: Leftism, Nationalism, Islamism

This was also the time when, apart from the cleavage between the CHP on the one hand and the DP and its successor parties on the other, a new cleavage between left and right became solidified and was expressed for the most part through the emergence of political radicalism. The industrial development and urbanisation trends, already in evidence in the 1950s, the growing student population and the more permissive climate fostered by the 1961 constitution, including the labour law of 1963, which legalised strikes and promoted trade unions, provided the conditions for the emergence of organised labour organisations and, more broadly, a left movement. Left-wing organisations started appearing in the political landscape, with most notable amongst them at the time, the Workers' Party of Turkey (Türkiye İşçi Partisi, TİP) founded as early as in 1961. A few years later, in 1967, the Confederation of Reformist Workers' Unions (Devrimci Işçi Sendıkalari Konfederasyonu, DİSK) was founded, while in 1969, the Revolutionary Youth Movement (Türkiye Devrimci Gençlik Federasyonu , or Dev Genç), and a little later, organisations such as the People's Liberation Party-Front of Turkey (Türkiye Halk Kurtuluş Partisi-Cephesi, THKP.C) and the Revolutionary Workers' and Peasants' Party of Turkey (Türkiye İhtilalci İşçi Köylü Partisi, TİİKP) – a Dev Genç splinter group – followed suit. Alongside these, an array of student and labour organisations and groups, and cycles of intellectuals engaging with left publications such as the weekly *Yön* ('Direction') made up a lively and diverse socialist movement (see Zürcher 2017:267–9; Christophis 2021:111–49). Soon, political disagreements gave rise to militancy, partly inspired by similar developments globally, and this often took the form of confrontations in the streets, and eventually kidnappings and other forms of violence.

The return, in 1963, of Alparslan Türkeş, one of the main instigators and leaders of the 1960 coup, from his effective exile as an attaché at the Turkish embassy in New Delhi, and his intention to play an active role in politics, was a significant milestone in the politics of the right in Turkey. In 1965, Türkeş, together with some of the other fourteen radical officers who had participated in the coup and the MBK until their marginalisation, joined the Republican Peasant Nation Party (Cumhuriyetçi Köylü Millet Partisi, CKMP), the first far-right party in Turkey, and within a few months took over its leadership as elected chairman (Özkırımlı and Sofos 2008:139). Under Türkeş, the party was transformed into a more radical nationalist and pan-Turkist organisation characterised by strict hierarchy and discipline under a powerful leader, eventually renamed in 1969 Nationalist Action Party (Milliyetçi Hareket Partisi,

MHP). The MHP sought to combine its pan-Turkist nationalism with an anti-communist direction and an appeal to the conservative Muslim elector-ate (Landau 1995:185; Özkırımlı and Sofos 2008:140), but also to radicalise its supporter base. Associated (although this association was never officially acknowledged) with the revamped party and this new orientation was Ülkü Ocakları Eğitim ve Kültür Vakfı (Idealist Hearths Educational and Cultural Foundation), a putatively cultural and educational youth organisation also known as idealists (*ülkücüler*) or the Grey Wolves (Bozkurtlar). The *ülkücüler* mustered at the time close to 100,000 members based in Hearths, not only in East and Central Anatolia where the majority of the MHP support base was located, but also in the major urban centres of the country where they were one of the key participants in the street violence of the late 1960s and 1970s, targeting leftist groups.

An added element to these political fissures came from the mobilisation of activists and some of the electorate around the idiom of Islam. Although the AP, and before it the DP, had utilised Islam as a means of coming closer to voters alienated by the aggressive secularism of the CHP, it was only in the late 1960s that a vision of a non-secular Turkey oriented towards the Islamic world was proposed by Necmettin Erbakan and his close associates in his Millî Görüş ('National Vision') manifesto. The tensions within the AP, the distortive role of party representation structures and of clientelism, had prepared the ground for the formation of a new space, and eventually party, with a clear Islamic, conservative character. Erbakan, an engineer and academic-turned-politician articulated a language and provided a frame-work that brought together a network of informal grassroots institutions, activists and disaffected segments of Islamist right elites who had previously been dispersed in several parties, or organised informally and often locally (see Sezgin 2013). After several years of convergences and exchanges, the *mukaddesatçılar* (advocates of sacred values), as the Islamist circles identified themselves, gained a sense of distinctiveness from other right-wing groups with which they had coexisted, such as the conservative nationalists of the AP and the pan-Turkist and ultra-right nationalists further to the right. As, among these circles, their faith that the AP would listen to their concerns and aspirations had faded by the late 1960s, activism outside the AP seemed a much better option. In January 1970, the National Order Party (Millî Nizam

Partisi, MNP) became the first of a series of political parties that adopted, or were influenced by, the ideology underpinning the Millî Görüş manifesto rendering the movement espousing Erbakan's principles a significant actor in Turkish politics and an additional pole in the political landscape.

As already pointed out, despite the AP's landslide victory in 1965, internal divisions limited Demirel's ability to provide effective leadership and tackle the increasing violence of the late 1960s. Although the general election of 1969 returned him and his party once more with a parliamentary majority, the AP was soon affected by the unwillingness of the banned DP's erstwhile leadership to accept Demirel as anything more than a temporary 'caretaker' leader of their party. At the same time, the conservative wing of the AP became increasingly vocal against Demirel's taxation and development policy proposals that would place a financial burden on the wealthier landowners of Western Anatolia and other professionals who formed the base of the party. An eventual split left the prime minister with a fragile majority in the National Assembly in February 1970, a time of considerable unrest as violence erupted among student groups on university campuses and among workers' organisations and, more importantly, between the far right and the far left.

Part of the military leadership saw in Demirel's woes confirmation that the politicians were unable to lead effectively especially as the unchecked street violence and the spread of radicalism in the country's Kurdish regions posed, in their view, dangers to the survival and unity of Turkey. In addition, as the officer corps itself was not impervious to the societal divides of the time, senior officers acted pre-emptively issuing a warning to an embattled Demirel in March 1970. As the Prime Minister was unable to tackle the crisis in his party, a galloping recession, and social unrest and violence, the armed forces stepped in again on 12 March 1971. Two of the relative newcomers in the political arena, the Islamist MNP and the left, provided the spectre of the threat that could suppress and conceal the divisions within the military and the different interpretations of Kemalism held by different factions within its ranks. The MNP, with its barely concealed opposition to Mustafa Kemal's legacy, was accused of undermining the Republic, while TİP and youth organisations considered to have affinities with *Dev Genç* were held responsible for the violence in Turkey's cities and universities and were accused of carrying out communist propaganda and agitation and supporting Kurdish separatism. In an interesting statement, the armed forces leadership demanded an end to the 'anarchy, fratricidal strife, and social and economic unrest' and the implementation, inspired by Atatürk's views, [of] the reformist laws envisaged by the constitution' (Ahmad 1993:147–9; Zürcher 2017:258). The authors of the military ultimatum, partly attempting to endow their repressive project with legitimacy, distanced themselves from liberal democratic principles and evoked the *auctoritas* of Atatürk, while deploying the language of unity, fraternity and horizontal camaraderie mixed with some vague references to democracy. Attempting to avoid the problems faced by the perpetrators of a coup across the Aegean in Greece, who had opted for the formation of a military government four years earlier, they chose to oversee the creation of a supra-party government of technocrats under Professor Nihat Erim, a veteran CHP politician deemed by the armed forces chiefs to be neutral enough for the job. Although Erim's appointment was unacceptable to the emerging left faction of the CHP led by party Secretary General Bülent Ecevit, it was accepted by the CHP establishment and the AP leadership, whom Demirel had advised to provide a measured response to the military takeover. Over the next couple of years, under the watchful eye of the military, Turkey was ruled by a succession of hybrid governments while the armed forces pursued their version of the restoration of unity and fraternity by establishing martial law in parts of the country, establishing special courts, confronting guerrillas, proscribing and shutting down parties and organisations, including the MNP, initiating a constitutional reform restricting personal freedoms and securing their political role by reinforcing the powers of the National Security Council. Interestingly, the orderly Turkey sought by the military had no place for the left but was still inhabited, alongside the two major parties – the CHP and the AP – by the ultra-nationalist MHP and its affiliated *ülkücüler*, who had been responsible for much of the disorder and violence that had prompted the coup and who contributed to the violent suppression of the left in the 1970s. The proscription and shutting down of the Islamist MNP in May 1971 was not as harsh as that of left organisations, as Necmettin Erbakan was not prosecuted and was eventually allowed to return to politics in 1973 to take over the reins of the National Salvation Party (Millî Selâmet Partisi, MSP), which, in October 1972 took the place of its predecessor, the banned MNP. Indeed, such was the rehabilitation of the Millî Görüş-aligned party that, after a brief interval of an Ecevit-led CHP–MSP coalition government in 1973, both the MHP and the MSP cohabited the corridors of power in Ankara together with the AP as part of the so-called Nationalist Front (Milliyetçi Cephe) government, which was allegedly formed to stem 'the advance of the left' (referring to both the CHP and the student and workers' movements). The MSP took advantage of the social opportunity structure that presented itself at the time. A decade of rapid urbanisation had swelled the ranks of the urban poor who lived in the Gecekondu – the shanty towns in the country's major cities – and neighbourhoods left dilapidated and abandoned by their original inhabitants. These new urban dwellers were in dire need of essential services that were not provided by the state as their neighbourhoods were 'off the grid' at a time when welfare provision was rudimentary at best. After over a decade of societal engagement, Millî Görüş possessed the necessary human capital and infrastructure to provide food, medical and educational services and, as the MSP participated in the ruling coalitions of the 1970s, access to work and 'nationwide distribution of favours', thus also amassing obligations (see White 2014) and an electoral base that rendered it one of the main political actors of the time.

Although the authors of the 1971 ultimatum maintained their oversight of politics and repeatedly declared their determination to bring about reforms, they lacked the radical vision of the younger officers who, a decade earlier, had toppled the DP government. Their reform programme was not aimed so much at society but mainly targeted civil–military relations, ensuring that the military had institutionalised powers and autonomy, and awarding themselves the role of arbiter and overseer. Apart from the violent repression of mainly left activism, and the curtailment of individual rights, their social vision did not encompass land redistribution programmes or other radical measures that could have a tangible impact in the livelihoods of ordinary citizens, such as the admittedly frustrated plans of their radical predecessors.

The 1970s were marked by a succession of weak coalition governments whose survival rested on the inclusion of ultra-nationalist and Islamist parties. Some of these parties tacitly tolerated or, as suggested by the cases of the MHP and, to a lesser extent, the MSP, played a major role in violence directed against the left or minority groups such as the Alevi and the Kurds.

Street violence continued unabated in the biggest cities while atrocities were committed in cities such as Çorum, Konya, or Maraş, where over 100 Alevi Kurds were killed by the Grey Wolves and Islamists (Bianet 18 December 2015). The response of the Turkish and Kurdish left to this onslaught by state agencies and the ultra-nationalist and Islamist right was perceived as an 'anti-fascist' struggle – a term that became current especially due to its being embraced by Dev Yol (The Revolutionary Way), one of the largest organisations of the time. However, the ideological and national divisions within the left did not let it develop a shared voice and avoid violent confrontations among different left groups, allowing the government and far right to blame them for the violence that they themselves were party to.

The Multiple Iterations of 'The People' in the 1960s and 1970s

Although a return to the course set by Atatürk was one of the main reasons put forward by the perpetrators of the military interventions of 1960 and 1971, the two turbulent decades that transpired after the violent and abrupt end of the Menderes prime ministership were a time when global trends and local dynamics changed the Turkey built by Atatürk and the early republican elite in ways they had not anticipated. The post-war era had forced the political class that had presided over the early Republic to make a choice between becoming integrated into one of the emerging global alliances or pursuing a path of isolation. Integration into the Euro-Atlantic alliance provided security and the potential for economic development but was incompatible with the single-party state that the founders of the Republic had envisaged. Party competition and regular elections seemed to provide Turkey with the democratic credentials that its international political alignment necessitated but were also unavoidable as the dissent within the CHP itself could no longer be managed through compromise or coercion.

Yet as already pointed out, 'the people' who were expected to exercise their sovereignty were not deemed quite ready to do so. According to the narrative of those who attempted to disrupt the system of party competition or supported these disruptions, the people were naïve, susceptible to the demagoguery of unscrupulous politicians, prone to reverting to values and lifestyles that the Republic had strived to eradicate. Each military intervention attempted to 'reset' the political process after introducing a number of 'corrective' measures:

banning political parties or forcing them to enter unviable coalitions, forcing unity over political processes that rested on competition, curtailing individual rights for the sake of a vaguely defined collective good. Turkey has not been the only example of a society transitioning towards a competitive multiparty political system without having necessarily developed values that legitimise particularistic interests and individual rights – one of the cornerstones of liberal democracies. Examples of several societies globally are characteristic of this incongruence that eventually shapes different understandings of who bears rights – the abstract individual, different groups (classes, groups advancing identity claims, an abstract notion of 'the people' or 'the nation' or another entity that expresses the equally abstract notion of the General Will) – and, by extension, affects 'democracy' and the ways it is understood, practised and lived in different social contexts. '

In Turkey, the army, the judiciary, parts of the state bureaucracy and segments of the political class have experienced competition between political parties with some degree of discomfort as it went against the grain of their own socialisation, which revolved around the sanctity of the unity of 'the people' and the indivisibility of the nation and the state that Kemalism elevated as the organising principles of the state. Beyond the aversion of these actors to competitive politics, another significant element of their 'sociology' of Turkish society was their mistrust of 'the people', who, despite the advent of the franchise and competitive politics, were still considered to possess infantile qualities and to be easily misled and confused. Military coups, ultimata and judicial interventions in politics were justified on the putative lack of maturity displayed by the electorate and their tendency to be led on the road to division. A formal political field structured along the lines of liberal democracy was not considered suitable for 'the people' of the Republic as it was deemed to be irrelevant to the particularities of the Turkish societal framework, and served to (re)produce a fragmented voice. In the absence of the idealised tutor and 'father figure', Mustafa Kemal, the military had to exert its influence although, lacking *auctoritas* of the magnitude of Atatürk's charisma, the armed forces were unable to normalise their involvement in politics and maintain it indefinitely, and therefore eventually had to hand power over to politicians who enjoyed an alternative legitimacy through their election to office, as happened after both the 1960 and 1971 military interventions.

The 1960s was a period of further transformations in Turkish society. A timid process of industrialisation created new jobs in the big economic centres of the Republic. Migration from the countryside and from less developed parts of the country to the large cities, primarily in Western Turkey, resulted in the formation of urban poor strata on urban peripheries but also in inner city areas, while the expansion of education resulted in an increase of a student population that was both aware of rural and urban poverty and in tune with the global waves of protest that emerged in the era of decolonisation, US interventions in Vietnam, Cuba, nearby Greece and the 1968 student and worker mobilisations. These conditions contributed to the emergence of both a vibrant, yet fragmented left and a right that was progressively divided into ultra-nationalist and Islamist segments.

The left, which had already emerged in the 1960s, and despite being identified as state enemy by the military after their 1971 ultimatum, retained a notable presence in Turkish society and politics. From the so-called left turn of the CHP under Bülent Ecevit, to the multitude of left organisations of workers, students and intellectuals, an underlying popular anti-imperialist stance permeated left activism. Instances of national resistance to US imperialism sustained a revolutionary paradigm that focused less on Soviet communism and more on the national–popular struggles in the decolonising world. This orientation prompted many on the left to look for a national path to socialism that also fused the anti-imperialist legacy of the independence war associated with Kemalism (see Döşemeci 2013:56–76, Bora 2017:162–5; 615–22; 633–4). The left, for the most part, was captive of the narrative that posited Kemalism as an anti-imperialist liberation movement pursuing an equitable society. As such, it embraced key elements of the Kemalist 'sociology'. Bulent Ecevit's attempt to combine the anti-imperialist and nationalist elements of Kemalism with an emphasis on equity and social justice is a case in point. The attempt to incorporate some of the Kemalist tenets into the socialist discourse of the time led to the articulation of a narrative whereby analysis of Turkish society was not based on Marxist or Western socialist categories, notably the concept of class divide. Echoing a long discursive tradition in Turkish politics, instead of understanding politics in terms of class struggle or of a society where different identities and interests compete for recognition, Turkish socialism reached out to a society organised not on the basis of class divisions but of popular unity. 'The people' in this narrative are one, indivisible and marked by horizontal equality and a common interest to fight a *comprador* elite, external to the people, advancing the interests of global imperialism (see, for example, Bora 2017:162–5). Despite exceptions such as that of TKP/ML and its leader, Ibrahim Kaypakkaya, which disavowed Kemalism as a reactionary role model with a hollow anti-imperialist mission, this Turkish exceptionalism permeating left visualisations of the 'social' blurred the boundaries between the latter and Kemalism, and has allowed left parties and intellectuals to consider Kemalist nationalist anti-imperialism and corporatism as part of their own tradition.[1]

Paradoxically, this affinity to, or echoes of, these elements of Kemalism on the left were also present in the ultra-right nationalism of the MHP, who claimed to be the 'true adherents' to the vision of Mustafa Kemal, especially his view of Turkish society being indivisible and his emphasis on a corporatist model of organisation and 'solidarity' at a time when his own party, the CHP, had embarked on a divisive route. For the MHP the left was not part of the indivisible body of the nation; it was external to it together with its internal enemies (minorities) and external foes.

The Islamist right was similarly averse to visualising society in classes or groups with particularistic interests as its worldview stemmed from a tradition viewing society as an organic whole, whereby membership in the community was underpinned by collective morality and responsibility, equality, justice, fairness and solidarity. Although Necmettin Erbakan and the Millî Görüş activists were critical of Kemalism, particularly on account of its aggressive secularism and irreverence, their understanding of 'the people' and 'the nation' converged with regard to the unity and the radical equality that permeated them.

A visualisation of society where class divides and conflicts, particularistic interest groups and diverse identity claims had no place, and a distinction between (internal) friend and (externalised) foe, formed the core of a discursive tradition that cut across left/right and secular/religious dichotomies. In addition, the left's understanding of the revolutionary vanguard as reminiscent of the understanding of the republican vanguard in Kemalism, and to some extent in the activism of the ultra-nationalist and Islamist, right juxtaposed 'the people' as a moral subject that needed nevertheless to be educated, enlightened, tutored and the elites who had been tasked with educating and deciding for them.

These iterations of the people have played an important role with regard to how not only ordinary people but also the political class, the state bureaucracy and the military have understood and positioned themselves vis-à-vis party competition, democracy and the question of who is the bearer of rights. The unstable coalition governments, the unrest in the streets, the corruption of politicians and party mechanisms, undermined the societal appeal of party competition – understood by many as democracy – and had paradoxically contributed to seeing military interventions in politics as motivated by their commitment to societal unity. This, interestingly, has led the army to have been historically ranked as the most highly respected and trusted institution (Jenkins 2007:339).

Thus, I would argue, that for many ordinary Turks, the bearer of rights was not the individual, or a group defined by class position or ethnic, gender or sexual identity, but whoever or whatever was conveyed by the abstract notions of 'the nation' or 'the people', both imagined as loci of solidarity and equality.

The 1980 Coup and the Transformation of Turkey's Political and Social Topography

Unprecedented polarisation, weak government coalitions unable to address a persistent balance of payments deficit, the shocks inflicted by the oil price crisis of the 1970s, industrial unrest, an array of social problems of the country, and the escalation of violence, partly instigated by actors within the state – the MHP proved extremely effective in infiltrating security agencies – and the failure of martial law, imposed on just under a third of the country, to bring any sense of peace, created the preconditions for yet another intervention.

Nine years after the 1971 military ultimatum, the leadership of the Turkish armed forces staged another coup, using the constitutional fig leaf of acting on behalf of the National Security Council (Milli Güvenlik Konseyi, MGK), an institution established by the 1961 constitution that allowed the military to be involved in the exercise of executive power together with the Council of Ministers (Sakallioğlu 1997:157–8). Despite this, the new regime, headed by General Kenan Evren, invoked the Kemalist tradition of state secularism and its emphasis on the unity of 'the nation' as the source of its *auctoritas*, adding its opposition to communism, fascism, separatism and religious sectarianism as elements that diluted this unity. At a time when Turkey was undergoing a severe economic crisis, the country was in dire need of a social and political model. Given the lack of consensus among the political elite, forging a hegemonic project became an impossible task. The weakness of the public institutions that had not grown organically out of the needs of society and had not had time to root themselves due to their short life span and the military interventions that disrupted their consolidation, and their limited capacity, hampered government's efforts to contain the radical movements that had plunged society into chaos. The armed forces saw in the widespread unrest and social fatigue an opportunity: basing the legitimation of their intervention on the need for security and their ability to provide it, they were welcomed by a population weary of the ineptitude of the political class, the government's inability to put an end to the conflict tearing the cities of the Republic apart, let alone its inability to provide solutions to the economic crisis.

The coup perpetrators were driven in the execution of their plans by their mistrust of 'the people' and the putative proclivity of the latter to making the 'wrong choices'. The military regime moved swiftly to abolish the Grand National Assembly and the government, suspend the constitution and ban all political parties and trade unions. The toll of this intervention was enormous: between 95 and 120 people were killed or died as a result of the coup, 650,000 were arrested, over 1.5 million people found themselves included on blacklists, not to mention those tried and denied passports or even their citizenship (TBMM 2012). This time, the military leadership was intent on not leaving what they deemed important reforms in the hands of politicians. Although the coup leaders eventually devolved power to a civilian government in 1983, they ensured that the civilian administration would operate under severe restrictions and close supervision. The armed forces reserved a number of 'security-related domains' for the exclusive oversight of the revamped and National Security Council, endowed with more powers and now dominated by the military. Although the coup banned political activities and organisations, its ideological bias was visible in the swift action taken against the left; its activists bore the brunt of the executions and arrests, while the regime embarked on a cultural campaign to steer Turkish society in a more conservative direction while striving to symbolically annihilate the left, as indicated by their interventions in the urban environment seeking to eliminate any memory of urban left culture (see Gül 2017:153–82). Its anti-communist zeal notwithstanding, the National Security Council also turned against the MHP and the Hearths of the *ülkücüler*, not so much because of their ideology but because of the potential challenge such an organised force, posed as their leader, Alparslan Türkeş, was a charismatic personality followed by the members of close to 1,700 Hearths, many of whom were experienced veterans of the street violence period. And finally, although the generals put an end to the political career of Necmettin Erbakan's MSP and prosecuted him alongside Süleiman Demirel, Bulent Ecevit and Alparslan Türkeş, they realised the need to check the potency of Islam as a mobilising force, and harness and integrate it in the conservative state ideology that they intended to propagate, as I argue in Chapter 6.

After 1983, the military once more initiated a process of cautious democratisation that was intended to ensure that politicians and political parties would remain under the oversight of the armed forces. Initially, the military junta leader, General Kenan Evren, assumed the presidency of the Republic and thus maintained an institutionalised position in Turkish politics. In accordance with the 1982 constitution (Türkiye Cumhuriyeti Anayasasi 1982), the military retained some oversight capacity and reserved a key executive role through its dominance on the National Security Council, which acquired a pivotal place in the Republic's institutional architecture. The Council proved an important instrument for the control of civilian political life, especially after Kenan Evren's retirement from the presidency in 1989. The 1982 constitution represented an expression of the mistrust of 'the people' displayed among the higher echelons of the military and their scepticism of electoral politics and politicians. As a result, it incorporated mechanisms of control and supervision, largely placing political institutions under the control of unelected ones and pitting governments against state institutions and bureaucracies. Some of the tutelary mechanisms put in place entailed judicial review of parliamentary decisions and government policies, thus rendering the country's higher courts overseers and opponents of parliament and political parties and curtailing various forms of political expression. These mechanisms kept contention at bay for the best part of two decades, but also set in motion convergences of social and political forces that eventually undermined the institutional arrangements the coup set in place as I discuss later.

Turkey's process of transition from the Kemalist one-party regime to a multiparty system in 1946 was not the product of a genuine belief in the value and merits of democracy. Despite widespread popular discontent with the CHP and its authoritarian management of the country, the move to multiparty politics was due largely to Turkey's alignment with the coalition of democracies that emerged victorious after the Second World War under US leadership and to the elite's effort to achieve the country's integration into the Western alliance (Hale 1990:56–7). In this new international context, the republican elite deemed that embracing elements of liberal democracy and experimenting with economic liberalism might facilitate Turkey's participation in the post-war international political and economic reconstruction and maximise the benefits that it might entail. Democratic transition was thus the offspring of necessity. It was also a restricted one in the sense that the guiding principles of Kemalism represented a number of limitations, especially in the expression of opinions or political activity that might be perceived to threaten the secular or unitary character of the state and nation. What is more, they provided the grammar of extra-institutional legitimation and political action that competed with democratic politics, however imperfect. Admittedly, restrictions to such activities have not always been implemented to the letter and political actors have managed to operate within the system, often bypassing official obstacles (Sofos 2000:250). However, since 1960, the military have intervened in Turkish politics through a variety of means on numerous occasions when they deemed that the democratic political process was posing a threat to the state's Kemalist principles or was undermining the country's political stability and social order. The Turkish experiment with a limited form of liberal democracy was thus interrupted by direct military interventions and military ultimata, when a series of legal measures such as court part closure orders were not effective. In addition, the army retained different forms and degrees of presence in political life, even after handing power to civilians, through a variety of means, some of which are discussed later. Whereas the litany of coups were undoubtedly inspired by a variety of factors, including the political leanings, status and preoccupations of their leaders and of course Turkey's increasing attachment to the Atlantic alliance and the US,[2] they all showed that the armed forces had responsibility and licence to take corrective action by suspending the time and space of politics whenever they deemed it necessary and that such decisions were invested with the *auctoritas* of Atatürk.

In the series of moments of exception that these military interventions represent, the idiom of crisis, of division and unity, of the imperfect people and the transcendental nation, of extra-institutional as opposed to institutional legitimacy, has been deployed, as Göçek suggests, constituting a pattern 'that was to repeat itself approximately once every decade thereafter: 12 March 1971; 12 September 1980 and 28 February 1997' (2011:27). What is more, as Zürcher notes, the senior officers in the armed forces found the independent action by junior officers problematic and, to avoid repetition of such events, founded the Armed Forces Union (Silâhli Kuvvetler Birliği), which itself interfered in politics repeatedly during 1961 and 1962. issuing memoranda warning civilian politicians not to return to pre-27 May politics (Zürcher 2017:247). The army and state bureaucracy have tended to consider civilian democratic rule to be riddled with problems. From their perspective, multiparty democracy fragmented the body politic, led to selfish, misguided governments unable to discern the public good; they thus considered that a tutelary model of limited democracy was most suitable in order to avoid 'the excesses of democratic' politics.[3]

Although the armed forces were usually quick to relinquish the powers they usurped (with the exception of the 1980s coup perpetrators who developed a legal-institutional framework for the longer-term oversight of politics and 'correction' of the choices made by 'the people'), the public seems to have maintained high levels of trust in the military, as various public trends studies seem to suggest (Aydin et al. 2020; Konda Barometer 2010–19, to mention two of them). The extension of this trust notwithstanding, the short 'corrective interventions', the occasional lack of a blueprint for the longer-term presence of the coup perpetrators in politics, or the search for legal and institutional avenues to achieve the 'normalisation' or 'routinisation' of the army's supervision of political life revealed the limitations of the *auctoritas* the army could derive from the trust of 'the people'. Claiming to speak 'for the people in spite of the people', keeping Atatürk's flame alive without getting burnt, proved a hard act to maintain.

Notes

1. Interestingly, this rejection of Kemalism by only the fringes of the Turkish left opened the space for a critique of the mainstream Turkish left by Kurdish left organisations. As Kemalism had been experienced as an oppressive and alienating force in Kurdish communities, the Kurdish left sought to distance itself from this tradition and attempted to develop its own identity and ideology that combined socialism and addressed the Kurdish issue as one of national liberation.

2. For a detailed discussion of the diverse factors that led to the coups, see Dorronsoro and Gourisse 2015.

3. From the 1960s, the military gradually acquired the opportunity to define threats to the regime by mastering a security-focused discourse that articulated the threat of a conservative reactionism (*irtica*) opposed to the gains of the Kemalist revolution, and that of domestic Communist or Kurdish-nationalist enemies.

6

A DIFFICULT DEMOCRACY: POPULISM AND 'THE PEOPLE' IN TURKISH POLITICS

Islam: Between Pacification and Mobilisation

In the field of ideology, the 1980 coup invested in and systematically propagated Kemalism – the ideology that the coup perpetrators used to legitimise the suspension of multiparty democracy. This shallow version of Kemalism, premised primarily on the idolisation of Mustafa Kemal's personality and authority, became ubiquitous throughout the country, without however interfacing with the actual challenges faced by Turkish society (Göçek 2011:31). To complement its ideological armour and to shield the country from the 'communist menace', which the coup leadership identified as one of the enemies of 'the people' and 'the nation', the National Security Council governing the country saw in Islam the potential to provide the legitimacy it needed, and to counter the left's popularity among the youth who, they believed, had led the country into chaos in the second half of the 1970s. General Kenan Evren, the coup protagonist, was reported to suggest that the 'rational' Turkish Islam he wanted to propagate would be 'an element in the service of the nation and nationalism' and not in competition with either secularism or nationalism'; open to Western modernity and change and compatible to the secularism underpinning the Republic, it could buttress the Turkish state and society against Kurdish separatism and Marxism, which he considered to be the threats that his coup would eliminate (Yavuz 2003:70).

Accordingly, article 1924 of the 1982 constitution made religious education compulsory in primary and secondary schools as a means of propagating their version of a Turkish–Islamic Synthesis and instilling conservative values among the youth (Bora and Can 1999:174–5; Üstel 2004:290). The Diyanet (Directorate of Religious Affairs) embarked on a mosque-building programme (Morris 2005:73), and was reorganised in order to play a role in a campaign to propagate the regime's ideology and its version of Islam as a factor of societal and national cohesion especially in the southeast, where Kurdish separatism and the Kurdish left were seen as representing threats to the unity of Turkey (Yavuz 2003:70). The importance of, and new role attributed to Islam after the 1980 coup is even more obvious if one takes into account the expansion of religious television programmes, and the massive expansion of Imam Hatip schools and the recognition of their status as avenues to employment in the public sector (Baran 2010:36).

This rehabilitation of religion may have been intended to be cautious, integrated into the regime's nationalist ideology and under state control, but it created a space where Islam was looked at positively and even propagated by the educational system as a positive aspect of Turkishness. This shift succeeded in shifting social values in a more conservative direction but also further injected Islamic values into conservative politics and opened the way for an Islamic political space and civil society (see White 2002), taking a circuitous route to the eventual formation of the Justice and Development Party (Adalet ve Kalkınma Partisi, AKP) and, I would argue, to its electoral acceptability by constituencies beyond the traditional constituencies of its predecessor Islamist parties.

The 1983 parliamentary elections – the first after the coup and under the 1982 constitution introduced by the generals – returned a government, not of their preferred Popular Party (Halkçı Parti), housing the conservative wing of the banned CHP, but of the Motherland Party (Anavatan Partisi), a new party established and led by Türgüt Özal. Özal, a former World Bank employee and lecturer, had run unsuccessfully in the 1977 general election as an MSP candidate for the Grand National Assembly. He had not hesitated to point out that he was a practising Muslim and had completed the *hajj* pilgrimage to Mecca during his time as prime minister and, although his government had to tread cautiously as it operated under military tutelage, he had challenged a number of decisions taken by the military, most notably the appointment of a new chief of the General Staff, which he had vetoed (Morris 2005:44). During his 1983 election campaign, Özal made references to 'the long repressed Muslim identity of the Turks' and the neglect of religious issues that his government would be more sensitive to (Baran 2010:39). During his time as prime minister, and from November 1989 as president, Özal displayed a much more positive attitude to the role of Islam but also to the heritage of the Ottoman Empire whose memory had been marginalised in the Republic's ontological narrative.

Similarly, despite its emphasis on the centrality of Kemalism, the regime permitted, and the civilian governments that ensued pursued, policies that contradicted Mustafa Kemal's emphasis on statism (*devletçilik*) and his caution with regards to economic liberalisation. As discussed earlier, Atatürk favoured an economic system that gave primacy to state control, which, he believed, was the only actor that could drive development and economic independence. Turkey's mixed economy had been dominated by state monopolies, and a state-protected domestic market (Göçek 2011:31; Buğra 1994:35–93) that left very little space for domestic entrepreneurs to develop their businesses. In order to reheat the economy, the regime initiated a process of liberalisation that was presided over by Turgut Özal, head of the Motherland Party (Anavatan Partisi) and former World Bank employee (Aral 2001:72–4). As Aral notes, the policy envisaged an opening of the Turkish market to the global economy, and effectively lifting the protective cocoon to which the local industrial and commercial sectors, unprepared for such a change had grown accustomed (Aral 2001). This sea change in economic policy, although painful for the traditional secular industrialists, introduced two new social forces into Turkish society: 'a newly empowered civil society, which came about with the abolition of state control over communications [and] the provincial Anatolian bourgeoisie, which arose in response to the opportunity to establish direct contact with global businesses without the mediation of the state' (Göçek 2011:31–2). The civil society that emerged over time included secular and liberal organisations that shared unease with the tutelage of politics and society by the military regime, and eventually with organisations that expressed the concerns and values of the Anatolian bourgeoisie (White 2002:178–212). This religious bourgeoisie, unlike the secular entrepreneurs who had developed as a result of state protectionism and support, grasped the opportunities of the liberalisation and carved a space for itself in the new economic environment, accumulating economic resources (Göçek 2011:32) and contributing to the development of the Anatolian cities where it was based, thus contributing to the development of an 'Islamist' civil society and demanding to become accepted as part of the mainstream after decades of suppression of Islam and its social and political expressions. As Taspinar argues,

> These 'Islamic Calvinists' have been more concerned about maximizing profits, creating access to international currency markets, and ensuring political stability than about introducing Islamic law or creating a theocracy. Turkey now has thousands of such small and medium-sized export-oriented businesses, often referred to as 'Anatolian tigers'. (Taspinar 2012)

Islamist activism in the context of municipalities, supported by the new Anatolian bourgeoisie, contributed to the 'training' of valuable human capital that would be instrumental in building a party that would express the values and interests of the new Anatolian entrepreneurs. The Welfare Party (Refah Partrisi), established by Ali Türkmen, Ahmet Tekdal and the founder and leader of the banned MNP and MSP, and the Millî Görüş movement (Necmettin Erbakan) benefited in 1983 from both the more tolerant atmosphere towards Islam and the emergence of the Anatolian Tigers, as the new entrepreneurs were called, to denote their dynamism and aspiration, as their support allowed it to establish itself in municipal politics in the first instance and develop support structures for its constituency (see White 2002 and 2013), and for newcomers seeking help that the state could not provide or was not interested in providing. Whereas the 1980 coup had disrupted the political operation of the MSP, the Millî Görüş's charitable work continued, so much so that upon its establishment the Welfare Party already enjoyed links with the social networks that the movement's charitable and mutual support work had created over time both at the level of the Anatolian conservative bourgeoisie and that of the conservative urban poor. Without underestimating the Welfare Party's Islamic character, it is important to point out that the party connected with these constituencies in complex ways: by appealing to their conservative values, which it linked with Islamic piety, by endorsing their aspirations and, in the case of the urban poor, by addressing their needs.

However, the upward trajectory of the Welfare Party, becoming the largest party in the 1996 elections and leading a government coalition, with Necmettin Erbakan taking the office of the prime minister, was fairly abruptly terminated with the military memorandum of 28 February 1997, which forced Erbakan's resignation and led to the party's banning and eventual closure in January 1998. Although, the memorandum effectively sealed the fate of the Welfare Party, which was eventually banned just like its predecessors, the National Order Party (Millî Nizam Partisi) and the National Salvation Party (Millî Selâmet Partisi), the main target appears to have been Erbakan's secular coalition partner and leader of the centrist True Path Party (Doğru Yol Partisi), Tansu Ciller, who had been implicated in a number of scandals (Goltz 1997:M-2). Nevertheless, the army's intervention led to the purge of hundreds of Welfare Party-associated appointees in government ministries and agencies, and the withholding of substantial government funds earmarked for Welfare Party-controlled municipal governments, such as Istanbul, Ankara and Izmir, in an apparent attempt to stem the rising influence of Islamist politics. As Jenny White demonstrates, municipalities controlled by the Welfare Party had supported the development of an Islamic civil society as well as Islamist mobilisation (White 2002). And, more importantly, the evocation of concerns that stemmed from the Kemalist legacy of secularism tells of the perceived power of Mustafa Kemal's enduring *auctoritas* through his continually evoked legacy, albeit in the pursuit of ulterior goals. The statement made by General Çevik Bir, one of the masterminds of the memorandum, reminiscent of Atatürk's paternal(ist) metaphors, constitutes an eloquent – in its rhetorical awkwardness – summary of the prevalent thinking of the time: 'In Turkey we have a marriage of Islam and democracy. (. . .) The child of this marriage is secularism. Now this child gets sick from time to time. The Turkish Armed Forces is the doctor which saves the child. Depending on how sick the kid is, we administer the necessary medicine to make sure the child recuperates' (*Kıbrıspostası* 13 July 2011). Although Bir does not refer explicitly to 'the infant people', and does not assume the role of the father on behalf of the military, he nevertheless replicates the underlying paternal(istic) gaze typical of the early republican elite. The infant not only needs to mature and be trained, but also be medicated and nursed for its childhood illnesses.

The political space left by the ban on Welfare was soon to be filled by a new party that aspired to take the mantle from its predecessor, but also to actively reach out to a broader section of the society. The Justice and Development Party (AKP) was the product of a convergence of broader culturally conservative but economically liberal forces, including the reformist faction of the Islamist Virtue Party (Fazilet Partisi), which succeeded the Welfare Party for a brief period until it, too, was banned, as well as eminent members of Turgut Özal's Motherland Party (Anavatan Partisi), and others without previous party affiliations. In a sense, as I suggested earlier, the AKP has been a beneficiary of the cultural, political and economic transformations set in motion by the 1980 coup. The rehabilitation of Islam, even in the controlled manner in which it took place, created a space for different forces and constituencies that did not include Islam as part of their value system. The Motherland Party did not originate in the 'traditional' Islamist space that had tried on several occasions, and in several reincarnations, to challenge the Kemalist forces and institutions placing obstacles to their participation in the political arena. It represented a different political culture, less offensive to secularist sensitivities and more acceptable to the political gatekeepers – the courts and the military. Its constituency, too, was different from that of the Welfare Party and its predecessors. The unstable coalition governments and the political crises instigated by the army and the courts pave the way for these disparate forces to join and form the AKP. Their diverse backgrounds and trajectories and different relationships with Islam played a significant role in the articulating the party's ideological coordinates, which were the product of a compromise that could enable the founding members to find a modus vivendi with each other, but also to develop a different rapport with broader segments of society.

Since its founding in 2001 the AKP has won all but one electoral contests. It was able to form governments on its own in 2002, 2007, 2011 and November 2015, while, although attracting the votes of 40.87 per cent of the electorate in June 2015 and coming first in preferences, it did not have the necessary parliamentary majority to form a government. In 2018, as the presidential system introduced encouraged the formation of party coalitions, the AKP, together with the MHP, received 42.56 per cent of the vote and now commands the majority of delegates in the Grand National Assembly, while its leader was elected as the country's first president under the new presidential system, endorsed in a constitutional referendum in 2016 with 52.59 per cent (YSK Seçim Arşivi).

From early on, the party leadership, aware of the suspicions of the military and the bureaucratic elites as well as those of the secular establishment and intent on avoiding the fate of its banned predecessors, refused to be labelled as Islamist and preferred the label 'conservative democratic' party. In a speech in 2005, then Prime Minister Recep Tayyip Erdoğan, a former member of the Welfare and Virtue parties, former mayor of Istanbul and recognised for his pragmatic leadership of the city, avoided painstakingly using the word Islam in his description of the party. 'We are not an Islamic party, and we also refuse labels such as Muslim-democrat', Erdoğan pointed out, and went on to say that the AKP's agenda was nothing more than one befitting 'conservative democracy' (Taspinar 2012). Erdoğan had already been closely associated with Islamist militancy at the time of the ban of the Welfare Party, when he participated in protests as a public speaker (Yeşilada 2002:67–8). In a speech he gave in December 1997 in the town of Siirt while holding the office of mayor of Istanbul, he attempted to inspire his audience by reciting a poem written by Ziya Gökalp whose work, as discussed earlier, shaped much of the National Movement's ideology. Erdoğan's recitation contained a set of modified verses that proved controversial – 'The mosques are our barracks, the domes our helmets, the minarets our bayonets and the faithful our soldiers'– and led to his prosecution, a short prison sentence and a political ban, which forced him to step down from the Istanbul mayoral office, prevented him from participating in parliamentary elections (Al Jazeera 2018) and thus stopped him from taking up the office of prime minister when his party won the parliamentary elections of 2002 and was able to form the first non-coalition government in over a decade.

Hegemony beyond Islamism

Despite repeated declarations disavowing the party's Islamist heritage by party officials, the party was subjected to the scrutiny of the secularist establishment and, in order to avoid following the footsteps of its predecessors, it needed to shield itself through not only words, but also practice that would, on the one hand, disarm its critics, and on the other, enable it to strengthen its appeal to parts of the electorate that lay outside the traditional Islamist and Motherland Party constituencies. Responding to these exigencies, the AKP exploited an already existing split in the country and its elites into supporters of reform, often rallying around the banner of Europeanisation, and supporters of a statist view of Turkey under the tutelage of a suspicious and possessive military elite (Sofos 2000:256) in order to root itself in the political arena. It launched an agenda of democratic reform, coupled with the intensification of Turkey's EU accession bid, essentially situating itself at the centre of the political spectrum in its ambition and commitment to a mainstream agenda (Adak and Turan 2016). Coupling its democratic reform and EU accession policies gave the party a significant advantage; no longer could it be accused of an anti-Western orientation, as its Islamist predecessors were, as it integrated into its domestic politics the EU democratisation and human rights agenda – restricting the military's supervisory role (Cizre 2008) and its capacity to take extra-institutional action – which became part and parcel of the country's drive to fulfil a goal that was popular among the Kemalist establishment.[1] The AKP introduced measures, as part of a series of democratisation packages, that effectively redefined the role of the military in the exercise and supervision of executive power by trimming down the role of the National Security Council (NSC) from a supervisory to an advisory one. This redesignation was packaged together with a reduction of the staff and the departments of the NSC, thus reinforcing the message that the institution was no longer compatible with a democratic political system. A combination of substantive and symbolic measures presaged the eventual reversal of fortunes of the armed forces and their submission to civilian oversight, but not without resistance from the military.

The promise of a more democratic polity, apart from being an essential part of AKP's route to autonomy from the military–bureaucratic establishment, had intrinsic value for parts of the electorate who were secular and liberal in outlook, and thus provided an interface between them and the party. The AKP's democratic 'coup' enabled the party to increase its share of the vote, but also to challenge the divides that had solidified as a result of the Kemalists' uncompromising emphasis on the unity of 'the nation' and its mistrust of 'the people'.

Decades of suppression of Islam had spread mistrust, and indeed separated those with a secular outlook from those who had adopted conservative, Muslim values, while the practice of turning anyone who challenged the narrative of the homogeneous nation into 'political abjects' had given rise to disgruntlement among the country's Kurdish population, which had partly taken the form of an armed insurgency led by the outlawed Kurdistan Workers' Party (Partiya Karkerên Kurdistanê, PKK) and other groups that had been demanding secession, autonomy or political and cultural rights for the Kurdish citizens of Turkey. The progressive desecuritisation of the Kurdish issue, and countenancing the possibility of a non-military solution after years of suppressing any voice that supported dialogue and compromise, especially as the main opposition party, the CHP, considered this a non-negotiable red line, represented a sea change and also cast the CHP as an inflexible, fossilised institution with no forward-looking solutions. Even before any mention of a peace process, the AKP displayed unprecedented tolerance that opened up a space for a 'more self-conscious Kurdish associational life' (Öktem 2011:141; Turan 2019:196). The adoption of a politically liberal agenda gave rise to opportunities for dialogue and convergences on both fronts, thus challenging the hegemony of the military and secularist establishment that had been secured through the uncompromising 'othering' and securitisation of both Islam and the Kurdish issue.

While the AKP committed to the economic liberalisation premises of the Özal period and of the post-Erbakan era, it also deployed a social justice idiom that it had inherited from the Welfare Party and its emphasis on providing essential services for the urban and rural poor (see White 2002), without, however, explicitly acknowledging the lineage of this commitment. Just as its predecessor Islamist parties had done whenever they had gained control of municipalities, under the AKP, state institutions assumed new 'redistributive and allocative' functions, partly as an attempt to provide resources to its previously excluded Islamist constituency. The party improved the infrastructure of poorer urban districts, expanded health service provision for those who could not afford it, took initiatives to improve housing for the poor and provide accessible housing credits, provided financial support for students, and mobilised and funded initiatives to distribute food and provide emergency service to populations forgotten by the state and left behind in the years of economic development. This reaching out to the impoverished underclass, upon which the fantasy of Kemalist egalitarianism was built, gave the party a considerable advantage as it mobilised on its behalf previously disenfranchised parts of the population with limited life chances. Apart from reaching out to the poorest parts of the population, the AKP did not attempt, during its first years to mobilise them discursively or in other ways as it sought to project an image of a mainstream conservative party.

As Öniş (2015) points out, this early period of the AKP in office was characterised by a stint of economic growth, significant democratisation reforms and improved foreign relations. However, as he suggests, the party proved to be adaptable to new circumstances and challenges to such an extent that one cannot understand its nature and role without attempting a periodisation that goes beyond the first years of the AKP trajectory. And, indeed, Öniş discerns a second phase of the AKP's incumbency that spans from 2007 to 2011. This is a period during which a number of external variables change, potentially limiting the party's autonomy and prompting it to respond accordingly. Five years after the AKP took office, the original euphoria started dissipating as it was eclipsed by the stagnation of the country's EU accession bid, a slowdown in the democratisation drive and an economic standstill. It is in this context that the armed forces felt emboldened and attempted to revitalise their extra-institutional capacity to influence the political process. In April 2007, the armed forces General Staff, incensed at the selection of Abdullah Gül, whom the AKP had put forward as its candidate for the presidency, as they found the fact that his wife wore the headscarf offensive, issued a bold, barely concealed threat, on their website in which they attempted to recast the AKP as an enemy of the Republic, evoking, once more, the legacy of Atatürk:

> It is observed that some circles who have been carrying out ceaseless efforts to disturb the fundamental values of the Republic of Turkey, especially secularism, have escalated their efforts recently . . . Those activities include . . . a redefinition of the fundamental values and attempts to organize alternative celebrations instead of our national festivals symbolizing the unity and the solidarity of our nation . . . Those who are opposed to the Great Leader Mustafa Kemal Ataturk's understanding expressed in 'How happy is the one who says I am a Turk' are enemies of the Republic of Turkey and will remain so. The Turkish Armed Forces maintain their sound determination to carry

out their duties stemming from laws to protect the unchangeable characteristics of the Republic of Turkey. (BBC Türkçe in Turan 2019:197)

In this so-called e-coup (as it was staged through a statement on the armed forces website), the armed forces explicitly evoked the Atatürk's *auctoritas* in order to isolate and weaken the AKP government, and to reinstate their wounded claim to the custodianship of the values of the Republic. The AKP, calculating that the military would not risk the EU accession process, as a suspension was the most likely outcome in the case of any derailment of the democratic process, decided to respond firmly and go ahead with the Gül candidacy for the presidency, but, in addition, to use its majority in the Assembly to bring the parliamentary election forward, as the Assembly in session could not muster the necessary majority to elect a president. The vote saw the AKP returned to office with a significantly enhanced majority (46 per cent of all the votes and an absolute majority in the parliament, as opposed to just over 34 per cent in the previous election), and the new Assembly elected Abdullah Gül as the new President of the Republic (YSK Seçim Arşivi). The dilemmas the military sought to mobilise in order to isolate and delegitimise the AKP were turned against them. The AKP adeptly used the polarisation of the political field orchestrated by the leadership of the armed forces to its own advantage by juxtaposing the Kemalist discourse that had clearly lost its hegemonic appeal, if it ever had any, with the voice of the emerging majority that it claimed to represent. Characteristically, in the debates on the character of the presidency, the AKP proposed constitutional amendments that stipulated direct popular election of the president, while Erdoğan put across the argument that the president's office is too significant politically to leave it to the machinations of political parties and suggested that the president should be elected directly by the public, deriding his opponents as seeing the election of the Turkish president by popular vote as a problem for the regime and then having the audacity to ask votes from the people. Referring to a comment which, in an apparent reference to the presidential palace, described the secularists' 'last fortress' as 'fallen', he said:

Those who can say this are disrespectful of the people's will . . . Çankaya, which is said to have 'fallen,' does not belong to any one person or an elite group, but to 70 million, to the Republic of Turkey . . . Where is this fortress that is said to have fallen? Whose is this Çankaya? Does it belong to some, or to 70 million children of the motherland? Who are the people in power? Where did we come from? We were born and raised in the land of this motherland. We are the citizens of this country. Those who trusted power in our hands are the children of this land. (*Today's Zaman* 29 August 2007)

In another instance, he took the opportunity to articulate his own definition of the AKP:

The AK Party is equidistant to every person living in this country, every legitimate idea, every belief, and every ideal, and it is a center party that defines itself not with respect to a specific faction in society but with respect to the entire society. (*Today's Zaman* 28 September 2007)

The party, displaying its growing self-confidence, positioned itself as a champion of 'the people', who were denied the right to select the person to occupy the country's highest political office in their entirety, and juxtaposed itself with those who mistrusted the people they are supposed to serve and who talked of the country's institutions as if they were their own. Although Erdoğan was careful to make reference to the plurality of ideals nurtured by the people, he insisted on his party seeking to represent, not factional, particularistic interests, but those of the society in its entirety. Although this reference may be interpreted as part of the party leadership's effort to represent their party as open to everyone, as a catch-all party (see Kirchheimer 1966), the particular circumstances of the political confrontation surrounding the 2007 elections indicate that the AKP was fleshing out an alternative discourse centring on the inclusion of 'the repressed', sharply contrasting with the discourse of the CHP, its rival and ally of the military, thus abandoning a period of caution and of evading confrontation with the leadership of the armed forces. More importantly, perhaps, this was one of the instances where Erdoğan expressed the importance of the unity of 'the people' and its precedence over particularistic interests whose representation was detrimental to the 'unity, solidarity and brotherhood' of 'the people' (*Hürriyet Daily News* 2019).

Indeed, although the AKP, prior to its consolidation, was an ardent supporter of the country's fragile parliamentary system, it has slid rapidly and violently towards adopting a personalised presidential leadership model and has pursued legitimation avenues free of the mediation of parliamentary procedural 'niceties', as shown in Recep Tayyip Erdoğan's appeals to the abstract notion of a homogeneous people's National Will to contest supreme court decisions (*Hürriyet Daily News* 2016), to mention a telling example of prioritisation of the rights of the nation/people as a collectivity over those of individual citizens. In view of this change of course by the AKP leadership, there seem to be broad consensus among commentators that Turkey has been undergoing a process of de-democratisation and has evolved into a competitive authoritarian regime, especially since 2015 (Esen and Gümüşçü 2017; Somer 2017).

The tense relationship of the AKP, the military and the judiciary polarised the political scene in the summer of 2007 when the Ergenekon case was brought to court. The case involved a group of military personnel who were investigated on suspicion of planning to destabilise the country through the use of violence, and soon encompassed journalists, businessmen, academics and politicians (Kalaycıoğlu 2012). Although it eventually transpired that the allegations were fabricated by the Gülen movement which, at the time, was cooperating with the AKP, it provided a pretext for the government to purge officers and judges it considered inimical to it, and to gave it the opportunity to intimidate the AKP's opponents within the bureaucracy and civil society (Akkoyunlu and Öktem 2016; Somer 2017). When civil society organisations criticised the investigations and lawyers criticised the violations of due process and inconsistencies in the evidence, the AKP brushed off their objections accusing them of providing moral and political support to 'coup plotters' in ways reminiscent of the 'othering' of abjects who had criticised the authoritarianism of the early Republic (Kalaycıoğlu 2012). Media outlets that were friendly to the government cast the Ergenekon trials as the government's reaction to the 'deep state' conspiracies.

March 2008 saw another serious challenge to the AKP, this time by the Republic's judiciary, as the chief prosecutor of the Supreme Court of Appeal filed a lawsuit in the Constitutional Court demanding that the AKP be closed down and its leadership be banned from politics. Reminiscent of the early republican treason court cases, the AKP leadership was accused of turning the party into 'a focal point of anti-secular activities'. The Court acknowledged evidence supporting the charges, but voted narrowly against closure of the party.

In 2010 the AKP turned to the judiciary. At a time of heightened tensions between the government and the high judiciary, the AKP proposed a series of constitutional amendments aimed at challenging the dominance of secularist judges in the Constitutional Court and the High Council of Judges and Public Prosecutors (Kalaycıoğlu 2012; Özbudun 2014:156). The constitutional amendments were supported by 58 per cent of the voters thus completing a series of reforms that removed the means that the civil and military bureaucracy had at its disposal to challenge the AKP. After the AKP's electoral victory in 2011, Erdoğan seemed to have firmly consolidated his political power, with 47 per cent of the popular vote and a weak and divided opposition that was unable to challenge him (YSK Seçim Arşivi). On 29 July 2011, the armed forces chief of staff resigned after a disagreement with the Prime Minister over staff promotions, followed by the heads of the army, navy, and air force, enabling Erdoğan to extend his government's control over the military. The emboldened AKP consolidated its gains through shrewd manoeuvring and discursively pitting 'the people' against the 'usurpers of their sovereignty'. Duran describes the shift of political strategy from the early AKP years to what Öniş distinguishes as the second phase of the AKP's development (Öniş 2015) in terms of a move of the party from a 'politics of patience' to one of 'controlled tension' (Duran 2013:98). In this polarised political landscape, the AKP leadership claimed that they represented 'the repressed' (without necessarily attributing an Islamic connotation to them), who had long not been entrusted with the sovereignty that was promised to them. The party, largely though not exclusively due to the charisma of Erdoğan, mobilised the dominant divides in Turkish society to its own advantage, once these were made relevant by the military's attempt to force the government to resignation or, at best, to change course.

The Politics of Indignation and the Moment of the People

Zooming in, just off Taksim Square in Istanbul, a modest protest event in May 2013, which aimed to denounce government plans to demolish central Istanbul's Gezi Park and make room for the construction of a shopping mall in the form of a replica of a nineteenth-century Ottoman artillery barracks, would become a defining moment of the AKP's period in office – little known to its participants at the time.

Despite its initial emphasis on the park itself, the protest constituted the expression of a more widespread grievance, a sense of 'moral indignation', that far exceeded environmental concerns. The protests soon focused on Prime Minister Recep Tayyip Erdoğan and the authoritarian character of his and his party's politics. The symbolic violence exercised by the government and the overwhelming material violence deployed by the riot police dispatched to suppress the protests had a 'constitutive' role, sparking and providing direction to the emotions of the protesters and providing the raw material for the construction of injustice frames (Gamson 2011:464). They facilitated the mobilisation of a diverse crowd of protesters who invented novel and more dynamic forms of solidarity to openly confront the police. 'As common as the images of police firing tear gas into crowds' were, Paul notes, were 'the images of people picking up the canisters and throwing them back, of people using antacid solutions to wash off each other's faces and neutralise the effects of the gas, and of people sprinting into the clouds to help wounded protesters escape' (Paul 2013). Interestingly, solidarity did not depend on the co-presence of protesters in the same physical space. The fact that, in the absence of a traditional organisational structure, protest and the forms of solidarity that sustained it were extended through the use of cyberspace and information/communications technology constitutes a prime example of what Bennett and Segerberg call 'connective action' (2012).

The sense of solidarity engendered by 'resisting together', of collectively transcending the precariousness of bodily existence (Gambetti 2014) has also precipitated the stitching together of diverse grievances and the formation of injustice frames. Environmental concerns (protecting the park and the trees); issues of urban space; perceived interference with ways of life and creeping moralism; Erdoğan's paternalistic rhetoric and antagonistic style; general frustration with the political system, including the opposition – all mixed in and gave expression to a wide gamut of grievances, fears and aspirations and, interestingly, led those who uttered them to listen to others doing the same.

The carnivalesque character of the protest, its multi-centrality, the celebration of diversity in a moment of unity united all these people. Participants seemed willing to talk, to tell each other why they were part of this moving crowd sprawling from Taksim Square, along the side streets and through İstiklal Caddesi where groups of students stood still against the flow of pedestrians browsing shop windows and read books, magazines, newspapers or contemplated the facades of buildings in a protest against the commercialisation of the public spaces of the area. Back in Taksim, others voiced their concerns at what they perceived as the authoritarian tendencies of the government as they prepared to stand still facing the Atatürk Cultural Center until the police removed them, following the example of Erdem Gündüz who first staged this act of non-violent protest and immediately became a trending topic on Twitter as 'the standing man' (*duran adam*). Irrationality and sober analysis, emotion and calculation, the local and the national, everyday concerns and *long-durée* vision, the profound and the mundane found expressions in the words or even the silences in the townscape that the movement inhabited and claimed as its own. And beyond the confines of the physical space, social media transmitted the discussion far away into remote neighbourhoods and towns and even into the diaspora. In this context, participants attempted to articulate grievances from different quarters that made sense to them and resonated with their own experiences, and integrated them into narratives of injustice. What united these narratives, *the point de capiton* (see Lacan 1977:267–8) of these injustice threads, was a sense of disenchantment, 'a shared feeling of being cheated', which blurred, even if temporarily, the rigid boundaries separating the rich and the poor, the Turk and the Kurd, the Sunni and the Alevi, and so on, prompting them, in Mishra's (2013) apt description, to revolt 'against their own previous apathy'.

The protesters had no concrete predetermined agenda other than stopping the demolition of Gezi Park, and this was nowhere more visible than in the ever-changing list of demands presented to the government by Taksim Solidarity Platform (Taksim Dayanışma Platformu), the only body with the semblance of representing a movement that was multipolar, multifaceted, leaderless and disorganised. Having said that, the Gezi protests did not occur in a void; they were certainly not the product of the convergence of hitherto isolated individuals; informal and loose networks often provided the building blocks of the mobilisation as friends, neighbours and colleagues from work descended on Taksim or arranged to meet there at the end of the working day or during the weekends.

The protest opened up spaces for exchange and translation, where the pious met the secular, the libertarian encountered the conservative, where different traditions and practices were shared and often translated and experienced collectively. It was marked by a yearning for the warmth and solidarity, for the 'homeliness' and 'sisterhood/brotherhood' of an idealised community. Despite the external risk presented by police violence, Gezi provided a 'safe' and 'egalitarian' space for protesters to experiment with and articulate their views and identities. Drawing upon the work of Victor Turner on liminality (1974), one can see participation in the protests as a *rite de passage*, a 'liminal moment', a moment when individuals, free from the constraints and rules of daily life can experiment with their identities. Turner suggests that in such liminal moments, ritual participants find themselves within an egalitarian social field that he calls 'communitas', that is, a community marked by a sense of equality and freedom. This admittedly temporary 'egalitarian' dimension of Gezi has been crucial in enabling protesters to come together, indeed work together, in articulating their grievances and demands, but also organising daily routines, modes of coexistence and the sharing of resources and duties. These popular mobilisations had a plebeian, not a populist character. Irreverent, carnivalesque, expressing a sense of malaise, yet anti-political, in the sense of lacking any will to intersect with the formal political arena and of the participants adamantly refusing to associate themselves with any political party. Gezi represented a form of collective action, a plebeian event, geared towards self-expression, and experiencing a momentary sense of freedom and solidarity, a fluid movement/moment characterised by a multicentric culture of contestation, a shared and constantly and openly negotiated universe of discourse and action. As I argued in Chapter 1, Gezi was a veritable 'outsider', with its participants not interested in translating their energy and mobilisation into political capital, not fuelled or tempted by the aspiration of the gain of political power, and many of its protagonists indeed resisted the beckoning of the opposition parties. Operating outside the linear time and the conventional topography of Turkish politics, the urban plebs that engaged in the carnivalesque action of resistance for almost a month fought to restore or reclaim their rights to the urban commons they felt they were losing, as the state and its commercialisation and gentrification policies were encroaching on them and setting claim on new common goods, public services, transport, health, access to knowledge and to work. Not just Gezi itself, but also the squares, the green spaces, the streets, the spaces of leisure and encounter, became their confrontation grounds in this struggle.

The AKP government, seasoned when it came to staving off the political manoeuvres of the military and the judiciary, was taken aback by the vitality and contagiousness of the protests. Not only were they unexpected, but they also constituted the first extensive challenge to the AKP and its increasingly arrogant policies, especially the big construction and urban regeneration projects that its leadership considered the symbols of its modernism, whereas, for middle-class and a segment of poor city dwellers, such projects infringed on their living space and everyday life.

The composition and structure of the movement represented a puzzle; most of the AKP leadership had grown up in the midst of conventional politics whose logics obeyed the contours of particular divides in Turkish society that they saw as perennial in nature, and whose action repertoires were very different from what was unfolding. Whereas political challenges were expected to come from more conventional political actors, such as parties or trade unions, the protest took shapes and forms that were hard to anticipate and contain. Without clear leadership or any understanding of the hierarchies and structures of this popular outpouring in Turkey's streets, the police were also at a loss, unable to determine a course of action other than the wholesale deployment of brutal force, especially as it became evident that arresting the 'usual suspects' – mainly left-wing activists – did not pay any dividends (Sofos 2018a).

The AKP initially attempted to discredit the action in the eyes of its own conservative constituency. Erdoğan chose to deny the agency of the demonstrators by dismissing them as 'thugs' (*çapulcular*), a 'menace' to society. These terms were intended to effectively facilitate the 'misreading' of the protests as wanton acts of vandalism and destruction by irresponsible youth. Yet I suggest that Erdoğan's and other AKP leaders' discourse during the days of the crisis was not only intended to define the protesters and cast them in a negative light, but was also instrumental in defining their constituency, 'the people', who defined the National Will (*milli irade*). Thus, beyond these characterisations, a fortnight after the start of the protests, in the 'Respect for the National Will' rallies his party held in Ankara and Istanbul (*Today's*

Zaman 2013) to demonstrate that it was their constituency and not the protesters that represented 'the people' and expressed the National Will, Erdoğan claimed that a conspiracy and 'terrorists' were involved in the protests, which were designed to tarnish Turkey's international reputation. Trying to appeal to the proclivity of Turkish society for *komplo* (conspiracies), he claimed that the protests were orchestrated by a vaguely defined murky 'interest lobby' and its internal collaborators (primarily members of the Armenian, Greek minority communities and the Kurdish movement). Yiğit Bulut, financial commentator and later chief economic advisor to Erdoğan, suggested that the protests 'were engineered by an "interest rate lobby" to bring down the Turkish economy. Bulut also implied that the protesters were organised and compensated by unnamed foreign agents' (Taş 2015:784). The use of the conspiracy idiom has always been a potent one, and has been reused since then by the AKP leadership to achieve the externalisation of the protesters and the protest from the body politic. As Guida (2008:37) notes, 'according to a striking survey, 72 per cent of Turks believe that there are some countries that would like to divide Turkey, a view shared by a great proportion of the population as well as by politicians' (see also Kuzmanovic 2012). At the same time, the transformation of the protesters into 'national abjects' was matched by their physical suppression as the government eventually ordered the riot police to step in and violently disperse the protests with an assortment of pepper gas, water cannons and plastic bullets. The protests themselves came to stir the stagnant waters of Turkish politics as they went against the governing party's hitherto perceived prevalence for over a decade over Turkish political life and the opposition's inability to articulate a credible and inspiring voice (Sofos 2014).

This disquiet was clearly expressed on 11 June 2013 when Recep Tayyip Erdoğan used his address at the AKP Grand National Assembly to express his exasperation with the protesters:

> According to them we don't understand politics. According to them we don't understand art, theatre, cinema, poetry. According to them we don't understand aesthetics, architecture. According to them we are uneducated, ignorant, the lower class, who has to be content with what is being given; meaning, we are a group of negroes [*zenci*]. (AK Parti TBMM Grup Toplantısı 2013)

This excerpt from his speech constitutes a culmination of previous attempts to position his party and his constituency, timidly at first and more outspokenly later, in the context of what he represented as a perennial divide running through the Turkish body politic as well as the country's society and culture. Erdoğan's address reproduced and reinforced the trope of the 'downtrodden' and their indignation at the contempt shown to them and, at the same time, conjured the image of the contemptuous 'other' of the downtrodden 'people'. As in his comments about the 'fall of the Çankaya presidential residence' during the presidential crisis of 2007, Erdoğan maps Turkish society in terms of two camps: the 70 million hard-working, wholesome native (*yerli*) Turks, whose *Çankaya*, whose country and Republic, has been usurped by the small minority of arrogant, 'cultured' (*kültürlü*) upper-class urbanites with their impeccable Istanbul accents who looked down on them.

Targeting the 'cultured' elite and uncovering its disdain for 'the people' did not represent a couple of isolated instances, as these examples indicate, but a more pervasive element of the AKP discourse, especially after its first five years in office. In his address at the Fatih Sultan Mehmet Vakıf University graduation ceremony in 2016, Erdoğan, now Turkey's president, reminded his audience of the intellectual elite's ugliness and its disrespect for the people:

> If you do not give up the fight with the people, with the people's values, history, culture and their representatives, you will drown in your own ugliness . . . What kind of men are these? Who cares if you are an artist, a professor? First you will respect this people; you can never look down on this people. (*Sabah* 22 June 2016)

To go back to June 2013 statements, to strengthen the vastness of distance and the sense of the irreconcilable difference between 'them' and 'us' that he is trying to convey, he uses the racialised term *zenci*, translatable as negroes but originating in the Ottoman era, referring to enslaved and emancipated African Ottoman subjects. Often used as a racial slur, the term carries within it a strong connotation of slavery and of being at the bottom of the social hierarchy (see also the interesting genealogy of the term in Ferguson 2014; also Acemoğlu and Robinson 2013). To compound his condemnation of the protesters, Erdoğan cast the protesters as sacrilegious secularists, who displayed their immorality and impiety by bringing alcohol into the Dolmabahçe Mosque where they were seeking refuge from the teargas used by the police to disperse the crowds (*Hürriyet* 2013).

And, reportedly, when a female AKP supporter, alleged to have been 'insulted, kicked and pissed on by 100 men half-naked wearing leather gloves and black bandanas' by protesters on account of her headscarf, Erdoğan, in one of his National Will meetings, used the reported assault of a 'sister' to instil his audience with indignation:

> 'they dragged my covered sister on the streets near my office and attacked her and her child.' He also contrasted the impious acts of the Gezi crowd with 'his covered sisters who never resorted to rebellious acts despite being treated as outcasts, not being allowed into the universities. They showed patience knowing that patience brings salvation.' (Özkazanç 2020)

Such rhetorical devices, including the trope of 'our threatened women', reinforced the dividing lines and contributed to his attempt to redesignate the AKP constituency as that of outcasts, of the repressed (see on this Sofos 1996a:82). Uninterested in the diversity of the participants in the Gezi protests, as his aim was to isolate and delegitimise them, Erdoğan bundled them all into the small cultured arrogant minority, simultaneously adding layers such as their irreverence, their servitude to foreign masters, their contempt for rules and order, that turned them into abjects and confirmed their 'alienness' to 'the ordinary people'. Culture, disdain and condescension served here as boundary-making mechanisms, magnifying emotional distance between those of Erdoğan's audience who found that such a divide resonated with them and their life experiences. These boundary-making processes did indeed resonate with their intended audience, as conservative interviewees talking about Gezi about thirty days after the protests expressed in no unambiguous terms their feeling of alienation from what Gezi represented, even when they expressed misgivings about the AKP government.

> 30-year-old Hassan, a mechanic from Üsküdar said characteristically 'I do not trust them [the protesters]. They want to turn the clock back [to the Kemalist era]. I worked hard to improve my life and to gain dignity but people like them would not even think about my problems and hopes.' Similarly, Fatmanur, a

23-year-old student from Balat ironically dismissed Gezi as a 'party of over-privileged arrogant youngsters gone wrong'. Clearly such responses highlight the enormous chasm between parts of Turkish society whose political concerns and priorities as perceived as mutually incompatible. (Sofos 2018a:91)

Referring to the discursive strategy of mobilising this feeling of rejection, Ferguson suggests that '[t]his trope is well-worn ground for Erdoğan, a staple of his self-branding as the great outsider, disinterested and removed from the politics of twentieth-century one-party rule and corruption, just a simple man trying to get things done for Turkey' (Ferguson 2014:78). He sees this as evidence of a class divide that is best encapsulated in the popular distinction between 'White Turks' and 'Black Turks':

> White Turks are considered to be educated, working mainly in the upper reaches of the state bureaucracy, the army and business world, while Black Turks are their opposite: uneducated, lower classes or people with peasant backgrounds. What Erdoğan was doing in this speech, then, was trying to emphasize that he and his party have been discriminated against by their opponents, whose views have been more fuelled [sic] by prejudice than logic. (2014:79)

Although I find this evocation of the 'White Turk/Black Turk' (also see Acemoğlu and Robinson 2013) divide very astute and relevant, I think that its designation as a class divide misses the point of its being a composite and malleable divide, inhabiting the space between the structural and the contingent, continuously reordering and remapping Turkish society, making some differences relevant and others redundant at different moments, as I discuss later. The composite and malleable character of the 'White Turk/Black Turk' divide is especially useful as a resource at this particular populist 'moment', when the name of 'the people' is explicitly uttered in the context of their antagonistic relationship (see Laclau 1990:92) with those who look down on them. As Arditi reminds us,

> the populist 'us' remains conveniently vague . . . It is a deliberate vagueness, for it enables it to blur the contours of 'the people' sufficiently as to encompass anyone with a grievance structured around a perceived exclusion from a

public domain of interaction and decision hegemonized by economic, political, or cultural elites. (2007:75)

The different layers that Erdoğan and his associates added to demonstrate the distance between the people and the protesters effectively constitute examples of redrawing the contours of the divide using resources such as status, culture, religion, education and class, and are part of the broader and much longer-term processes under way. Leaving this aside, the mobilisation of this binary and the inequalities it denotes is significant and by no means accidental. Erdoğan presented himself and his party as the true representatives of 'the people', often resorting to 'low' sociocultural and political performative codes, as defined by Ostiguy (2017). Erdoğan's 'outsider' status and humble socioeconomic background when he first rose to power facilitated his use of anti-establishment appeals (Aytaç and Öniş 2014). As Acemoğlu and Robinson (2013) point out, Erdoğan reminded his audiences where he, and they, belonged when he said, reportedly on more than one occasion, 'In this country there are White Turks and Black Turks. Your Brother Tayyip comes from the Black Turks', thus turning a term that used to designate social abjects into a badge of honour, a genealogy to be proud of.

Mobilising the Black/White Turk binary, Erdoğan brought together experiences of exclusion and inequality in modern Turkey and discursively reconstructed them in the shape of a cultural trauma (see Alexander et al. 2004, Demertzis 2020)). Turning the anxiety this trauma has evoked – its affective dimension – into the threat of undermining what 'the people', together with *their* party and *their* father-figure-as-Brother Tayyip, had achieved loomed large, has time and again produced emotional responses in the form of fear and anger. Rekindling this constructed yet productive crisis and these powerful emotions has been at the centre of Erdoğan's communicative and performative repertoire, which he and his associates have repeatedly deployed.

The polarisation around the Gezi events provided the raw material for the performative, discursive, cognitive and affective construction of threat and set the tone and language that prevailed towards the end of the turbulent year 2013 and beyond, as the government was shaken by corruption probes, and the pro-AKP media continued to represent the party representing 'the people', locked into a struggle with powerful international actors who wanted the AKP experiment to fail (Reuters 2013). The general election of June 2015, resulted in a hung parliament, the first since the 1999 general election. Although the AKP was returned as the largest party, having won 258 seats with 40.9 per cent of the vote, it lost its parliamentary majority (YSK Seçim Arşivi) and was clearly short of the two-thirds majority needed for the implementation of its plan to introduce constitutional amendments for an executive presidency that would considerably strengthen the president's powers at the expense of those of the Assembly and the rest of the executive. The new left-wing People's Democratic Party (Halkların Demokratik Partisi, HDP), whose platform included the promotion of Kurdish and minority rights, managed to exceed the 10 per cent election threshold winning 13.1 per cent of the vote and eighty seats (YSK Seçim Arşivi), eroding the AKP's support in the predominantly Kurdish southeast. The loss of its Assembly majority was a moment of reckoning for the AKP leadership which saw in HDP a potential threat, despite its relatively low electoral support. The AKP was not interested in a coalition government at such a significant juncture. The shocks of the Gezi protest and the corruption probes of late 2013 had convinced Erdoğan that a strong presidential executive was the only way to dispense with the weaknesses of parliamentary-style democracy, enable him to push ahead with his blueprint of Yeni Türkiye (New Turkey) and shield himself and his associates from attacks like the corruption allegations. Erdogan dismissed the prospect of a coalition, characteristically saying that such governments belonged to the days of 'old Turkey'. He called new elections for November 2015, which took place after ceasefire negotiations between the government and the Kurdistan Workers' Party (PKK) collapsed in July of that year, leading to a resumption in conflict in the southeastern provinces. The AKP won a majority in the Assembly with 316 delegates and 49.4 per cent of the popular vote. The HDP saw less support compared to June, polling 10.7 per cent of the vote, just above the 10 per cent threshold and winning fifty-nine seats, while the MHP saw approximately 4 per cent of its voters expressing support for the AKP (YSK Seçim Arşivi). The victory of the AKP, its comfortable control of the Assembly and the emergence of its key opponents weaker from this contest produced a sense of triumphalism. The party pushed forward President Erdoğan's plans for constitutional amendments, causing discontent among critics who felt that the country lacked an opposition.

On 15 July 2016, a group of armed forces officers attempted an ill-fated coup d'état. The coup involved a fairly limited but efficiently deployed number of units and military hardware. Although manpower and materiel came from several locations in the country, the main thrust of the military takeover was focused in Istanbul and especially Ankara, where key state institutions are located. As a helicopter raid on the Marmaris hotel where President Erdoğan was spending his holidays was unfolding, the armed forces' website featured a statement declaring that a Peace Council had taken control to restore democracy, human rights and 'peace at home' – a reference to one of Atatürk's cornerstones of modern Turkey's orientation (Sofos 2016). Erdoğan, narrowly missed by the soldiers who raided his hotel, decided to fight back. Using facetime to address the public, declaring the government's determination to resist and calling 'the people' to get out in the streets and defy the curfew that was meanwhile declared, he boarded a business jet to Istanbul. A series of errors and bad timing, combined with the resolute expression of defiance by the government and condemnation by the opposition, did not convince key players in the military and the civil service to lend their support to what they considered a potentially moribund rebellion. The government had managed to take advantage of the chaos the coup had caused and provided its own organising narrative of the moment. The failed coup attempt and its aftermath have allowed Erdoğan to shrink the political space for dissenting opinions and to juxtapose them to the National Will. Erdoğan's defiant response to the coup attempt and his ability to mobilise thousands of people to face the putschists on the streets have elevated his popularity to 'mythic proportions among significant portions of Turkey's population' (Akkoyunlu and Öktem 2016:520).

President Erdoğan appealed to the public to fill the streets and squares, while the country's Presidency of Religious Affairs (Diyanet) issued instructions to imams to make similar calls from the mosques, and the ruling AKP party networks started mobilising their members. Despite the condemnation of the coup by major political, military and civil institutions, the government decided to base its fight back partly on mobilising loyal military units and a heavily armed police – the product of a long, slow process of militarisation of the latter under the aegis of the AKP – and partly by recourse to extra-institutional means, notably mobilising 'the people'. Soon enough, the combined determined response of military and police, and the crowds who heeded the calls of the government, had sealed the fate of the coup.

Although we have no hard evidence of who went out in the streets to defy the coup – it will take a long time to get a clear picture – I think we have sufficient indication to suggest caution when trying to make sense of the popular mobilisations that took place both during the coup and after its defeat. It is clear that 'the people' out in the streets comprised different actors. First, where violent clashes took place, often next to the police forces, one could discern lightly armed angry mobs who, on occasion, relished the spilling of their opponents' blood. Then, among the defiant crowds who came out on to the streets to express their opposition to the coup through their mere physical presence, one could recognise government supporters, mobilised by the appeals of their political leaders either through the AKP or the mosque networks, or merely the calls of the imams from the mosque speakers and minarets.

Claims that 'the people' in their 'entirety' filled the country's streets and squares may sound appealing and have a romantic quality, but are untrue. Indeed, footage and interviews from the night of the coup with participants in the demonstrations and clashes with the rebel units, but also the soundscape and visual repertoire of the post-coup celebrations, indicate that the crowds making up 'the people' were mainly though not exclusively supporters of the governing party. Nevertheless, the mobilisations of the day, and the days that followed the coup, were important elements in the construction of the people's and the government's majoritarian ideology. Just as mass rallies before elections, on occasions organised by the government to demonstrate the continued support by 'the people', provided visibility but also, and more crucially, tangibility of that support for the AKP (see Baykan 2018:162), so the response of party supporters and sympathisers to the AKP leadership's calls could be seen as 'plebiscitary' moments where the people's rapport and bond with the leadership are manifested and confirmed. Indeed the AKP had already invested considerably in the organisation of such plebiscitary moments; before the 2007 general elections, it was reported that Erdoğan visited fifty-four provinces out of eighty-one (*Hürriyet* 2007), while according to Zaman, in 2009, he had visited fifty-seven provinces. The reason for this intensive effort to bring the party leader to his constituents had to do with the AKP's reliance on a politics of direct rapport, of immediacy, related to

Manin's discussion of the metamorphoses of representation (1997). Although Manin focuses on the media which, he claims, provide a semblance or simulacrum, of immediacy that gives momentum to an alternative mode of representation, I would argue that the constituents' exposure to the presence of the charismatic leader, however briefly, can dissimulate asymmetrical relations under the guise of a dialogic interaction and the imaginary identification of 'constituents as the people' with the leader. And, more importantly, the party had invested considerable effort and resources to organise the National Will meetings after the Gezi protests to provide proof of the legitimacy afforded to it by 'the people'.

Turning to Erdoğan's decision to appeal to 'the people' to resist, and later to celebrate night after night in the country's public spaces, such as Ankara's Kızılay Meydanı, Istanbul's Taksim Meydanı and Izmir's Konak Meydanı, to name but a few, I would argue that the move echoes the mobilisations choreographed by Slobodan Milošević in former Yugoslavia. According to Sofos (1996b) Milošević used the 'moral panic' (see Cohen 1974), which had been cultivated in Serbia and Montenegro over the sensitive issue of the alleged 'Albanisation' of Kosovo – a Serbian autonomous province at the time – to justify the need for constitutional reform and to launch the notorious 'anti-bureaucratic revolution', a campaign aimed to cleanse the party and the state apparatus of inefficient and 'treasonous' bureaucrats. To support his anti-constitutional 'reform' programme, which entailed purges and intimidation of the opposition and the suppression of dissenting voices, Milošević and his collaborators encouraged a series of public rallies and demonstrations between 1987 and 1989 that became known as instances of 'street democracy' (*ulična demokracija*). These mass mobilisations acquired the character of impromptu plebiscites, forms of theatrical activation and exercise of popular sovereignty, 'endowing' Milošević with the authority to bypass legal niceties in the pursuit of his plans and providing cover for violent mobs to gate-crash meetings of elected authorities, demand the resignation of their members or terrorise those whose opinions they disapproved of. In both Serbian and Turkish cases the mobilisation of the people had a noteworthy performative dimension. The outpouring of 'the people' in the streets and squares in the face of adversity, the expression of indignation and determination at the face of danger constitutes a visual and material manifestation of the notion of the people, of the abjects that the AKP and its leader have mentioned time and again in addresses, rallies and interviews, and who, once called on by Erdoğan made their presence felt. This liminal moment, where fear and wonder in the streets and squares of Ankara and Istanbul converged, was, or was so represented by Erdoğan and his party, the moment when the Republic and its public spaces were symbolically/theatrically reclaimed by its people, who had previously been excluded, mistrusted and unheeded. This visual, aural and tangible dimension of the populist moment of the night of the fifteenth and the early morning of the sixteenth of July created a representation of unity of purpose and will of 'the people', while displacing the reality of a deeply divided and unequal society, giving the former a materiality that discourse, in its strict sense, could not give it. The sights and sounds of the people who had until that moment found themselves, or so they were painstakingly told, on the receiving end of disdain from 'arrogant' elites, were now validating their existence as 'one', and constituted the raw material for a memory and mythology of resistance, as the multitude of forms of commemoration of the Demokrasi ve Birlik Gün (Democracy and Unity Day) indicate.

Apart from the physical spaces occupied by 'the people' who responded to the call of Erdoğan and his party, this outpouring of masses in the streets and squares of the country instituted and inhabited a symbolic, extra-institutional space that allowed them to feel directly in control, and to enjoy unmediated contact with their leader and protector of *their* democracy. It is at moments possessing a plebiscitary quality like these – the various AKP mobilisations, the National Will meetings and the Democracy and Unity Days – that populist 'democracy' is affirmed and the institutionalised structures of representation are bypassed and supplanted by the direct communication between Erdoğan and 'his people' in a way reminiscent of the extra-institutional relationship of Atatürk and 'his people' discussed earlier.

Even though 'the people' were not really *sovereign*, the president's decision a day later to institute a state of emergency proved, according to this mythology, that the abjects of the Republic could resist the interruption of the political process of 'their' democracy by those who wanted to usurp their sovereignty and to refuse the institution of a state of exception (Schmitt 1985:13). The mobilisation of 'the people' in the country's streets not only confirmed their putative sovereignty, but also the unity of their 'will'. This 'will' was mobilised at another moment of national crisis during the Gezi protests, when the AKP organised counter-demonstration rallies to prove that the party and its leader – who was the speaker and enjoyed a privileged connection with the people that was displayed during their asymmetrical dialogic interaction – were endowed with popular legitimacy. These meetings, tellingly named 'Respect for the National Will' (Milli İradeye Saygı), alluded to the suggestion that the only bearer of rights in the New Turkey envisaged by Erdoğan is 'the people'. It is in this light that one can see the AKP/MHP 'People's Coalition', which emerged victorious in the last presidential and parliamentary elections, advocating without any inhibition a host of punitive administrative, judicial and extra-institutional measures to effectively destroy, symbolically and/or physically, anyone who contradicted the National Will, which supersedes the expression of individual and particularistic rights. The same conclusion can be deduced from the party's search for legitimation avenues free from the mediation of parliamentary procedural 'niceties' as Recep Tayyip Erdoğan appeals to the abstract notion of a National Will of a homogeneous people to contest supreme court decisions, to mention a telling example of prioritisation of the rights of 'the nation'/'the people' as a collectivity over those of individual citizens.

The carnivalesque atmosphere of 'street democracy' that followed the 15 July coup constituted a manifestation of this one indivisible will, in contrast to the diversity displayed in another liminal moment of plebeian expression: that of the Gezi protests (Sofos 2014). In some ways, the effect of the AKP's polarisation strategy was maximised in the failed coup d'état of 2016. The divide that the military attempted to recreate and exploit back in 2007 was appropriated by Erdoğan and represented as a perennial fissure in the Republic's body politic. Little did it matter that the Black Turks of 2016, of today, were not the same after 100 years as the colonised people in the early Republic. The memory of the divide and its most recent reincarnations with the 2007 and 2016 coups were sufficient for the president to rekindle his charisma and prove to his constituency that he had protected 'his people' from the tangible manifestation of the disdain and contempt of the cultured secularist elites and their allied interests. In the populist fantasy he cultivated, Erdoğan provided the image of 'the father' that was once represented by Atatürk and which, after decades of inculcation, was not alien to even the most religious of his constituents. What is more, the AKP leadership exploited the deficiencies of the parliamentary process over years of coalition governments under the tutelage of the army to promote their majoritarian, plebiscitary (institutionalised and extra-institutional) vision. The dejected Black Turks responded to the call of their leader to protect 'their' Republic and to reclaim their place, which had been denied to them since the foundation of modern Turkey.

Erdoğan's message promised a strong and effective leadership that would make the Turkish people feel sovereign. Yet in his authoritarian populist vision, popular sovereignty, the sovereignty of the abjects of the Republic, is a 'deflected' one. It to be experienced solely in the realm of emotion, in the form of solitary instances where a sense of loss, displacement and marginalisation is theatrically reversed, and vindication is momentarily enjoyed without challenging the very authoritarian structures that he and his party have blamed all along and simultaneously reproduced. How sustainable this delicately orchestrated divorce of emotion from 'empowerment' is remains to be seen. Emotions cannot be circumscribed or rescripted in isolation from their materiality, and their separation from it and from the lived experience of politics cannot be sustained.

Note

1. Indeed, Sofos points out that on 25 March 1981, at the very early stages of the 1980s military takeover, at one of the meetings of the National Security Council, the generals attempted to demonstrate their commitment to an open and democratic Turkey by resolving that, once democracy was restored, Turkey should file an official application for EEC membership (2000:256).

7

LIFE AFTER POPULISM?

Standing on Precarious Divides

At a time when the term 'populism' is used indiscriminately to describe an array of phenomena that characterise contemporary politics, from authoritarianism to nativist politics and charismatic leadership, to forms of collective action such as the Occupy movement, or the Tahrir Square and the Gezi protests, developing an understanding of the concept that retains its theoretical and analytical utility and that provides us with the tools to demarcate populism from other forms of mobilisations and politics is paramount. In this book I attempted to ground the particular case of Turkey in social-historical terms as I have argued that current sociopolitical constellations also have a historical dimension in social memory, historically conditioned emotional economies and repertoires of action and discourse.

In the preceding pages I suggested that 'the Turkish nation' and 'the people' were born in response to a state of ontological insecurity. The diverse population of an imploding homeland whose territory was coveted by numerous suitors was forced literally to make up its mind on fundamental issues of identity that would determine the future, wellbeing and security of generations, and often go against the grain of vernacular traditions, profane and sacred alike. I used the term 'forced', as becoming Turkish was not a matter of a *long-durée* process that might entail encounters with relative strangers, cultural and political convergences or less abrupt and violent processes of assimilation. It was also forced as the population was made to 'choose', to support an unclear project, by a humiliated yet ambitious elite believing it had a mission to build a new nation. Although the nation-building enterprise was by no means planned in detail, it was nevertheless inspired by the project of Turkism espoused by the CUP, which steered the Ottoman Empire to its defeat. The imperative of building and consolidating a strong modern nation state and the negative experience of Ottoman experiments with parliamentary politics tilted the balance decisively to a project of selective modernisation from above. This envisaged the establishment of formally democratic, but in essence authoritarian, political institutions that would safeguard the unity and modernisation of Turkey. It also entailed what I called, drawing on Habermas's assessment of the encroachment of the contemporary welfare state into domains that had hitherto been located outside its reach, the colonisation of lifeworlds (Habermas 1987:318–25), which took the form of the appropriation, policing and suppression of plebeian cultures (Barkan 1948).

To the question 'who are "the people"?', or even 'who is a Turk?', the answer was more complex than most of the literature seems to suggest. Leaving aside the obvious others, the Christian minorities, dwindling in numbers, whose very religion rendered them unassimilable second-rate citizens and unwelcome in their country, 'the republican people' who were called on to be part of the national project, were not 'of this time', did not exist, but were 'to become', as I argued in Chapters 2 and 3. Those reluctant to embrace Turkishness became 'abject', effectively expendable and certainly undesirable. The transformation of those citizens of the Republic who were open to being convinced into Turks, not only ethnically, but also in their civic culture, attitudes and behaviour, was essential to their recognition as members of 'the Turkish people'. Despite the obvious commitment to Turkish nationalism displayed by the nationalist elite, the latter showed, as I indicated in the preceding chapters, openness to non-Turks embracing Turkishness. Perhaps paradoxically, the nation on whose behalf the independence war had been waged, whose immemorial past the Republic celebrated, was not yet in place. Senior government officials never hid their resolve to 'make' their compatriots Turkish in public speeches and encouraged others to contribute to this drive; those embarked on work in the literacy campaigns or who staffed the Halkevleri, or nationalist educators such as Sıdıka Avar, were in no doubt that they were propagating Turkishness. But most of the people who would be the living vessels of this idealised nation, whose labour would bring about the recognition of the Turkish nation's place beside that of other civilised nations, were not in place either. Being simply 'Turkish' was not sufficient. It is true that some of the reforms the Republic initiated encouraged assimilation in terms of linguistic uniformity, and that the a priori exclusion of Christians from substantive citizenship had brought the populace close to uniformity, at least in the eyes of an unsuspecting observer. But 'the people' were expected to conform to the 'republican citizen ideal' set for them. The nation-building project relegated the entire 'people', who were supposed to be the Republic's source of power and sovereignty, to an inferior position as it posited them as subservient to 'the nation' – at least the elite's ideal of the nation – and the Republic. This introduced a duality, or rather a tension, in the way of visualising 'the people' and 'the nation' that is worth noting as it went against the grain of the assumption that the two are coterminous, despite the frequently interchangeable use of the terms – *halk* ('people') and *millet* ('nation').

This contradicted the principles upon which the new Republic was built, especially republicanism, nationalism and populism, which contained a vision of a polity that would replace the elitist Ottoman social order with a more just system, closer to 'the people'. The nationalist movement had already mobilised the principle of self-governance and the sovereignty of 'the people' in its struggle to retain and recapture as much of what it considered the territory of the nation as possible and had claimed the moral high ground over the sultan and his government precisely because it claimed that in a post-imperial future sovereignty should lie with 'the people'. Although never equated to democracy, 'populism' in the republican ideology addressed 'the people' as an active subject that would build the Republic, and recognised them as the locus of legitimacy, if not sovereignty, as well as the focus of the new state's efforts and energies. Atatürk's articulation of the foundational myth of the Turkish Republic, as already seen, partially hinged on an essentially anti-colonial premise: 'the Turkish people' had not been listened to and had no bonds with an Ottoman political class that had behaved selfishly and without any empathy for the plight of the Anatolian peasant, who had to endure war and poverty and was held captive to superstition and backwardness.

However, expressing dissent and deviating from the prescribed path meant challenging the unity of the nation and questioning the path chosen by the leadership. Political divergence was tantamount to setting oneself apart from the body politic of the Republic. But even after these multiple externalisations, those citizens who were not considered to belong to the 'other' in terms of ethnicity or religion, or to the 'dissident other', and who were deemed not to antagonise the pursuit of the vision of the Republic, were considered to be the raw material upon which compliant, trustworthy and committed citizens could be built. However, even for them, this did not mean empowerment or representation. Their putative liberation from the Ottoman Empire did not mean their emancipation, despite the promise of their independence struggle leaders.

The populace of Anatolia, the homeland reserved for the new nation, was effectively seen by the nation-building elites as noble savages, to be colonised and civilised by their Republic. Through a prism of disdain and paternalism, 'the people' of the Republic were seen as infants, susceptible to confusion and unable to discern that their interests needed protection from dissident influences and occasional disciplining and rehabilitation. This lack of trust and the intolerance of the expression of oppositional voices, of dissent, but also of behaviours and practices that were deemed inappropriate, meant that 'the people' were constantly under suspicion and surveillance, subjected to consecutive campaigns to reform them, to teach them the history of the nation, to suggest to them how to dress and behave, which political choices to make and which to avoid, and ultimately how to think like Turks. This arduous process of inculcation of cultural norms, of radical transformation of the habitus of those interpellated as 'the people', rested on the suppression, if not eradication, of the *vernacular* and colonisation by the *official*. The Turkish nation-building project was based on a sociopolitical divide created by mistrust and disdain that reproduced multiple partially overlapping patterns of exclusion; the rural versus urban divide ran more or less the same course as the secular versus religious one but diverged on occasion in different regions, while it was complicated by the Turkish versus Kurdish cleavage. Other divides were premised on socioeconomic, educational and other status differentials that mattered in a society that was tormented by ontological insecurity and the feeling of lagging behind societies whose civilisational and cultural achievements it was expected to surpass. Interestingly, the deliberate effort of the state to police or breach some of these divides had the effect of further politicising them: Islam became a vehicle of opposition that was expressed in politics in the success of conservative parties, and Kurdish identity defined itself in starker opposition to the Kemalist state once the latter tried to subsume it to its republican one-nation fantasy.[1]

Overall, 'the people' were expected to be loyal to the republican ideology and the leadership of the Republic. Communists, Islamists and others who were not disciplined, and were undistracted by false ideologies and allegiances, also found themselves of the wrong side of the political divide. These outcasts, or abjects, and to a lesser extent all citizens, were subjected to active moral regulation by the state by a combination of moral leadership, propaganda, surveillance and disciplining.

The civic culture that the leadership sought to impart on 'the people' emphasised the unity and indivisibility of the state, its territory and its people. The single 'popular' voice and a sense of collective interest, both expressions of the 'general will' underlying the republican philosophy (Mardin 1997a), posited 'the nation', and, by extension 'the state', as a bearer of rights. As Keyder points out, this process of authoritarian political modernisation, combined with the economic modernisation that Turkey has undergone, has not led to the development of individual autonomy or legal rights (1997:41). And as the republican elite treated the modernisation project of Turkey as one of indefinite duration, thus justifying their unwillingness to allow democracy in the first instance, or, after the end of the one-party state, anything more than experiments with variants of tutelary democracy. This has further reinforced the conceptual distinction between 'the people' and the 'national' interest (usually equated with the preservation of the Republic and its underlying Kemalist principles) and the precedence of the latter over particularistic interests, the expression of which has often been seen in republican Turkey as a threat to the unity of state and nation.

The lack of trust, inherent in the logic of the Republic, combined with the intrusiveness of a continual Turkifying, civilising, modernising mission, impacted significantly in the way the Republic was experienced and visualised by many of its citizens. The state was perceived as a colonising force, remote and yet overbearing, generating fear and indignation.

Turkish democracy was therefore established from above by a coalition of reformist bureaucracy and the military. The Kemalist conception of the state as standing outside and above society and intervening to protect the national interest has often been used to legitimise authoritarian policies and military interventions 'with the armed forces claiming to be the embodiment of the state and the nation' (Ahmad 1993:17). The military elite has used this assumption as the ideological cover for its interventions in social and political life and the overall role of 'the sovereign' assumed by the military, even in periods of civilian control.

In addition to this tendency to see the country's political life through the prism of a near-perpetual exception, the republican elite tended to see alternative spaces of belief and expression as threats that needed to be colonised and controlled by the state, or a core within it: a sinister manifestation of the republican principle of statism. The so-called civil society of the early Republic comprised organisations that were effectively controlled by or coordinated with the state. Thus, as I pointed out earlier, the nominally civil society-based, yet, in actuality, semi-official Türk Tarih Kurumu (the Turkish Historical Society) and the Türk Tarihi Tetkik Cemiyeti (the Society for the Study of Turkish History), to name two examples, that were responsible for the development and substantiation of the historical narrative of the genealogy of the Republic and the Turkish nation, and their linguistic counterpart, the Türk Dili Tetkik Cemiyeti (the Turkish Linguistic Society) remained high-brow institutions, as were the nominally independent Türk Ocakları and the less high-brow Halkevleri, an institution intended to tap into local plebeian cultures in order to propagate republican ideology. The core instrumentalist attitude that the early republican elite demonstrated during the aborted 'liberalisation experiments' (one unwitting and the other designed) and the establishment of an official communist party, or even the acceptance by it of the multiparty system in the mid-1940s, has also been evident in the way in which Islam was incorporated into the system (through the Turkish–Islamic synthesis). The emphasis on the unity of 'the nation' and 'the people' left very little space for autonomy and the public expression of particularism or individuality. The colonisation of 'the vernacular' and 'the plebeian' was just one manifestation of a broader pattern that marked Turkey's experiment with democratic politics for most of the twentieth century, under the scrutiny of the military, which stood ready to 'correct' or cancel 'transgressions'. This peculiar symbiosis of a suffocated civil society and electoral democracy with regular ultimata and, where these were not heeded, military coups character-ised Turkey's 'tutelary democracy', where the prospect of activating citizen-ship rights has been treated with suspicion.

Full Circle

The process of cautious democratisation initiated after the 1980 coup by the military did not challenge any of this combination of the cultural and structural elements of political life. The tutelary mechanisms it put in place were a reminder of their underlying mistrust of politicians, but also of 'the people' they claimed to represent and who elected them. The judicial safe-guards in place were intended to ensure that politicians and political parties would remain under the oversight of the armed forces which, in any case, reserved their self-awarded but culturally sanctioned 'right' to mount extra-institutional interventions. The military continued intervening in politics as it had been doing roughly every decade, in unison with the judiciary, thus not allowing democratic institutions, including political parties, to consoli-date and mature. The tradition of weak parties and coalition governments further weakened the institutionalisation of democracy, which was perceived by many as a cacophony of uncoordinated voices, and the grounding of a democratic political culture.

As already mentioned, in the field of ideology, the 1980 coup invested in, and systematically propagated Kemalism, usually a pop-culture version of it, marked by an excess of symbols idolising the personality of Mustafa Kemal as well as the idea of strong leadership, but also turned to Islam as it saw its potential to provide the legitimacy it needed. This partial and controlled rehabilitation of a healthy dose of Islam further injected Islamic values into conservative politics. The intention of controlling Islam and channelling its energy in ways that would benefit the regime had an unintended conse-quence. as I pointed out in Chapter 6, as its toleration, or even promotion, opened the way for a political space and civil society where Islam occupied a prominent place. The parallel process of economic liberalisation facilitated the emergence of and emboldened a middle class of entrepreneurs from the opposite side of the secular/religious, low/high, and geo-cultural divides splitting Turkey. This constellation of circumstances led to the eventual formation of the Justice and Development Party (AKP) and to its electoral acceptability by constituencies beyond the traditional constituencies of its predecessor Islamist parties. As already seen, the electoral victory of the AKP brought a sea change in the politics of the country. After a succession of weak coalition governments, an ultimatum that deposed a prime minister from the 'wrong side' of the secular/religious divide prior to the party's electoral success was swept away by its command of an absolute majority in parliament. The AKP's initial 'politics of patience', intended not to provoke the military, switched to one of 'controlled tension' (Duran 2013:98) after 2007, as the party managed to fend off a military ultimatum and an attempted ban by the judiciary and emerged strengthened.

Compared to other political actors in Turkey who attempted to mobilise the secular/religious divide partly and isolate the AKP by resorting to rhetorical antagonistic tropes (Erdoğan and Uyan-Semerci 2018), the AKP has been much more effective in constructing an atmosphere of crisis, as indeed populist actors are adept at doing (Moffitt 2016:113–32), and injustice frames (Gamson 2011), discussed in Chapter 6, as the party and its leader have consistently raised the issue of contempt and marginalisation of their constituency by the Kemalist establishment and the intellectual elite, thus raising its anti-elitist profile and turning the intellectual elites' cultural capital into a liability. The party made use of the polarised political landscape that the armed forces' attempts the against it had rekindled, relaunching itself as a party of the repressed – the Black Turks, as Erdoğan has said on more than one occasion. Erdoğan himself drew on such tropes effectively to contain a mass protest movement (the Gezi protests) and emerge with his supporter base emboldened after another coup attempt in July 2016. As I tried to indicate, although clearly more research needs to be conducted on this, the AKP leadership claimed they represented 'the repressed', but have gone to great lengths not to attribute an exclusively Islamic connotation to their constituency (although references to covered women and the mockery of piety have been increasingly present in the party discourse), referring to conservative values in general and to status disparities. They drew effectively on the themes of state and elite mistrust as well as disdain, and represented their confrontations with various opponents, imaginary and real, as a fight for the protection and empowerment of their constituency. Owing to Erdoğan's charisma, the party largely, though not exclusively, mobilised the dominant divides in Turkish society to its own advantage, once they were made relevant by the military's attempt to force the government to resign or, at best, to change course back in 2007.

In the field of formal politics, the message that the party has shared with its audience has been one that points out the ineffectiveness of parliamentary politics especially when juxtaposed with the presidential system, which provides strong and effective leadership. When the AKP lost its parliamentary majority in 2015, Erdoğan and his party leadership dismissed the possibility of a coalition government, indicating their preference for majoritarian politics. Erdoğan often expressed his preference for a strong, presidential-type leadership on account of the past experience of Turkish society with coalition governments. This anti-institutional, but also anti-particularistic emphasis of the party (given that the Assembly constitutes a reminder of the diversity of 'the people' whose unitary will Erdoğan claims to express) is highly significant. Aversion to assertions of social diversity was also demonstrated during the Gezi protests, which were instances of plebeian mobilisations that were permeated by a complex interplay between particularistic and shared vistas constructed by the participants. Instead, the party and its constituency seem to be more in tune with populist conceptualisations of the people and their emphasis on the 'general will' as indicated by recurrent identifications of democracy to the will of the majority by Erdoğan and key party officials, which were construed as overriding the 'selfish interests' of social minorities. The 'Respect for the National Will' (Milli İradeye Saygı) meetings of 2013, clearly organised to provide a response to the performative aspects of the Gezi protests, placed considerable emphasis on the size of the events and their quasi-dialogic character, in a way reminiscent of the 'virtual' interactions between Atatürk and 'his people', discussed in Chapter 4. Similarly, leaving aside the gruesome situation in which it took place, the mobilisation of the people on the early hours of the morning of 16 July 2016, as discussed in Chapter 6, constituted an instance of a performative, liminal moment, a direct, unmediated yet highly 'mediatised' plebiscitary event. Erdoğan's populism, just like populism in general, rests on the promise of sovereignty to 'a people' posited as deprived of this fundamental right. But as sovereignty is not linked to actual social individuals but to an abstract collectivity, hard to locate empirically, whose 'will' is impossible to decipher, popular sovereignty, the sovereignty of the 'abjects' of the Republic is a 'deflected' one, theatrically activated, experienced in emotional terms. Divorced from the material universe of empowerment, the sense of emotional vindication that populism portends renders its democratic promise deceptive.

Conclusion: Life after Populism?

Soon after the June 2019 Istanbul mayoral election, a rerun of the earlier election of March 2019, which saw opposition candidate Ekrem İmamoğlu win with a very narrow margin only to be annulled by the Supreme Electoral Council (YSK), İmamoğlu's landslide gave hope to supporters of the opposition as well as commentators who saw in the election results the possibility that this period of polarisation could end. Various media hailed the results as an indication that they were witnessing the 'beginning of the end' for Erdoğan (*Washington Post* 2019; *World Politics Review* 2019), and predicting a potential İmamoğlu candidacy in the next presidential election (see, for example Lowen 2019). Implicit in such thinking is the assumption that the departure of a 'charismatic' leader from the political scene, or, of a skilful political entrepreneur like Erdoğan would mean the end of the country's long populist moment.

Although I have focused on the impact of Erdoğan's charismatic personality in what preceded, I tried to heed Marsden and Snow's warning against such facile explanations as far as charismatic personalities are concerned (Marsden and Snow 1991:5), and to situate his charisma in its social context. I suggest that just like Atatürk's, Erdoğan's charisma, and indeed the AKP's success as a populist organisation, cannot be considered in a social void. I have tried to identify the contours of key discursive traditions that have been informing and circumscribing Turkish politics and its lived experience, as well the largely cultural, but certainly underpinned by tangible, material disparities that have served as fault lines structuring social and political life in Turkey. The politics of the past two decades in Turkey, the transition of the AKP from a 'tame', socially liberal and inclusive party to an organisation that has solidified around its leader's personality, shoring itself up on the polarisation that has consumed Turkish society, are the product of the structural and cultural conditions I tried to identify earlier.

Even before the AKP abandoned its 'politics of patience', which informed and shaped its first five years in office, the tensions between the military and the judiciary on the one hand, and the party on the other, were hard to ignore. They were not the product of coincidence or caprice, but were deeply embedded in a political culture that had shaped the contours of what was permissible and what was not, and of who could and who could not inhabit the prime ministerial office. The rumours that were circulating among political circles in Ankara just before the presidential election of 2007, that the Çankaya presidential residence was about to 'fall', were part of a pervasive discourse that made possible the categorisation of the AKP as an outsider, a temporary presence in Ankara's government offices. This very same discourse had contributed to the identification of the constituency of the AKP as outcasts and abjects. In a discussion I had with an eminent intellectual at the campus of Boğazici University in June 2000, I was told, while gazing at the Asian shores of Istanbul, that the hinterland of what we were looking at constituted a 'factory of fascists'. The categorisations that Erdoğan used in his speeches, the binary representations of the social, the contrasts between pious and infidel, native (*yerli*) and cultured (*kültürlü*), 'Black' and 'White' Turks, belonged to the same discourse my interlocutor used. They have been part and parcel of the politics of 'the popular' in Turkey for the best part of a century. To be sure, those who make up 'the people' have changed in their provenance, education, religiosity, insertion in consumer society and the like, but the divides have remained, not immutable but an established part of the social landscape of the Republic. The divides upon which the Republic has been built have fed a politics of 'the popular' for decades. On some occasions, plebeian cultures would become the backbone of communities, infused with a mixture of pride and solidarity, as well as defiance of the 'bad state' and its continuous demands, the erection of barriers, the limiting of life chances. On other occasions, and, increasingly nowadays, as the contradictions stemming out of a system premised on economic disparities and sociocultural marginalisation have manifested themselves in the dejection of the abject, the same plebian cultures would feed a politics of 'the popular' premised on antagonism, resentment and indignation. The time of populism is here and now, with Erdoğan or without.

Note

1. Özbudun (2013), taking his cue from Lipset and Rokkan (1967), uses the concept of 'cleavage structures' to describe these divides. As, despite their durability, these divides have not, until very recently, been underlined by an institutionalised relationship between political and social actors, I think that the use of the notion of cleavage merely reifies particular visualisations of a near-irreparably divided Turkish society that are reflected in much of the literature on populism, and therefore I prefer the term 'divide'.

REFERENCES

Adak, Hülya. 2003. 'National Myths and Self-Na(rra)tions: Mustafa Kemal's Nutuk and Halide Edib's Memoirs and The Turkish Ordeal', *South Atlantic Quarterly* 102(2/3): 509–27.

Adak, Sevgi and Ömer Turan. 2016. 'Is "Dialogue among Civilizations" a True Remedy for "Clash of Civilizations"? Rethinking Civilizationist Categories with Reference to Turkey–EU Relations', pp. 305–16 in *Towards Dignity of Difference?: Neither 'End of History' nor 'Clash of Civilizations'*, edited by Mojtaba Mahdavi and Andy Knight. London: Routledge.

Adorno, Theodor. 1982 [1952]. 'Freudian Theory and the Pattern of Fascist Propaganda', *The Essential Frankfurt School Reader*. New York: Continuum.

Agamben, Giorgio. 2005. *State of Exception*. Chicago: University of Chicago Press.

Ahmad, Feroz. 1993. *The Making of Modern Turkey*. New York: Routledge.

Akça, Kemal. 1946. 'Seferberlik Destanı', *Folklor Postası* 19: 11–14.

Akçam, Taner. 2006. *A Shameful Act: The Armenian Genocide and the Question of Turkish Responsibility*. New York: Holt.

Akçuraoğlu Yusuf (Yusuf Akçura). 2009. *Türk Yılı 1928*. Ankara: Türk Tarih Kurumu Yayınları.

Akın, Yiğit. 2018. *When the War Came Home: The Ottomans' Great War and the Devastation of an Empire*. Stanford: Stanford University Press.

Akkoyunlu, Karabekir and Kerem Öktem. 2016. 'Existential Insecurity and the Making of a Weak Authoritarian Regime in Turkey', *Southeast European and Black Sea Studies* 16(4): 505–27.

Akşit, Elif Ekin. 2005. *Kızların Sessizliği: Kız Enstitülerinin Uzun Tarihi*. Istanbul: Iletisim.

Akşit, Elif Ekin. 2013. 'Girls' Institutes and the Rearrangement of the Public and the Private Spheres in Turkey', pp. 133–52 in *A Social History of Late Ottoman Women*, edited by Duygu Köksal and Anastasia Falierou. Leiden: Brill.

Aktar, Ayhan. 1996. 'Economic Nationalism in Turkey: The Formative Years, 1912–1925', *Boğaziçi Journal of Economic and Administrative Sciences* 10(1–2): 263–90.

Aktar, Ayhan. 2000. *Varlık Vergisi ve 'Türkleştirme' Politikaları*. Istanbul: İletişim.

Aktar, Ayhan. 2004. 'Homogenising the Nation, Turkifying the Economy: The Turkish Experience of Population Exchange Reconsidered', pp. 79–95 in *Crossing the Aegean: An Appraisal of the 1923 Compulsory Population Exchange Between Greece and Turkey*, edited by Renée Hirschon. New York and Oxford: Berghahn Books.

Akural, Sabri M. 1984. 'Kemalist Views on Social Change', pp. 125–52 in *Atatürk and the Modernization of Turkey*, edited by Jacob Landau. Boulder, CO: Westview Press.

Alaranta, Toni. 2008. 'Mustafa Kemal Atatürk's Six-Day Speech of 1927: Defining the Official Historical View of the Foundation of the Turkish Republic', *Turkish Studies* 9(1): 115–29.

Alber, Jan Henning. 2017. 'Indigeneity and Narrative Strategies: Ideology in Contemporary Non-Indigenous Australian Prose Fiction', *Storyworlds: A Journal of Narrative Studies* 9(1/2): 159–81.

Alexander, Jeffrey C., Ron Eyerman; Bernard Giesen; Neil J. Smelser; and Piotr Sztompka, eds. 2004. *Cultural Trauma and Collective Identity*. Berkeley: University of California Press.

Alighieri, Dante. 1966–7. *Commedia*. Milano: Mondadori.

Almond, Gabriel and Sidney Verba. 1963. *The Civic Culture: Political Attitudes and Democracy in Five Nations*. Boston: Little, Brown and Company.

Alp, Tekin. 1970. 'The Restoration of Turkish History', pp. 207–24 in *Nationalism in Asia and Africa*, edited by Elie Kedourie. London: Frank Cass.

Anderson, Benedict. 1991. *Imagined Communities: Reflections on the Origin and Spread of Nationalism*. London: Verso.

Andrews, Peter Alford (ed). 1989. *Ethnic Groups in the Republic of Turkey*. Wiesbaden: Dr Ludwig Reichert Verlag.

Aral, Berdal. 2001. 'Dispensing with Tradition? Turkish Politics and International Society during the Özal Decade, 1983–1993', *Middle Eastern Studies* 37(1): 72–89.

Arar, Ismail. 1963. *Atatürk'ün Halkgilik Programi ve Halkcilik Dkesinin Tarihcesi.* Istanbul: Baha Matbaasi.

Arat, Zehra. 1994. 'Kemalism and Turkish Women', *Women and Politics* 14(4): 57–80.

Arditi, Benjamin. 2007. *Politics on the Edges of Liberalism: Difference, Populism, Revolution, Agitation.* Edinburgh: Edinburgh University Press.

Arnold, Matthew. 2006. *Culture and Anarchy.* New York: Oxford University Press

Aslan, Senem. 2007. '"Citizen, Speak Turkish!": A Nation in the Making', *Nationalism and Ethnic Politics* 13: 245–72.

Aslan, Senem. 2011. 'Everyday Forms of State Power and the Kurds in the Early Turkish Republic', *International Journal of Middle East Studies* 43: 75–93.

Aşkun,Vehbi Cem. 1945. *Sivas Kongresi.* Sivas: Kamil Matbaası.

Atabay, Mithat. 2002. 'Anadoluculuk', pp. 515–32 in *Modern Türkiye'de Siyasi Düşünce: Milliyetçilik*, edited by Tanıl Bora. Istanbul: İletişim.

Ataöv, Türkaya. 1960. 'The 27th of May Revolution and Its Aftermath', *Turkish Yearbook of International Relations 1960–61*: 13–22.

Ataöv, Türkaya. 1981. 'The Principles of Kemalism', *Turkish Yearbook of International Relations 1980–1981*: 19–44.

Atillasoy, Yüksel. 2002. *Atatürk: First President and Founder of the Turkish Republic.* Woodside, NY: Woodside House.

Avar, Sıdıka. 1999. *Dağ Çiçeklerim.* Ankara: Öğretmen Dünyası Yayınları.

Aydemir, Sevket Süreyya. 1973. *Ihtilalin Mantigi ve 27 Mays Ihtilali.* Istanbul: Remzi Kitabevi.

Aydin, Mustafa, Mitat Celikpala, Banu Hawks, Murat Can Güvenç and Deniz Tığlı, eds. 2020. *Quantitative Research Report on Social-Political Trends in Turkey – 2019.* Istanbul: Kadir Has University & Akademetre.

Aydın, Suavi. 2005. 'İsimler Milli Birliği Nasıl Bozar? "Bak Şu Tilkinin Ettiğine . . .'", *Toplumsal Tarih* 143: 90–7.

Aydın, Suavi. 2010. 'The Use and Abuse of Archaeology and Anthropology in Formulating the Turkish Nationalist Narrative', pp. 36–46 in *Nationalism in the Troubled Triangle: New Perspectives on South-East Europe*, edited by Ayhan Aktar, Niyazi Kızılyürek and Umut Özkırımlı. London: Palgrave Macmillan.

Aytaç, Erdem and Ezgi Elçi. 2019. 'Populism in Turkey', pp. 89–108 in *Populism Around the World*, edited by Daniel Stockemer. Cham: Springer.

Aytaç, Erdem and Ziya Öniş. 2014. 'Varieties of Populism in a Changing Global Context: The Divergent Paths of Erdoğan and *Kirchnerismo*', *Comparative Politics* 47(1): 41–59.

Baban, Feyzi. 2007. 'The Public Sphere and the Question of Identity in Republican Turkey', pp. 75–99 in *Remaking Turkey: Globalization, Alternative Modernities, and Democracy*, edited by Fuat Keyman. Lanham, MD: Rowman and Littlefield.

Badiou, Alain. 2005. *Being and Event*. New York: Continuum.

Baer, Marc. 2010. *The Dönme: Jewish Converts, Muslim Revolutionaries, and Secular Turks*. Stanford: Stanford University Press.

Bale, Tim, Stijn van Kesse and Paul Taggart, 2011. 'Thrown Around with Abandon? Popular Understandings of Populism as Conveyed by the Print Media: A UK Case Study', *Acta Politica* 46(2): 111–31.

Bali, Rıfat N. 1999. *Cumhuriyet Yıllarında Türkiye Yahudileri: Bir Türkleştirme Serüveni (1923–1945)*. Istanbul: İletişim.

Bali, Rıfat N. 2008. *1934 Trakya Olayları*. Istanbul: Kitabevi.

Baran, Zeyno. 2010. *Torn Country: Turkey between Secularism and Islamism*. Stanford: Hoover Institution Press.

Barkan, Ömer Lütfi. 1948. 'Türkiye'de Muhacir İskânı ve Bir İç Kolonizasyon Plânına Olan ihtiyaç', *Istanbul İktisat Fakültesi Mecmuası'ndan Ayrı Basım* (C. X, Nos 1–4): 204–23.

Baykan, Toygar. 2018. *The Justice and Development Party in Turkey: Populism, Personalism, Organization*. Cambridge: Cambridge University Press.

Bennett, Lance W. and Alexandra Segerberg (2012) 'The Logic of Connective Action', *Information, Communication & Society*, 15(5): 739–68.

Beresford, Alexander, Marie E. Berry and Laura Mann. 2018. 'Liberation Movements and Stalled Democratic Transitions: Reproducing Power in Rwanda and South Africa through Productive Liminality', *Democratization* 25(7): 1231–50.

Berger, Lutz. 2020. 'The Leader as Father: Personality Cults in Modern Turkey', pp. 119–28 in *Kemalism as a Fixed Variable in the Republic of Turkey: History, Society, Politics*, edited by Lutz Berger and Tamer Düzyol. Baden-Baden: Ergon Verlag.

Berman, Marshall. 1988. *All that is Solid Melts into Air: The Experience of Modernity*. London: Verso.

Beşikçi, İsmail. 1990. *Tunceli Kanunu (1935) ve Dersim Jenosidi; Bilim Yöntemi Türkiye'deki Uygulama – 4*. Istanbul: Belge Yayınları.

Bhabha, Homi K. 1990. 'Introduction: Narrating the Nation', pp. 1–7 in *Nation and Narration*, edited by Homi K. Bhabha. London: Routledge.

Biglieri, Paula, and Luciana Cadahia. 2021. *Seven Essays on Populism: For a Renewed Theoretical Perspective*. Cambridge: Polity.

Billig, Michael. 1995. *Banal Nationalism*. London: Sage.

Bilmez, Bulent. 2009. 'Shemseddin Sami Frashëri (1850–1904): Contributing to the Construction of Albanian and Turkish Identities', pp. 341–71 in *We, the People: Politics of National Peculiarity in Southeastern Europe*, edited by Diana Mishkova. Budapest: Central European University Press.

Blickle, Peter. 2004. *Heimat: A Critical Theory of the German Idea of Homeland.* Rochester, NY: Camden House.

Bora, Tanil. 2017. *Cereyanlar Türkiye'de Siyasî İdeolojiler.* Istanbul: İletişim Yayınları.

Bora Tanıl, and Kemal Can. 1999. *Devlet, Ocak, Dergâh: 12 Eylül'den 1990'lara Ülkücü Hareket.* Istanbul: İletişim.

Botelho, Austin. 2019. 'The Short End of the Stick: Income Inequality and Populist Sentiment in Europe', *Issues in Political Economy* 28(1): 39–78.

Bourdieu, Pierre. 1990. *In Other Words: Essays Towards a Reflexive Sociology.* Stanford: Stanford University Press.

Bowman, Glenn. 2003. 'Constitutive Violence and the Nationalist Imaginary. Antagonism and Defensive Solidarity in Palestine and Former Yugoslavia', *Social Anthropology* II (3): 319–40.

Brash, E. T. 1974. 'Prejudice towards Aborigines in Australian Literature', pp. 35–42 in *Racism: The Australian Experience, vol. 2: Black versus White*, edited by F. S. Stevens. Sydney: ANZ.

Breaugh, Martin. 2013. *The Plebeian Experience: A Discontinuous History of Political Freedom.* New York: Columbia University Press.

Breuilly, John. 1982. *Nationalism and the State.* Manchester: Manchester University Press.

Brockett, Gavin. 1999. 'Collective Action and the Turkish Revolution: Towards a Framework for the Social History of the Atatürk Era, 1923–38', pp. 44–66 in *Turkey Before and After Atatürk: Internal and External Affairs*, edited by Sylvia Kedourie. London: Frank Cass.

Brubaker, Rogers. 2017. 'Why Populism?', *Theory and Society* 46: 357–85.

Buğra, Ayşe. 1994. *State and Business in Modern Turkey.* Albany, NY: SUNY Press.

Burghart, Richard. 1996. *The Conditions of Listening: Essays on Religion, History and Politics in South Asia*, edited by C. J. Fuller and J. Spencer. Delhi: Oxford University Press.

Busky, Donald F. 2002. *Communism in History and Theory: Asia, Africa, and the Americas.* Santa Barbara: Praeger Publishers.

Butler, Daniel Allen. 2011. *Shadow of the Sultan's Realm: The Destruction of the Ottoman Empire and the Creation of the Modern Middle East.* Washington, DC: Potomac Books.

Butler, Judith. 1993. *Bodies that Matter: On the Discursive Limits of 'Sex'*. New York: Routledge.

Butler, Judith. 1997. *The Psychic Life of Power: Theories in Subjection*. Stanford: Stanford University Press.

Cagaptay, Soner. 2006. *Islam, Secularism, and Nationalism in Modern Turkey: Who is a Turk?* London: Routledge.

Çağlayan, Ercan. 2018. '"Kemalizm" in "Medeniyet Fabrikası": Kız Enstitüleri', *Tarih ve Gelecek Dergisi* 4: 8–35.

Camus, Jean-Yves and Nicolas Lebourg. 2017. *Far-Right Politics in Europe*. Cambridge, MA: Harvard University Press.

Canovan, Margaret. 1999. 'Trust the People! Populism and the Two Faces of Democracy', *Political Studies* 47(1): 2–16.

Canovan, Margaret. 2002. 'Taking Politics to the People: Populism as the Ideology of Democracy', pp. 25–44 in *Democracies and the Populist Challenge*, edited by Yves Mény and Yves Surel. London: Palgrave Macmillan.

Casier, Marlies and Joost Jongerden. 2011. *Nationalisms and Politics in Turkey: Political Islam, Kemalism and the Kurdish Issue*. London: Routledge.

Castoriadis, Cornelius. 1987. *The Imaginary Institution of Society*. Cambridge, MA: MIT Press.

Chatterjee, Partha. 1993. *The Nation and Its Fragments: Colonial and Postcolonial Histories*. Princeton, NJ: Princeton University Press.

Christophis, Nikos. 2021. *Από τον κεμαλισμό στον ριζοσπαστισμό. Το τουρκικό φοιτητικό κίνημα, 1923–1980*. Athens: Topos.

Ciddi, Sinan. 2008. *Kemalism in Turkish Politics: The Republican People's Party, Secularism and Nationalism*. London: Routledge.

Cizre, Ümit. 2008. 'The Justice and Development Party and the Military: Recreating the Past after Reforming It?', pp. 133–7 in *Secular and Islamic Politics in Turkey: The Making of the Justice and Development Party*, edited by Ümit Cizre. London: Routledge.

Clark, Bruce. 2006. *Twice a Stranger: How Mass Expulsion Forged Modern Greece and Turkey*. London: Granta.

Cohen, Stanley. 1972. *Folk Devils and Moral Panics: The Creation of the Mods and Rockers*. London: MacGibbon & Kee.

Cohen, Stanley. 1974. *Folk Devils and Moral Panics: The Creation of the Mods and Rockers*. Basingstoke: Macmillan.

Corrigan, Philip and Derek Sayer. 1985. *The Great Arch: English State Formation As Cultural Revolution*. Oxford: Blackwell.

Corten, André. 2012. 'Nouvelle langue politique ou souveraineté instantanée de la plèbe?', pp. 35–54 in *L'interpellation plébéienne en Amérique latine*, edited by André Corten, Cathérine Huart and Ricardo Peñafiel. Québec: Karthala-Presses de l'Université du Québec.

Croft, Stuart. 2012. 'Constructing Ontological Insecurity: The Insecuritization of Britain's Muslims', *Contemporary Security Policy* 33(2): 219–35.

Deleuze, Giles and Felix Guattari. 1987. *A Thousand Plateaus: Capitalism and Schizophrenia, II*. Minneapolis: University of Minnesota Press.

De Mauro, T. 1960. *Storia linguistica dell'Italia unita*. Milan: A. Guiffré,

Demertzis, Nicolas. 2020. *The Political Sociology of Emotions: Essays on Trauma and Ressentiment*. London: Routledge.

Deren, Seçil. 2002. 'Türk Siyasal Düşüncesinde Anadolu İmgesi', pp. 533–40 in *Modern Türkiye'de Siyasi Düşünce: Milliyetçilik*, edited by Tanıl Bora. Istanbul: İletişim.

Deringil, Selim. 2003. '"They Live in a State of Nomadism and Savagery": The Late Ottoman Empire and the Post-Colonial Debate', *Comparative Studies in Society and History* 45 (2): 311–42.

Derrida, Jacques. 1982. *Positions*. Chicago: University of Chicago Press.

Dilipak, Abdurrahman (1991). *Ihtilaller Donemi*. Istanbul: Dogan Ofset.

Di Tella, Torcuato S. 1965. 'Populism and Reform in Latin America', pp. 47–74 in *Obstacles to Change in Latin America*, edited by Claudio Véliz. Oxford: Oxford University Press.

Dinç, Pınar. 2020. 'Euro-Who? Competition over the Definition of Dersim's Collective Identity in Turkey's Diasporas', *Turkish Studies* 1–25. DOI: 10.1080/14683849.2019.1708738.

Dodd, Clement. 1991. 'Atatürk and Political Parties', pp. 24–41 in *Political Parties and Democracy in Turkey*, edited by Metin Heper and Jacob M. Landau. London: I. B. Tauris.

Dorronsoro, G. and B. Gourisse. 2015. 'L'armée turque en politique: Autonomie institutionnelle, formation de coalitions sociales et production des crises', *Revue française de science politique* 65(4): 609–31.

Döşemeci, Mehmet. 2013. *Debating Turkish Modernity: Civilization, Nationalism, and the EEC*. New York: Cambridge University Press.

Durakbaşa, A. 1998. 'Cumhuriyet Modern Kadın ve Kimliklerinin Oluşumu: Kemalist Kadın Kimliği ve 'Münevver Erkekler', pp. 29–50 in *Bilanço '98: 75. Yılda Kadınlar ve Erkekler*, edited by A. B. Hacımirzaoğlu. Istanbul: Tarih Vakfı Yayınları.

Duran, Burhanettin. 2013. 'Understanding the AK Party's Identity Politics: A Civilizational Discourse and its Limitations', *Insight Turkey* 15(1): 91–109.

Eigler, Friederike. 2012. 'Critical Approaches to Heimat and the "Spatial Turn"', *New German Critique* 39(1/115): 27–48.

Eligür, Banu. 2019. 'Ethnocultural Nationalism and Turkey's Non-Muslim Minorities during the Early Republican Period', *British Journal of Middle Eastern Studies* 46 (1): 158–77.

Ellison, Grace. 1928. *Turkey Today*. London: Hutchinson.

Erçetin, Tuğçe and Emre Erdoğan. 2018. 'How Turkey's Repetitive Elections Affected the Populist Tone in the Discourses of the Justice and Development Party Leaders', *Philosophy & Social Criticism* 44(4): 382–98.

Erdoğan, Emre, Tuğçe Erçetin and Jan Philipp Thomeczek. 2018. 'How Populist Zeitgeist Controls Turkish Electoral Campaign 2018', http://bianet.org/english/politics/198440-how-populist-zeitgeist-controls-turkish-electoral-campaign-2018 (accessed 20 March 2020).

Erdoğan, Emre and Pınar Uyan-Semerci. 2018. *Fanusta Diyaloglar: Türkiye'de Kutuplaşmanın Boyutları*. Istanbul: Bilgi Yayınları.

Erogul, Cem. 1970. *Demokrat Parti, Tarihi ve Ideolojisi*. Ankara: Ankara Universitesi SBF.

Ersanlı, Büşra. 2003. *İktidar ve Tarih: Türkiye'de 'Resmi Tarih' Tezinin Oluşumu (1929–1937)*. Istanbul: İletişim.

Esen, Berk and Sebnem Gümüşçü. 2017. Turkey: 'How the Coup Failed', *Journal of Democracy* 28(1): 59–73.

Eyerman, Ron. 2001. *Cultural Trauma – Slavery and the Formation of African American Identity*. Cambridge: Cambridge University Press.

Eyerman, Ron. 2008. *The Assassination of Theo Van Gogh. From Social Drama to Cultural Trauma*. Durham, Duke University Press.

Fawaz, Leila Tarazi. 2014. *A Land of Aching Hearts: The Middle East in the Great War*. Cambridge, MA: Harvard University Press.

Ferguson, Michael. 2014. 'White Turks, Black Turks and Negroes: The Politics of Polarization', pp.78–88 in *The Making of a Protest Movement in Turkey: #occupygezi*, edited by Umut Özkırımlı. London: Palgrave Pivot.

Fink, Bruce. 1995. *The Lacanian Subject: Between Language and Jouissance*. Princeton: Princeton University Press.

Foucault, Michel. 1972. *The Archaeology of Knowledge and the Discourse on Language*. New York: Pantheon Books.

Foucault, Michel. 1977. *Discipline and Punish: The Birth of the Prison*. New York: Pantheon.

Foucault, Michel. 1991. *Discipline and Punish: The Birth of a Prison*. London, Penguin.

Foucault, Michel. 2003. *The Essential Foucault: Selections from Essential works of Foucault, 1954–1984*. New York: The New Press.

Freeden, Michael. 2003. *Ideology: A Very Short Introduction*. Oxford: Oxford University Press.

Freeden, Michael. 2017. 'After the Brexit Referendum: Revisiting Populism as an Ideology', *Journal of Political Ideologies* 22(1): 1–11.

Freud, Sigmund. 1923. *The Ego and the Id*. London: W. W. Norton & Company.

Freud, Sigmund. 1955. *Group Psychology and the Analysis of the Ego*, pp. 67–143 in *The Standard Edition of the Complete Works of Sigmund Freud*, edited by James Beaumont Strachey (Vol. 18). London: Hogarth Press.

Freud, Sigmund. 1961. 'The Future of an Illusion', pp. 3–56 in *The Standard Edition of the Complete Works of Sigmund Freud*, edited by James Beaumont Strachey (Vol. 21). London: Hogarth Press.

Freud, Sigmund. 1964a. 'New Introductory Lectures on Psycho-Analysis', pp. 3–182 in *The Standard Edition of the Complete Works of Sigmund Freud*, edited by James Beaumont Strachey (Vol. 21). London: Hogarth Press.

Freud, Sigmund. 1964b. 'Moses and Monotheism', pp. 3–137 in *The Standard Edition of the Complete Works of Sigmund Freud*, edited and translated by James Beaumont Strachey (Vol. 23). London: Hogarth Press.

Gambetti, Zeynep. 2014. 'Occupy Gezi as Politics of the Body', pp. 89–102 in *The Making of a Protest Movement in Turkey: #occupygezi*, edited by Umut Özkırımlı. Basingstoke and New York: Palgrave Macmillan.

Gamson, W. A. 1992. *Talking Politics*. Cambridge: Cambridge University Press.

Gamson, W. A. 1995. 'Constructing Social Protes', pp. 85–106 in *Social Movements and Culture*, edited by H. Johnston and B. Klandermans. Minneapolis: University of Minnesota Press.

Gamson, W. A. 2011. 'From Outsiders to Insiders: The Changing Perception of Emotional Culture and Consciousness among Social Movement Scholars', *Mobilization: An International Journal* 16(3): 251–63.

Gellner, Ernest and Ghiţa Ionescu. 1969. 'Introduction', pp. 1–5 in *Populism: Its Meanings and National Characteristics*, edited by Ernest Gellner and Ghiţa Ionescu. London: Weidenfeld & Nicolson.

Germani, Gino. 1963. *Politica y sociedad en una epoca de transicion*. Buenos Aires: Paidós.

Germani, Gino. 1978. *Authoritarianism, Fascism, and National Populism*. New Brunswick, NJ: Transaction Publishers.

Giddens, Anthony. 1991. *Modernity and Self-Identity*. Cambridge: Polity.

Giddens, Anthony. 2006. 'Misunderstanding Multiculturalism', *The Guardian*, http://www.guardian.co.uk/commentisfree/2006/oct/14/tonygiddens (accessed 12 December 2018).

Göçek, Fatma Müge. 2011. *The Transformation of Turkey: Redefining State and Society from the Ottoman Empire to the Modern Era*. London: I. B. Tauris.

Göknar, Erdağ. 2014. 'Reading Occupied Istanbul: Turkish Subject-Formation from Historical Trauma to Literary Trope', *Culture, Theory and Critique* 55(3): 321–41.

Göle, Nilüfer. 2000. 'Global Expectations, Local Experiences: Non-Western Modernities', pp. 40–55 in *Through a Glass, Darkly*, edited by Wil Arts. Leiden: Brill.

Goodwyn, Lawrence. 1976. *Democratic Promise: The Populist Moment in America*. New York: Oxford University Press.

Gramsci, Antonio. 1971. *Selections from the Prison Notebooks of Antonio Gramsci*, edited and translated by Quintin Hoare and Geoffrey Nowell-Smith. London: Lawrence & Wishart.

Gramsci, Antonio. 1977. *Quaderni del Carcere, vol. 1, Quaderni 1–5*. Turin: Giulio Einaudi editore.

Greenfeld, Leah. 1992. *Nationalism: Five Roads to Modernity*. Cambridge, MA: Harvard University Press.

Guida, Michelangelo. 2008. 'The Sèvres Syndrome and '*Komplo*' Theories in the Islamist and Secular Press', *Turkish Studies* 9(1): 37–52.

Gül, Murat. 2017. *Architecture and the Turkish City: An Urban History of Istanbul since the Ottomans*. London: I. B. Tauris.

Gunes, C., and Welat Zeydanlioğlu. 2014. *The Kurdish Question in Turkey: New Perspectives on Violence, Representation, and Reconciliation*. New York: Routledge.

Güneş-Ayata, Ayşe. 1992. *CHP: Örgüt ve İdeoloji*. Ankara: Gündoğan Yayınları.

Gurov, Boris and Emilia Zankina. 2013. 'Populism and the Construction of Political Charisma', *Problems of Post-Communism* 60(1): 3–17.

Gürsoy, Y. 2021. 'Moving Beyond European and Latin American Typologies: The Peculiarities of AKP's Populism in Turkey', *Journal of Contemporary Asia*, 51:1, 157–78.

Habermas, Jürgen. 1987. *The Theory of Communicative Action, Volume 2: Lifeworld and System: A Critique of Functionalist Reason*. Boston: Beacon Press.

Hale, Grace Elizabeth. 1998. *Making Whiteness*. New York: Vintage.

Hale, William. 1990. 'The Turkish Army in Politics 1960–73', pp. 53–77 in *Turkish State, Turkish Society*, edited by Andrew Finkel and Nükhet Sirman. London: Routledge.

Hale, William. 1993. *Turkish Politics and the Military*. London: Routledge.

Hall, Stuart. 1980. 'Popular-Democratic versus Authoritarian Populism', pp. 157–85 in *Marxism and Democracy*, edited by Alan Hunt. London: Lawrence & Wishart.

Hall, Stuart. 1985. 'Authoritarian Populism: A Reply to Jessop et al', *New Left Review* 1(151): 115–24.

Hall, Stuart, Charles Critcher, Tony Jefferson, John Clarke and Brian Roberts. 1978. *Policing the Crisis: Mugging, the State, and Law and Order*. London: Macmillan.

Hanioğlu, M. Şükrü. 2002. 'Turkish Nationalism and the Young Turks, 1889–1908', pp. 85–97 in *Social Constructions of Nationalism in the Middle East*, edited by Fatma Müge Göçek. New York: SUNY Press.

Hanioğlu, M. Şükrü. 2011. *Atatürk: An Intellectual Biography*. Princeton: Princeton University Press.

Hassan, Mona. 2011. *Longing for the Lost Caliphate: A Transregional History*. Princeton: Princeton University Press.

Hawkins, Kirk. 2010. 'Who Mobilizes? Participatory Democracy in Chávez's Bolivarian Revolution', *Latin American Politics and Society* 52(3): 31–66.

Healy, John H. 1972. 'The Treatment of the Aborigine in Early Australian Fiction, 1840–1870', *Australian Literary Studies* 5(3): 233–53.

Held, David. 1989. *Political Theory and the Modern State: Essays on State, Power, and Democracy*. Cambridge: Polity Press.

Helström, Anders. 2013. 'Help! The Populists Are Coming: Appeals to the People in Contemporary Swedish Politics', Malmö: Malmö Institute for Studies of Migration, Diversity and Welfare.

Herzfeld, Michael. 1986. *Ours Once More: Folklore, Ideology, and the Making of Modern Greece*. New York: Pella.

Herzog, Christoph and Raoul Motika. 2000. 'Orientalism alla turca: Late 19th/ Early 20th Century Ottoman Voyages into the Muslim "Outback"', *Die Welt des Islams* 40(2): 139–95.

Hirst, Paul. 1999. 'Carl Schmitt's Decisionism', pp. 7–17 in *The Challenge of Carl Schmitt*, edited by C. Mouffe. London: Verso.

Hobsbawm, Eric. 1959. *Primitive Rebels*. Manchester: Manchester University Press.

Hobsbawm, Eric and Terence Ranger (ed.). 1983. *The Invention of Tradition*. Cambridge: Cambridge University Press.

Hofstadter, Richard. 1948. *The American Political Tradition*. New York: A. A. Knopf.

Hofstadter, Richard. 1955. *The Age of Reform*. New York: Vintage Books.

Hofstadter, Richard. 1963. *Anti-Intellectualism in American Life*. New York: A. A. Knopf.

Horkheimer, Max and Theodor W. Adorno. 1944. *Dialectic of Enlightenment*. New York: Herder and Herder.

Hroch, Miroslav. 2007. 'Introduction: National Romanticism', pp. 4–18 in *Discourses of Collective Identity in Central and Southeast Europe, vol. II National Romanticism: The Formation of National Movements* edited by Balázs Trencsényi and Michal Kopeček. Budapest: Central European University Press.

Huart, Catherine. 2012. 'Interpellation plébéienne et subjectivation politique', pp. 55–68 in *L'interpellation plébéienne en Amérique latine*, edited by André Corten, Cathérine Huart et Ricardo Peñafiel. Québec: Karthala-Presses de l'Université du Québec.

İnan, Afet. 1999. *Atatürk Hakkında Hatıralar ve Belgeler*. 21st edn. Istanbul: İş Bankası Kültür Yayınları.

İnce, Basak. 2012. *Citizenship and Identity in Turkey: From Atatürk's Republic to the Present Day*. London: I. B. Tauris.

Issawi, Charles. 1982. *An Economic History of the Middle East and North Africa*. New York: Columbia University Press.

Jansen, Robert S. (2011). 'Populist Mobilization: A New Theoretical Approach to Populism', *Sociological Theory* 29(2): 75–96.

Jenkins, Brian and Spyros A. Sofos. 1996. 'Nation and Nationalism in Contemporary Europe: A Theoretical Perspective', pp. 7–29 in *Nation and Identity in Contemporary Europe*, edited by Brian Jenkins and Spyros A. Sofos. London: Routledge.

Jenkins, Gareth H. 2007. 'Continuity and Change: Prospects for Civil–Military Relations in Turkey', *International Affairs* 83(2): 339–55.

Kadioğlu, Ayse. 1996. 'The Paradox of Turkish Nationalism and the Construction of Official Identity', *Middle Eastern Studies* 32(2): 177–93.

Kalaycıoğlu, Ersin. 2012. '*Kulturkampf* in Turkey: The Constitutional Referendum of 12 September 2010', *South European Society and Politics* 17(1): 1–22.

Kandiyoti, Deniz. 1991. 'End of Empire: Islam, Nationalism and Women in Turkey', pp. 22–47 in *Women, Islam and the State* edited by D. Kandiyoti. Philadelphia: Temple University Press.

Kandiyoti, Deniz. 2015. 'The Gender Wars in Turkey: A Litmus Test for Democracy', Open Democracy, https://www.opendemocracy.net/5050/deniz-kandiyoti/gender-wars-in-turkey-litmus-test-of-democracy (accessed 20 January 2022).

Kaplan, İsmail. 1999. *Türkiye'de Milli Eğitim İdeolojisi ve Siyasal Toplumsallaşma Üzerindeki Etkisi*. Istanbul: İletişim Yayınları.

Karabekir, Kazim. 1990. *Kazim Karabekir Anlatiyor*. Istanbul: Tekin Yayınevi.

Karaömerlioğlu, M. Asim. 1999. 'The People's Houses and the Cult of the Peasant in Turkey', pp. 67–91 in *Turkey Before and After Atatürk: Internal and External Affairs*, edited by Sylvia Kedourie. London: Frank Cass.

Karpat, Kemal. 1959. *Turkey's Politics: The Transition to a Multi-Party System*. Princeton: Princeton University Press.

Karpat, Kemal. 1963. 'The People's Houses in Turkey: Establishment and Growth', *Middle East Journal* 17(1/2): 55–67.

Karpat, Kemal. 1991. 'The Republican People's Party: 1923–45', pp. 42–64 in *Political Parties and Democracy in Turkey*, edited by Metin Heper and Jacob M. Landau. London: I. B. Tauris.

Kastoryano, Riva. 2013. *Turkey Between Nationalism and Globalization*. New York: Routledge.

Keyder, Çağlar. 1997. 'Whither the Project of Modernity? Turkey in the 1990s', pp. 37–51 in *Rethinking Modernity and National Identity in Turkey*, edited by Sibel Bozdogan and Resat Kasaba. Seattle: University of Washington Press.

Kinnvall, Catarina. 2004. 'Globalization and Religious Nationalism: Self, Identity, and the Search for Ontological Security', *Political Psychology* 25(5): 741–67.

Kinnvall, Catarina. 2007. *Globalization and Religious Nationalism in India*. New York: Routledge.

Kinross, Patrick Balfour. 1964. *Atatürk: A Biography of Mustafa Kemal, Father of Modern Turkey*. London: William Morrow & Company.

Kirchheimer, Otto. 1966. 'The Transformation of the Western European Party Systems', pp. 177–200 in *Political Parties and Political Development*, edited by Joseph LaPalombara and Myron Weiner. Princeton: Princeton University Press.

Kitsikis, Dimitris. 1981. Ιστορία του Ελληνοτουρκικού Χώρου [History of the Grecoturkish Space] *(1928–1973)*. Athens: Βιβλιοπωλείο της Εστίας.

Klein, Melanie. 1975. *Envy, Gratitude and Other Works 1946–1963*. New York: Free Press.

Koçak, Cemil. 1986. *Türkiye'de Milli Şef Dönemi (1938–1945) Cilt I*. Istanbul: İletişim.

Koçak, Cemil. 2003. *Umumi müfettişlikler (1927–1952)*. Istanbul: İletişim Yayınları.

Koçak, Cemil. 2013. *Rejim Krizi Cilt: 3*. Istanbul: İletişim Yayınları.

Körükçü, Muhtar. 1950. *Köyden Haber*. Istanbul: Varlik.

Köymen, Nusret Kemal. 1934. *Köycülük ve Halkçilik*. Istanbul: Tarik Edip ve S. Kütüphanesi.

Köymen, Nusret Kemal. 1939. 'Düşünceler', *Ülkü* 13: 29.

Kriesi, Hanspeter and Takis S. Pappas, eds. 2015. *European Populism in the Shadow of the Great Recession*. Colchester: ECPR Press.

Kushner, David. 1977. *The Rise of Turkish Nationalism, 1876–1908*. London: Cass.

Kuzmanovic, Daniella. 2012. *Refractions of Civil Society in Turkey*. New York: Palgrave Macmillan.

Lacan, Jacques. 1977. *Écrits*. London: Tavistock.

Laclau, Ernesto. 1977. *Politics and Ideology in Marxist Theory*. London: New Left Books.

Laclau, Ernesto. 1990. *New Reflections on the Revolution of Our Time*. London: Verso.

Laclau, Ernesto and Chantal Mouffe. 1985. *Hegemony and Socialist Strategy*. London Verso.

Laing, R. D. 1990. *The Divided Self*. London: Penguin.

Landau, Jacob M. 1995. *Pan-Turkism in Turkey*. London: C. Hurst & Company.

Laue, Theodore H. von. 1954. 'The Fate of Capitalism in Russia: The Narodnik Version', *American Slavic and East European Review* 13(1): 11–28.

Le Bon, Gustave. 1897. *The Crowd: A Study of the Popular Mind*. Dunwoody, GA: Norman S. Berg.

Lees, Andrew. 2002. *Cities, Sin, and Social Reform in Imperial Germany*. Ann Arbor: University of Michigan Press.

Lellouch, Benjamin. 2013. 'Qu'est-ce qu'un Turc? (Égypte, Syrie, XVIe siècle)', *European Journal of Turkish Studies* 16: 1–23.

Leontis, Artemis. 1995. *Topographies of Hellenism; Mapping the Homeland*. Ithaca: Cornell University Press.

Levend, Agâh Sırrı. 1949. *Türk Dilinde Gelime ve Sadeleme Safhaları*. Ankara: Türk Tarih Kurumu Basımevi.

Lewis, Bernard. 1961. *The Emergence of Modern Turkey*. Oxford: Oxford University Press.

Lipset, Seymour and Stein Rokkan. 1967. *Party Systems and Voter Alignments: Cross-National Perspectives*. New York: Free Press.

Lundgren, Asa. 2007. *The Unwelcome Neighbour: Turkey's Kurdish Policy*. London: I. B. Tauris.

Lynch, Gabrielle. 2015. 'Democratization in Trouble: The Election Syndrome and the Return of Guided Democracies', *The Constitution* 15(1): 1–22.

McQueen, Humphrey. 1974. 'Racism and Australian Literature', pp. 143–50 in *Racism: the Australian Experience, v. 1: Prejudice and Xenophobia*, edited by F. S. Stevens. Sydney, ANZ.

Makdisi, Ussama. 2002. 'Ottoman Orientalism', *American Historical Review* 107(3): 768–96.

Mango, Andrew. 1999. *Atatürk: The Biography of the Founder of Modern Turkey*. London: John Murray.

Mango, Andrew. 2005. *The Turks Today*. London: John Murray.

Manin, Bernard. 1997. *The Principles of Representative Government*. Cambridge: Cambridge University Press.

Mardin, Serif. 1997a. 'Projects as Methodology: Some Thoughts on Turkish Social Science', pp. 64–80 in *Rethinking Modernity and National Identity in Turkey*, edited by Sibel Bozdogan and Resat Kasaba. Seattle: University of Washington Press.

Mardin, Serif. (1997b): 'The Ottoman Empire', pp. 115–28 in *After Empire: Multiethnic Societies and Nation-Building*, edited by Karen Barkey and Mark von Hagen. Boulder: Westview.

Markou, Grigoris. 2021. 'Anti-populist Discourse in Greece and Argentina in the 21st Century', *Journal of Political Ideologies* 26(2): 201–19.

Marsden, Douglas and Peter Snow. 1991. *The Charismatic Bond: Political Behavior in Time of Crisis*. Cambridge, MA: Harvard University Press.

Matthews, Sean. 2001. 'Change and Theory in Raymond Williams's Structure of Feeling', *Pretexts: Literary and Cultural Studies* 10(2): 179–94.

Mbembe, Achille. 2019. *Necropolitics*. Durham, NC: Duke University Press.

Melber, Henning. 2018. 'Populism in Southern Africa under Liberation Movements as Governments', *Review of African Political Economy* 45(158): 678–86.

Mercer, David. 1993. 'Terra Nullius, Aboriginal Sovereignty and Land Rights in Australia: The Debate Continues', *Political Geography* 12(4): 299–318.

Middleton, Stuart. 2019. 'Raymond Williams's "Structure of Feeling" and the Problem of Democratic Values in Britain, 1938–1961', *Modern Intellectual History*: 1–29.

Mishra, Pankaj. 2013. 'The World Returns to the Barricades', *Bloomberg*, http://www.bloomberg.com/news/2013-07-14/the-world-returns-to-the-barricades.html (accessed at 26 March 2014).

Mishra, Pankaj. 2018. *Age of Anger: A History of the Present*. London: Picador.

Moffitt, Benjamin. 2016. *The Global Rise of Populism: Performance, Political Style, and Representation*. Stanford: Stanford University Press.

Morin, Aysel and Ronald Lee. 2010. 'Constitutive Discourse of Turkish Nationalism: Atatürk's Nutuk and the Rhetorical Construction of the "Turkish People"', *Communication Studies* 61(5): 485–506.

Morris, Benny and Dror Ze'evi. 2019. *The Thirty-Year Genocide: Turkey's Destruction of Its Christian Minorities, 1894–1924*. Cambridge, MA: Harvard University Press.

Morris, Chris. 2005. *The New Turkey: The Quiet Revolution on the Edge of Europe*. London: Granta.

Morris, R. C., ed. 2010. *Can the Subaltern Speak? Reflections on the History of an Idea*. New York: Columbia University Press.

Morton, S., 2011. 'Subalternity and Aesthetic Education in the Thought of Gayatri Chakravotry Spivak', *Parallax* 17(3): 70–83.

Mouffe, Chantal. 2018. *For a Left Populism*. London: Verso.

Mouffe, Chantal. 2020. 'Why a Populist Left Should Rally around a Green Democratic Transformation', openDemocracy RethinkingPopulism, https://www.opendemocracy.net/en/rethinking-populism/left-populist-strategy-post-covid-19/ (accessed 22 January 2022).

Moulier-Boutang, Yann. 2014. 'La plèbe, la multitude et la rente', *Multitudes*, 56: 213–20.

Mudde, Cas. 2004. 'The Populist Zeitgeist', *Government & Opposition* 39(3): 549–63.

Mudde, Cas and Cristóbal Rovira Kaltwasser. 2011. '"Voice of the Peoples": Populism in Europe and Latin America Compared', Helen Kellogg Institute for International Studies. Working Paper #378: 1–47.

Mudde, Cas and Cristóbal Rovira Kaltwasser. 2012. 'Populism and (Liberal) Democracy: A Framework for Analysis', pp. 1–26 in *Populism in Europe and the Americas: Threat Or Corrective for Democracy?*, edited by Cas Mudde and Cristóbal Rovira Kaltwasser. Cambridge: Cambridge University Press.

Müller, Jan-Werner. 2014. 'The People Must Be Extracted from Within the People: Reflections on Populism', *Constellations* 21(4): 485–9.

Müller, Jan-Werner. 2016. *What is Populism?* Philadelphia: University of Pennsylvania Press.

Nalçaoğlu, Halil 2002. 'Devrimci Öğrencilerin Özgül Fantezi Uzamı', *Toplum ve Bilim* 933: 142–72.

Nereid, Camilla T. 2011. 'Kemalism on the Catwalk: The Turkish Hat Law of 1925', *Journal of Social History* 44(3): 707–28.

Nguyen, Christoph G. 2019. 'Emotions and Populist Support', *SocArXiv* 13 March, doi:10.31235/osf.io/e2wm6 (accessed 4 February 2022).

Öktem, Kerem. 2004. 'Incorporating the Time and Space of the Ethnic "Other": Nationalism and Space in Southeast Turkey in the Nineteenth and Twentieth Centuries', *Nations and Nationalism* 10 (4): 559–78.

Öktem, Kerem. 2011. *Angry Nation: Turkey since 1989*. London: Zed Books.

Olson, Robert W. 1989. *The Emergence of Kurdish Nationalism and the Sheikh Said Rebellion, 1880–1925*. Texas: University of Texas Press.

Öniş, Ziya. 2015. 'Monopolising the Centre: The AKP and the Uncertain Path of Turkish Democracy', *International Spectator* 50(2): 22–41.

Ostiguy, Pierre. 2017. 'Populism: A Socio-Cultural Approach', pp.73–97 in *The Oxford Handbook of Populism*, edited by Cristóbal Rovira Kaltwasser, Paul A. Taggart, Paulina Ochoa Espejo and Pierre Ostiguy. Oxford: Oxford University Press.

Özbudun, Ergun. 2000. *Contemporary Turkish Politics: Challenges to Democratic Consolidation*. Boulder, CO: Lynne Rienner.

Özbudun, Ergun. 2013. *Party Politics and Social Cleavages in Turkey*. Boulder, CO: Lynne Rienner.

Özbudun, Ergun. 2014. 'AKP at the Crossroads: Erdoğan's Majoritarian Drift', *South European Society and Politics* 19(2): 155–67.

Özbudun, Ergun and Ömer Faruk Gençkaya. 2009. *Democratization and the Politics of Constitution Making in Turkey*. Budapest: Central European University Press.

Özkazanç, Alev. 2020. 'Gender And Authoritarian Populism In Turkey: The Two Phases Of AKP Rule', OpenDemocracy, https://www.opendemocracy.net/en/rethinking-populism/gender-and-authoritarian-populism-turkey-two-phases-akp-rule/ (accessed 20 March 2020).

Özkırımlı, Umut and Spyros A. Sofos. 2008. *Tormented by History: Nationalism in Greece and Turkey*. New York: Oxford University Press.

Özoğlu, Hakan. 2009. 'Exaggerating and Exploiting the Sheikh Said Rebellion of 1925 for Political Gains', *New Perspectives on Turkey* 41: 181–211.

Özoğlu, Hakan. 2011. *From Caliphate to Secular State: Power Struggle in the Early Turkish Republic: Power Struggle in the Early Turkish Republic*. Santa Barbara: Praeger Publishers.

Öztürkmen, A. 1992. 'Individuals and Institutions in the Early History of Turkish Folklore, 1840–1950', *Journal of Folklore Research* 29(2): 177–92.

Özyürek, Esra. 2001. *Türkiye'nin Toplumsal Hafızası*. Istanbul: İletişim

Özyürek, Esra. 2006. *Nostalgia for the Modern: State Secularism and Everyday Politics in Turkey*. Durham, NC: Duke University Press.

Pappas, Takis S. and Hanspeter Kriesi. 2015. 'Populism and Crisis: A Fuzzy Relationship', pp. 303–26 in *European Populism in the Shadow of the Great Recession*, edited by Hanspeter Kriesi and Takis S. Pappas. Colchester: ECPR Press.

Parla, Taha. 1994. *Türkiye'de Siyasal Kültürün Resmî Kaynakları. Cilt. 1, Atatürk'ün Nutuk'u*. Istanbul: İletişim.

Parla, Taha. 1995. *Türkiye'de Siyasal Kültürün Resmi Kaynakları. Cilt. 3, Kemalist Tek-Parti İdeolojisi ve CHP'nin Altı Ok'u*. Istanbul: İletişim.

Paul, I. A. 2013. 'Resisting Tear Gas Together', http://www.ianalanpaul.com/resisting-tear-gas-together/ (accessed 23 March 2014).

Peñafiel, Ricardo. 2012. 'Les actions directes spontanées au-delà du virage à gauche: Les conditions de possibilité de l'interpellation plébéienne', pp. 11–31 in *L'interpellation plébéienne en Amérique latine*, edited by André Corten, Cathérine Huart and Ricardo Peñafiel. Québec: Karthala-Presses de l'Université du Québec.

Poggi, Gianfranco. 1978. *The Development of the Modern State: A Sociological Introduction*. London: Hutchinson.

Poulantzas, Nicos. 1978. *State, Power, Socialism*. London: New Left Books.

Provence, Michael. 2011. 'Ottoman Modernity, Colonialism, and Insurgency in the Interwar Arab East', *International Journal of Middle East Studies* 43(2): 205–25.

Przeworski, Adam. 1988. 'Democracy as a Contingent Outcome of Conflict', pp. 59–83 in *Constitutionalism and Democracy*, edited by J. Elster and R. Slagstad. Cambridge: Cambridge University Press.

Richardson E. B. 1969. 'The Aborigine in Fiction: A Survey of Attitudes since 1900', *Armidale and District Historical Society Journal and Proceedings* 12: 1–13.

Roberts, K. 2006. 'Populism, Political Conflict, and Grass-Roots Organization in Latin America', *Comparative Politics* 38(2): 127–48.

Rojek, Chris. 1995. *Decentring Leisure; Rethinking Leisure Theory*. London: Sage.

Ruysdael, Salomon. 2002. *New Trends in Turkish Foreign Affairs: Bridges and Boundaries*. iUniverse.

Sakallıoğlu, Cizre. 1997. 'The Anatomy of the Turkish Military's Autonomy', *Comparative Politics* 29(2):151–66.

Satan, Ali. 1985. *Halifeliğin Kaldırılması*. Istanbul: Gökkubbe.

Schmitt, Carl. 1985. *Political Theology: Four Chapters on the Concept of Sovereignty*. Cambridge, MA: MIT Press.

Schmitt, Carl. 1988. *The Crisis of Parliamentary Democracy.* Cambridge, MA: MIT Press.

Schmitt, Carl. 1996. *The Concept of the Political*. Chicago: University of Chicago Press.

Schmitt, Carl. 2007. *Theory of the Partisan: Intermediate Commentary on the Concept of the Political*. New York: Telos Publishing.

Sezgin, İpek Gencel. 2013. 'How Islamist Parties Emerge: The Case of the National Order Party', pp. 77–98 in *Negotiating Political Power in Turkey: Breaking the Party Apart*, edited by É. Massicard and N. F. Watts. Abingdon: Routledge.

Shaw, Stanford and Ezel Kural Shaw. 1977. *History of the Ottoman Empire and Modern Turkey: Volume 2, Reform, Revolution, and Republic: The Rise of Modern Turkey 1808–1975*. Cambridge: Cambridge University Press.

Shissler, Ada Holly. 2003. *Between Two Empires: Ahmet Agaoğlu and the New Turkey*. London: I. B. Tauris.

Sighele, Scipio. 1903. *L'intelligenza della folla*. Torino: Fratelli Bocca.

Şimsir, Bilal. 1992. *Türk Yazı Devrimi*. Ankara: Türk Tarih Kurumu Basımevi.

Smith, Peter H. 1969. 'Social Mobilization, Political Participation, and the Rise of Juan Peron', *Political Science Quarterly* 84(1): 30–49.

Sofos, Spyros A. 1996a. 'Inter-ethnic Violence and Gendered Constructions of Ethnicity in Former Yugoslavia', *Social Identities* 2(1): 73–92.

Sofos, Spyros A. 1996b. 'Culture, Politics and Identity in Former Yugoslavia', pp. 235–65 in *Nation and Identity in Contemporary Europe*, edited by Brian Jenkins and Spyros A. Sofos. London: Routledge.

Sofos, Spyros A. 1996c. 'Nationalism, Mass Communications and Public Rituals in Former Yugoslavia: The Case of Serbia', *Contemporary Politics* 2(1): 123–32.

Sofos, Spyros A. 2000. 'Reluctant Europeans? European Integration and the Transformation of Turkish Politics', *South European Society and Politics* 5(2): 243–60.

Sofos, Spyros A. 2014. 'In Lieu of Conclusion: Rallying for Gezi, or Metaphors of Aporia and Empowerment', pp. 134–41 in *The Making of a Protest Movement in Turkey: #occupygezi*, edited by Umut Özkırımlı. London: Palgrave Pivot.

Sofos, Spyros A. 2016. 'Turkey: Of Coups and Popular Resistance', OpenDemocracy, https://www.opendemocracy.net/en/turkey-of-coups-and-popular-resistance/ (accessed 20 March 2020).

Sofos, Spyros A. 2018a. 'A Momentary Lapse of Reason? Gezi in Social-Historical Perspective', *Journal of Historical Sociology* 31(1): 82–93.

Sofos, Spyros A. 2018b. 'The Turkish Election as a Warning against the Irresistible Charms of Populism', OpenDemocracy, https://www.opendemocracy.net/en/turkish-election-as-warning-against-irresistible-charms-of-populism/ (accessed 20 January 2022).

Sofos, Spyros A. 2000. 'Reluctant Europeans? European Integration and the Transformation of Turkish Politics', *South European Society and Politics* 5(2): 243–60.

Sofos, Spyros A. and Roza Tsagarousianou. 1992. 'The Politics of Identity: Nationalism in Contemporary Greece', pp. 51–66 in *The Resurgence of Nationalist Movements in Europe*, edited by José Amodia. Bradford: Bradford University Occasional Papers.

Sofos, Spyros A. and Roza Tsagarousianou. 2012. 'Introduction: Back to the Drawing Board: Rethinking Multiculturalism', *Journal of Contemporary European Studies* 20(3): 263–71.

Somer, Murat. 2017. 'Conquering versus Democratizing the State: Political Islamists and Fourth Wave Democratization in Turkey and Tunisia', *Democratization* 24(6): 1025–43.

Somers, Margaret R. 1994. 'The Narrative Constitution of Identity: A Relational and Network Approach', *Theory and Society* 23(5): 605–49.

Spivak, Gayatri Chakravorty. 1988. 'Can the Subaltern Speak?', pp. 271–315 in *Marxism and the Interpretation of Culture*, edited by C. Nelson and L. Grossberg. Urbana: University of Illinois Press.

Spivak, Gayatri C. 1999. *A Critique of Postcolonial Reason: Toward a History of the Vanishing Present*. Boston: Harvard University Press.

Stavrakakis, Yannis. 2014. 'The Return of "The People": Populism and Anti-Populism in the Shadow of the European Crisis', *Constellations* 21(4): 505–17.

Szurek, Emmanuel. 2015. 'The Linguist and the Politician: The Türk Dil Kurumu and the Field of Power in the 1930–40s', pp. 68–96 in *Order and Compromise: Government Practices in Turkey from the Late Ottoman Empire to the Early 21st Century*, edited by Marc Aymes, Benjamin Gourisse and Elise Massicard. Leiden: Brill.

Taggart, Paul A. 2000. *Populism*. Buckingham: Open University Press.

Tahir-Gürçağlar, Şehnaz. 2008. *The Politics and Poetics of Translation in Turkey, 1923–1960*. Amsterdam and New York: Rodopi.

Taine, Hippolyte. 1876–8. *Origines de la France contemporaine*. Paris: Hachette et Cie.

Tanör, Bülent. 2001. *Osmanlı-Türk Anayasal Gelişmeleri*. Istanbul: Yapı Kredi Yayınları.

Tanyol, Cahit. 1984. *Atatürk ve Halkcilik*. Ankara: Türkiye İs Bankasi Kültür Yayinlari.

Tarde, Gabriel. 1903. 'Inter-Psychology, the Inter-Play of Human Minds', *International Quarterly* 7: 59–84.

Taş, Hakki. 2015. 'Turkey – From Tutelary to Delegative Democracy', *Third World Quarterly* 36(4): 776–91.

Taylor, Frederick Winslow. 1947. *Scientific Management: Comprising Shop Management, the Principles of Scientific Management [and] Testimony Before the Special House Committee*. New York: Harper & Brothers.

Tekdemir, Omer. 2018. 'Turkey's Three-Dimensional Populism, Three Leaders and Three Blocs', OpenDemocracy, https://www.opendemocracy.net/en/can-europe-make-it/turkey-s-three-dimensional-populism-three-leaders-and-three-blocs/ (accessed 20 March 2020).

Tekeli, Ilhan. 1978. 'Türkiye'de Halkçılık İdeolojisinin Evrimi', *Toplum ve Bilim* 6–7: 65–71.

Theweleit, Klaus. 1989. *Male Fantasies, Volume II: Male Bodies: Psychoanalyzing the White Terror*. Minneapolis: University of Minnesota Press.

Thompson, E. P. 1963. *The Making of the English Working Class*. London: Penguin.

Thompson, E. P. 1971. 'The Moral Economy of the English Crowd in the Eighteenth Century', *Past & Present* 50: 76–136.

Thompson, E. P. 1974. 'Patrician Society, Plebeian Culture', *Journal of Social History* 7(4): 382–405.

Thompson, E. P. 1978. 'Eighteenth-Century English Society: Class Struggle without Class?', *Social History* 3(2): 133–65.

Thompson, E. P. 1991. *Customs in Common*. London: Merlin.

Thompson, John B. 1984. *Studies in the Theory of Ideology*. Berkeley: University of California Press.

Toktas, Sule and Dilek Cindoğlu. 2006. 'Modernization and Gender: A History of Girls' Technical Education in Turkey since 1927', *Women's History Review* 15(5): 737–49.

Tomlin, E. W. F. 1946. *Life in Modern Turkey*. London: Thomas Nelson.

Toprak, Zafer. 1984. 'Osmanlı Narodnikleri: 'Halka Doğru' gidenler', *Toplum ve Bilim* 24: 69–81.

Tunçay, Mete. 'Kemalism' in *The Oxford Encyclopedia of the Islamic World*. Oxford Islamic Studies Online, http://www.oxfordislamicstudies.com/article/opr/t236/e0440 (accessed 30 March 2020).

Tunçay, Mete. 1989. *T.C.'nde Tek-Parti Yönetimi'nin Kurulması (1923–1931)*. Istanbul: Cem Yayınevi.

Turam, Berna. 2012. *Secular State and Religious Society: Two Forces in Play in Turkey*. Basingstoke: Palgrave Macmillan.

Turan, Ömer. 2019. 'Return to the Status Quo Ante: Reloading Militarism Before and After 15 July Coup Attempt', pp. 198–241 in *The Dubious Case of a Failed Coup; Militarism, Masculinities, and 15 July in Turkey*, edited by Feride Çiçekoğlu and Ömer Turan. Singapore: Palgrave Macmillan.

Türköz, Meltem. 2007. 'Surname Narratives and the State–Society Boundary: Memories of Turkey's Family Name Law of 1934', *Middle Eastern Studies* 43(6): 893–908.

Türkyilmaz, Zeynep. 2016. 'Maternal Colonialism and Turkish Woman's Burden in Dersim: Educating the "Mountain Flowers" of Dersim', *Journal of Women's History* 28(3): 162–86.

Turnaoğlu, Banu. 2017. *The Formation of Turkish Republicanism*. Princeton: Princeton University Press.

Turner, Graeme. 2002. *British Cultural Studies: An Introduction* (3rd edn). London: Routledge.

Turner, Victor. 1967. *The Forest of Symbols: Aspects of Ndembu Ritual*. Ithaca: Cornell University Press.

Turner, Victor. 1974. *Dramas, Fields and Metaphors: Symbolic Action in Human Society*. Ithaca: Cornell University Press.

Tyler, Imogen. 2013. *Revolting Subjects: Social Abjection and Resistance in Neoliberal Britain*. London: Zed Books.

Unat, Faik R. 1961. 'Amassya Protokolleri', *Tarih Vesikaları* 3(18): 359–65.

Üngör, Uğur Ümıt. 2011. *The Making of Modern Turkey Nation and State in Eastern Anatolia, 1913–1950*. Oxford: Oxford University Press.

Ulgen, Fatma. 2010. 'Reading Mustafa Kemal Atatürk on the Armenian Genocide of 1915', *Patterns of Prejudice* 44(4): 369–91.

Üstel, Füsun. 1997. *Türk Ocakları (1912–1931): İmparatorluktan Ulus-Devlete Türk Milliyetçiliğiç*. Istanbul: İletişim.

Üstel, Füsun. 2004. *'Makbul Vatandaş'ın Peşinde: II. Meşrutiyet'ten Bugüne Vatandaşlık Eğitimi*. Istanbul: İletişim.

Van Bruinessen, Martin. 1992. *Agha, Shaikh and State: The Social and Political Structures of Kurdistan*. London: Zed Books.

Van Bruinessen, Martin. 1994. 'Genocide in Kurdistan? The Suppression of the Dersim Rebellion in Turkey (1937–8) and the Chemical War against the Iraqi Kurds (1988)', pp. 141–70 in *Conceptual and Historical Dimensions of Genocide*, edited by George J. Andreopoulos. Philadelphia: University of Pennsylvania Press.

Van der Lippe, John M. 2005. *The Politics of Turkish Democracy: Ismet Inonu and the Formation of the Multi-Party System, 1938–1950*. Albany: SUNY Press.

Vaner, Semih. 1987. 'The Army', pp. 236–65 in *Turkey in Transition: New Perspectives*, edited by Irvin C. Schick and Ertugrul Ahmet Tonak. New York and Oxford: Oxford University Press.

Weber, Eugene. 1976. *Peasants into Frenchmen*. Stanford: Stanford University Press.

Webster, Donald Everett. 1939. *The Turkey of Atatürk: Social Process in the Turkish Transformation*. Philadelphia: American Academy of Political and Social Science.

Weiker, Walter. 1973. *Political Tutelage and Democracy in Turkey: The Free Party and its Aftermath*. Leiden: Brill.

Weiner, Myron and Ergun Özbudun.1987. *Competitive Elections in Developing Countries*. Durham, NC: Duke University Press.

Weyland, Kurt. 2001. 'Clarifying a Contested Concept: Populism in the Study of Latin American Politics', *Comparative Politics* 34(1):1–22.

White, Jenny. 2002. *Islamist Mobilization in Turkey: A Study in Vernacular Politics*. Seattle: University of Washington Press.

White, Jenny. 2014. *Muslim Nationalism and the New Turks*. Princeton: Princeton University Press.

Williams, Raymond. 1954. 'Film and the Dramatic Tradition', pp. 1–55 in *Preface to Film*, edited by Raymond Williams and Michael Orrom. London: Film Drama: 1–55.

Williams, Raymond. 1977. *Marxism and Literature*. Oxford: Oxford University Press.

Williams, Raymond. 1983. *Keywords: A Vocabulary of Culture and Society*. London: Fontana.

Woodward, Comer Van. 1955. *The Strange Career of Jim Crow*. New York: Oxford University Press.

Yabanci, Bilge. 2016. 'Populism as the Problem Child of Democracy: The AKP's Enduring Appeal and the Use of Meso-Level Actors', *Southeast European and Black Sea Studies* 16(4): 591–617.

Yalgın, Ali Rıza. 1939. 'Cihan Harbi ve Halk Türküleri', *Görüşler: Adana Halkevi Dergisi* 22: 18–23.

Yavuz, Hakan. 2003. *Islamic Political Identity in Turkey*. New York: Oxford University Press.

Yeşilada, Birol A. 2002. 'The Virtue Party', pp. 62–81 in *Political Parties in Turkey*, edited by Barry Rubin and Metin Heper. London: Routledge.

Yeşil, Sevim. 2003. 'Unfolding Republican Patriarchy: The Case of Young Kurdish Women at the Girls' Vocational Boarding School in Elazığ', MA thesis, Middle East Technical University, Department of Gender and Women's Studies.

Yıldız, Ahmet. 2001. *'Ne Mutlu Türküm Diyebilene': Türk Ulusal Kimliğinin Etno-Seküler Sınırları (1919–1938)*. Istanbul: İletişim.

Yilmaz, Aybige. 2004. 'Victims, Villains and Guardian Angels: Batman Suicide Stories', *Westminster Papers in Communication and Culture* 1(1): 66–92.

Yilmaz, Hale. 2013. *Becoming Turkish: Nationalist Reforms and Cultural Negotiations in Early Republican Turkey*. Syracuse, NY: Syracuse University Press.

Young, Crawford. 2012. *The Postcolonial State in Africa: Fifty Years of Independence, 1960–2010*. Madison: University of Wisconsin Press.

Zeydanlıoğlu, Welat. 2008. '"The White Turkish Man's Burden": Orientalism, Kemalism and the Kurds in Turkey', pp. 155–74 in *Neo-colonial Mentalities in Contemporary Europe? Language and Discourse in the Construction of Identities*, edited by Guido Rings and Anne Ife. Newcastle upon Tyne: Cambridge Scholars Publishing.

Zölberg, Aristide R. 1966. *Creating Political Order: The Party-States of West Africa*. Chicago: Rand McNally.

Zürcher, Erik-Jan. 1991. *Political Opposition in the Early Turkish Republic: The Progressive Republican Party 1924–1925*. Leiden: Brill.

Zürcher, Erik-Jan. 1992. 'The Ottoman Legacy of the Turkish Republic: An Attempt at a New Periodization', *Die Welt des Islams* 32: 237–53.

Zürcher, Erik-Jan. 1996a. 'Between Death and Desertion: The Experience of the Ottoman Soldier in World War I', *Turcica* 28: 235–58.

Zürcher, Erik-Jan. 1996b. 'Little Mehmet in the Desert: The Ottoman Soldier's Experience', pp. 230–41 in *Facing Armageddon: The First World War Experienced*, edited by Hugh Cecil and Peter H. Liddle. London: Leo Cooper.

Zürcher, Erik-Jan. 2004. 'Institution Building in the Kemalist Republic: The Role of the People's Party', pp. 98–112 in *Men of Order: Authoritarian Modernization under Atatürk and Reza Shah*, edited by Touraj Atabaki and Erik-Jan Zürcher. London: I. B. Tauris.

Zürcher, Erik-Jan. 2017. *Turkey: A Modern History*. London: I. B. Tauris

Žižek, Slavoj. 2010. 'A Permanent Economic Emergency', *New Left Review* 64: 85–95.

Memoirs, Speeches and Addresses

Atatürk, Mustapha Kemal. 29 October 1933. Atatürk's 10th Anniversary Speech, http://www.ataturksociety.org/about-ataturk/ataturks-speech-at-the-10th-anniversary-of-the-turkish-republic/ (accessed 10 March 2020).

Atatürk, Mustafa Kemal. 1981. *A Speech Delivered by Ghazi Mustafa Kemal 1927*. Ankara: Başbakanlık Basımevi.

Atatürk, Mustafa Kemal. 1991. Atatürk'ün Tamim ve Telgrafları ve Beyannameleri (Atatürk's Circulars Telegrams and Declarations), Vol. IV. Ankara: Atatürk Araştırma Merkezi.

Atatürk, Mustafa Kemal. 1997. Atatürk'ün Söylev ve Demeçleri I–III. Vol. 1. Ankara: Atatürk Araştırma Merkezi.

Birinci Türk Tarih Kongresi, *Ankara, 2–11 Temmuz 1932: Konferanslar, Müzakere Zabıtları*. Istanbul: Maarif Vekaleti.

İnönü, İsmet. 1998. *İsmet İnönü'nün Hatıraları 2*. Istanbul: Yenigün Haber Ajansı Basın ve Yayıncılık AŞ.

Morgenthau, Henry. 1918. *Ambassador Morgenthau's Story*. Garden City, NY: Doubleday, Page & Company.

Turkish Official Archives and Publications (in chronological order)

Başbakanlık Cumhuriyet Arşivi (Prime Minister's Republican Archives)

Prime Minister's Republican Archives (BCA), Başbakanlık Muamelât Genel Müdürlüğü Evrakı (Prime Minister's Directorate of Transactions, BMGME), 490.01/1.14.15. 6 September 1930a.

Prime Minister's Republican Archives (BCA), BMGME, 490.01/1.14.16. 6 September 1930b.

Prime Minister's Republican Archives (BCA), BMGME, 030.10/72.470.2, 1 September 1937.

Prime Minister's Republican Archives (BCA), BMGME, 030.10/111.753.0, 1 November 1939.

Türkiye Büyük Millet Meclisi Arşivi (Turkish Grand National Assembly Archives)

Türkiye Büyük Millet Meclisi (TBMM) Zabit Ceridesi, vol. 5, session 99 (18 November 1920).

Türkiye Büyük Millet Meclisi (TBMM), Devre II, 3, Cilt 19 (1925).

Türkiye Büyük Millet Meclisi (TBMM) Zabit Ceridesi, vol. 2, session 71 (21 June 1934).

Türkiye Büyük Millet Meclisi (TBMM) Zabit Ceridesi, no. 2884, vol. 1, session 21: 175 (25 December 1935).

Türkiye Büyük Millet Meclisi (TBMM) Tutanak Dergisi, vol. 9, session 9/1 (1951).

Türkiye Büyük Millet Meclisi (TBMM). 2012. Ülkemizde Demokrasiye Müdahale Eden Tüm Darbe ve Muhtıralar ile Demokrasiyi İşlevsiz Kılan Diğer Bütün Girişim ve Süreçlerin Tüm Boyutları ile Araştırılarak Alınması Gereken Önlemlerin Belirlenmesi Amacıyla Kurulan: Raporu. Ankara: TBMM, https://www.tbmm.gov.tr/sirasayi/donem24/yil01/ss376_Cilt1.pdf (accessed 15 May 2020).

Türkiye Büyük Millet Meclisi Arşivi Basımevi (Turkish Grand National Assembly Publications)

Türkiye Cumhuriyeti Anayasasi.1982. Kanun no: 2709 Kabul Tarihi: 7 November 1982, https://www.tbmm.gov.tr/anayasa/anayasa2018.pdf (accessed 20 March 2020).

Yazıcı, Sefer, ed. 2015. *Milli Egemenlik Belgeleri*. Ankara: TBMM Basımevi.

TC Kültür Bakanlığı (Ministry of Culture, Turkish Republic)

TC Kültür Bakanlığı. 1990. *1920–1989 TC Hükümet Programlarında Kültür Politikası*. Ankara: TC Kültür Bakanlığı Araştırma ve Planlama Koordinasyon Kurulu.

TC Cumhurbaşkanliği Mevzuat Bilgi Sistemi (Turkish Republic Presidency Legislative Information System), Bazı Kisvelerin Giyilemeyeceğine Dair Kanunu (2596 / 3.12.1934), https://www.mevzuat.gov.tr/MevzuatMetin/1.3.2596.pdf (accessed 31 January 2022).

Yücel, Hasan Ali. 1993. *Milli Eğitimle İlgili Söylev ve Demeçler*. Ankara: TC Kültür Bakanligi Yayinlari.

Sagay, Esat. 1994. 'Son Yapilan Teftiç Neticesi Hakkmda Talimat', pp. 364–5 in *Türkiye'de Orta öğretim*, edited by Hasan Ali Yücel. Ankara: TC Kültür Bakanligi Yayinlari: 36TC.

TC Cumhurbaşkanliği Mevzuat Bilgi Sistemi (Legislative Information System, Turkish Republic)

Bazı Kisvelerin Giyilemeyeceğine Dair Kanunu (2596 / 3.12.1934), https://www.mevzuat.gov.tr/MevzuatMetin/1.3.2596.pdf (accessed 28 November 2022).

TC Anayasa Mahkemesi (Constitutional Court, Turkish Republic)

TC Anayasa Mahkemesi. 1924. Teşkilâti Esasiye Kanunu. Kanun No:491. Kabul Tarihi: 20/4/1340, https://www.anayasa.gov.tr/tr/mevzuat/onceki-anayasalar/1924-anayasasi/ (accessed 20 March 2020).

TC Anayasa Mahkemesi. 1961. Türkiye Cumhuriyeti Anayasasi. Kanun No:334. Kabul Tarihi: 9 July 1961, https://www.anayasa.gov.tr/tr/mevzuat/onceki-anayasalar/1961-anayasasi/ (accessed 20 March 2020).

Yüksek Seçim Kurulu (Supreme Election Council, Turkish Republic)

YSK Milletvekili Genel Seçimleri Arşivi: 1950–1977 Yılları Arası Milletvekili Genel Seçimleri, http://www.ysk.gov.tr/tr/1950-1977-yillari-arasi-milletvekili-genel-secimleri/3007.

YSK Seçim Arşivi, http://www.ysk.gov.tr/tr/secim-arsivi/2612 (accessed 20 March 2020).

Birinci Genel Müfettişlik (First General Inspectorate, Turkish Republic)

Birinci Genel Müfettişlik. 1939. *Güney Doğu: Birinci Genel Müfettişlik bölgesi*. Istanbul: Cumhuriyet Matbaası.

Cumhuriyet Halk Partisi (Republican People's Party)

Cumhuriyet Halk Partisi. 1935. *1935 Programı*. Ankara: Ulus Basımevi.

Adalet ve Kalkınma Partisi (Justice and Development Party)

AK Parti TBMM Grup Toplantısı, 11 June 2013. http://www.akparti.org.tr/site/video/45834/ak-parti-tbmm-grup-toplantisi-11-haziran (accessed 17 January 2022).

UK National Archives

Committee of the Congress, 'Manifesto of the Congress of the Vilayets of Eastern Anatolia at Erzerum', 7 August 1919, UKNA FO 371 / 4158.

Minister of Interior Affairs, Şükrü Kaya, UKNA FO 424 / 268 / E129.

Media

Acemoğlu, Daron and James Robinson. 2013. 'Beyaz Türkler, Siyah Türkler', Agos, 2 March 2013, http://www.agos.com.tr/tr/yazi/4460/beyaz-turkler-siyah-turkler (accessed 18 February 2020).

Al Jazeera. 25 June 2018. 'Profile: Recep Tayyip Erdogan', https://www.aljazeera.com/indepth/spotlight/turkeyelection/2011/05/2011526121054590355.html (accessed 29 January 2020).

Bianet. 18 December 2015. 'Maraş Katliamının Üzerinden 37 Yıl Geçti', https://bianet.org/bianet/siyaset/170307-maras-katliaminin-uzerinden-37-yil-gecti (accessed 1 September 2021).

Cupolo, Diego. 9 July 2018. 'For Kurds in Southeast Turkey, the urban conflict continues', *The New Humanitarian*, https://www.thenewhumanitarian.org/feature/2018/07/09/kurds-southeast-turkey-urban-conflict-continues. (accessed 22 October 2019).

Daily Sabah. 23 June 2018. 'Devastated by PKK terror, Diyarbakır's Sur district rebuilt with new projects', https://www.dailysabah.com/war-on-terror/2018/06/23/devastated-by-pkk-terror-diyarbakirs-sur-district-rebuilt-with-new-projects (accessed 10 March 2020).

Goltz, Thomas. 1997. 'As the "Coup" Turns: The Army's Real Target', *Los Angeles Times*, 13 July 1997:M-2.

The Guardian. 9 February 2016 'The destruction of Sur: is this historic district a target for gentrification?', https://www.theguardian.com/cities/2016/feb/09/destruction-sur-turkey-historic-district-gentrification-kurdish (accessed 10 October 2019).

Hürriyet. 10 November 1998. 'Atatürk'ün cenaze namazı', http://dosyalar.hurriyet.com.tr/hur/turk/98/11/10/gundem/04gun.htm (accessed 10 December 2014).

Hürriyet. 20 July 2007. 'Miting rekoru Erdoğan'ın', https://www.hurriyet.com.tr/gundem/miting-rekoru-erdoganin-6928772 (accessed 10 March 2020).

Hürriyet. 10 June 2013. 'Erdoğan 'camiye içkiyle girdiler' iddiasını tekrarladı', http://www.hurriyet.com.tr/gundem/23468860.asp (accessed 10 December 2014).

Hürriyet Daily News. 11 March 2016. 'Top court ruling on journalists was against the nation: President', https://www.hurriyetdailynews.com/top-court-ruling-on-journalists-was-against-the-nation-president---96338 (accessed 1 June 2016).

Hürriyet Daily News. 16 July 2019. 'No network of traitors will disrupt unity in Turkey: Erdoğan', https://www.hurriyetdailynews.com/no-network-of-traitors-will-disrupt-unity-in-turkey-erdogan-144990 (accessed 17 July 2019).

Kıbrıspostası. 13 July 2011. 'Türkiye'de "Demokrasi Ayarı" Şart!'.

Lowen, Mark. 24 June 2019. 'Can Erdogan bounce back from big Turkey defeat?', https://www.bbc.com/news/world-europe-48744733 (accessed 20 April 2020).

Reuters. 13 December 2013. 'Turkey's Erdoğan says 'dark alliances' behind graft inquiry', http://www.reuters.com/article/2013/12/21/turkey-corruption-idUSL6N0K002S20131221 (accessed 10 October 2019).

Sabah. 22 June 2016. 'Cumhurbaşkanı Erdoğan'dan o akademisyenlere sert tepki!', https://www.sabah.com.tr/gundem/2016/06/22/cumhurbaskani-Erdoğandan-o-akademisyenleresert-tepki (accessed 25 June 2016).

Today's Zaman. 29 August 2007. 'Prime minister expresses anger at Çankaya remarks', http://www.todayszaman.com/tz-web/detaylar.do?load=detay&link=120496 (accessed 28 May 2015).

Today's Zaman. 28 September 2007. 'AK Party closer to center as Abdüllatif Şener drops out', http://www.todayszaman.com/tz-web/detaylar.do?load=detay&link=112941 (accessed 28 May 2015).

Today's Zaman. 16 June 2013. 'Erdoğan Holds Second Rally as Taksim Clashes Continue', http://www.todayszaman.com/news-318456-erdogan-holdssecond-rally-as-taksim-clashes-continue.html (accessed 15 December 2014).

Washington Post. 15 December 2019. 'Turkey's political map is shifting. Is the country ready to shake off Erdogan's reign?', https://www.washingtonpost.com/opinions/2019/12/15/turkeys-political-map-is-shifting-is-country-ready-shake-off-erdogans-reign/ (accessed 19 December 2019).

World Politics Review. 27 June 2019. 'Is Turkey's Future in Play After the Opposition Won Istanbul's Election Rerun?', https://www.worldpoliticsreview.com/articles/27984/is-turkey-s-future-in-play-after-the-opposition-won-istanbul-s-election-rerun (accessed 19 December 2019).

Other

Konda Barometer 2010–19, https://konda.com.tr/en/konda-barometer/.

Türk Ocakları 2001. https://www.turkocaklari.org.tr/turk-ocagi-tarihi/turk-ocaklar-inin-kisa-tarihcesi-3496 (accessed 12 March 2020).

INDEX